CW01270463

1,000,000 Books

are available to read at

---◇---

www.ForgottenBooks.com

---◇---

Read online
Download PDF
Purchase in print

ISBN 978-1-333-85503-1
PIBN 10616239

English
Français
Deutsche
Italiano
Español
Português

www.forgottenbooks.com

Mythology Photography **Fiction**
Fishing Christianity **Art** Cooking
Essays Buddhism Freemasonry
Medicine **Biology** Music **Ancient**
Egypt Evolution Carpentry Physics
Dance Geology **Mathematics** Fitness
Shakespeare **Folklore** Yoga Marketing
Confidence Immortality Biographies
Poetry **Psychology** Witchcraft
Electronics Chemistry History **Law**
Accounting **Philosophy** Anthropology
Alchemy Drama Quantum Mechanics
Atheism Sexual Health **Ancient History**
Entrepreneurship Languages Sport
Paleontology Needlework Islam
Metaphysics Investment Archaeology
Parenting Statistics Criminology
Motivational

HE HERALD

OF

THE CROSS

178488
6/3/23

Published by PERCY LUND, HUMPHRIES & CO., Ltd.,
Bradford and London,
for "The Order of the Cross," Paignton, England.

In Memoriam.

In Memory of the late
MRS. JANE PURDON CLARKE,
of Larne, Ireland,
. and her sister,
MRS. ANNIE VIVIENNE PURDON JOYCE,

Whose noble gifts for the furtherance of the work of the Order of the Cross the Council gratefully acknowledge.

THE AIMS AND IDEALS OF
THE ORDER OF THE CROSS

(Formerly The Order of the Golden Age.)

To attain by mutual helpfulness, the realization of the Christ-life, by th path of self-denial, self-sacrifice, and absolute self-abandonment to the Divin will and service :—

It is of these things that the Cross as a symbol speaks. It stands for th Sign of the Order of the Cross because its three steps are those which have to b taken in order to arrive at that Estate which it symbolizes. It speaks of th quest after the humble spirit and the pure heart. It speaks also of that furthe state of realization, when the Soul gives itself in absolute abandonment for th Divine Service. The three steps are—

> Purity of Living.
> Purity of the Mind.
> Purity of the Soul.

Thus to endeavour by example and teaching to win all men to the love o ruth, Purity and Right-doing :

To proclaim the Brotherhood of Man, the essential one-ness of al eligious aspirations, and the unity of all living creatures in the Divine. T each the moral necessity for humaneness towards all men and all creatures.

To protest against, and to work for the abolition of, all national an ocial customs which violate the teachings of the Christ, especially such a nvolve bloodshed, the oppression of the weak and defenceless, the perpetuatio f the brutal mind, and the infliction of cruelty upon animals, *viz.*: ar, vivisection, the slaughter of animals for food, fashion and sport, an indred evils :

To advocate the universal adoption of a bloodless diet, and the return t imple and natural foods :

To proclaim a message of peace and happiness, health and purity pirituality and Divine Love.

ANNOUNCEMENTS.

This Journal is supplied regularly to many Public Institutions in this anc ther lands, such as Free Libraries, Institutes, University Colleges, etc.

All Official Correspondence in connection with the work of the Order ol he Cross should be addressed **TO THE SECRETARY,** to whom Cheques nd Postal Orders should be made payable.

"The Herald of the Cross" is published monthly. It can be obtained irect from Headquarters for 2s. 6d. per annum, post-free, or from the Publishers, Iessrs. PERCY LUND, HUMPHRIES & Co., LTD., 3, Amen Corner, London, E.C.

EXECUTIVE COUNCIL.

OBERT H. PERKS, M.D., F.R.C.S. (Eng.), *Secretary*, Ferndale,

CONTENTS.

THE HERALD OF THE CROSS.

| Vol v. New Series. | January, 1909. | No. I. |

WITHIN THE SANCTUARY.

The vision of the Adonai within the Sanctuary of the Soul which the Soul beholds when it reaches the Kingdom of the Divine :—

Behold there appeared unto one who was praying before the Altar within the Sanctuary of the Most High, the Sign of the Cross.

It was the Cross of the Divine Love and Wisdom, the Sign by which the Adonai is known upon the Kingdom of the Divine.

Each arm of the Cross expanded like a Radius Vector, sending forth its power and light in every direction, and was beautiful with all the tints of the wonderful spectrum of Elohim.

The whole Sanctuary became filled with the glory of the manifold light whose softened splendour was reflected everywhere, and which turned the Soul into a Heavenly Temple wherein the Divine Presence abides.

It was the vision within the Sanctuary of the Soul for which the Soul has ever prayed; "the Beauty of Holiness" where alone the Lord is truly worshipped, and where the Soul must needs inquire of the Lord; the inheritance which the Soul would fain obtain from the Divine Love and Wisdom,

CHRISTMAS.

THE new day breaketh and the long shadows of evil flee away ! As the Christmas Season comes and goes now, more and more are awakening to the new life which has come to the Earth, to behold its beauty and to share in its glory. More and yet more are men and women awakening to the terrible meaning of all the suffering and evil in the world, not only in the Human Kingdom, but also what they know to exist in the Animal Kingdom. The cry of the human life burdened with grievous chains and held fast in a bondage still more grievous, is heard and echoed from sphere to sphere until those who love to minister within these spheres of life through their own noble living and service come to know of the suffering, and send forth their healing thoughts and energies. And the cries of the greatly afflicted and oppressed creatures are also heard and responded to with such a fulness of service that the hour of the Deliverance of the creatures draweth nigh.

Soon shall it be that the Sanctuary of the body which should be fashioned, made and kept pure, no more shall be the receptacle for the mutilated remains of the oppressed creatures. Soon shall it be that no more the Sanctuaries shall have their Altars covered with these terrible oblations to make of them sacrifices unto the Mammon of unrighteous desires and inhuman tastes. For with the dawning of the new age the children of the Heavenly Father everywhere shall come to know how pure and beautiful is the life unto which He calls them ; how immeasurable is His Compassion and boundless His pity ; that as His Love knows no limits towards His children, neither does His merciful kindness towards the creatures. And then shall it be that through the purer and nobler vision of the Divine Love, and a more beauti_ ful exposition and realisation of the meaning of Christmas, and, consequently, that life of which the Angels are said to have sung of having become a reality in the very heart of society, the fearful and agonising cries of the suffering creatures will no longer be heard in our midst, nor sacrificed in thousands and hundreds of thousands in order to enable those who should now be like the Heavenly Father in compassion and pity, to keep the feast of the Season—a feast which should be one of such beautiful devotion and love that it would testify of the Soul reaching up unto the life of which it speaks. Then will the thoroughfares no longer be the scenes of the terribly barbaric exhibitions of the lifeless and mutilated forms of the slain creatures which have passed through the Abattoirs and laid down their burdened and afflicted lives as sacrifices unto the Moloch of inhuman desire and tastes ; for the bells upon the horses—the thoughts and purposes of the mind of the people which testify to the life within the heart—will ring out a world-wide message of peace unto all Souls (both Human Souls and Creature Souls). And they shall interpret the sweet pure music of the Heavens, and proclaim a nobler Song than now they ring—a song of a Divine Healing, making harmony where now there is discord, peace where now there is trouble, purity where now there is evil, and joy where now there is earth-born sorrow. They will ring out no mere meaningless music to please the outward senses and gratify the sensuous desires, for they will echo the harmonies of the Heavens whose sound is as the voice of the Divine Love when He speaketh unto His children. And so the Earth, now so distraught because of the wrong and evil ways of those who should be the Children of the Heavens in their life, will be made truly glad. The Christmas Season will then be one of pure and true joy for all who desire the life of goodness, and of loving and noble thoughtfulness toward all who require the manifestation of love, compassion and pity. The Christmas Season will then be a true prophecy of the Glorious Golden Age when the perfect life shall be lived by all, and all the creatures shall share in its blessing.

J. TODD FERRIER.

THE OLD AND THE NEW ORDERS.

THE day when the Earth was to be Redeemed from her mistake when she left the Kingdom of the Divine Father, has now come. That day when the Heavens would become changed and the Earth melt with fervent heat, is now at hand. The old order changeth and the new order taketh its place. Though with many it is still the reign of the darkness, the night in which they sleep and are unconscious of the wonderful and most glorious company from the Spiritual World, by which the Earth is now surrounded. yet to many others the day has broken, and the light from the Heavens of the Soul shines. The old order was one of darkness, fear and uncertainty ; the new order is one of light, trust and realisations. The old order was one lacking in true sympathy towards man and creature ; the new order is one in which compassion unto all men and pity towards all creatures make themselves manifest. In the old order even the Sanctuary was defiled by the impure sacrifices offered unto the Divine, for men and women sang and prayed unto Him with their hands stained with the blood of living creatures whom they had slain for their use ; but in the new order the life of the worshippers is purified from all such inhumanity, because the heart is full of true and beautiful love for all men and pity towards all the the creatures. In the old order men and women have sought the fulness of life through the power of the senses, in the new order they seek it through the power of the Divine in the Soul. In the old order the standard of life has been material, in the new it is spiritual. In the old order that standard was physical and social in its caste, in the new order it is only spiritual : The measure of man will be the measure of his true being, not as now the measure of his racial, blood and social conditions. For the day of the Redemption is come, and every one will now enter into his own land, from which all Souls went away when they went down into the Egypt of the sense-life.

J. TODD FERRIER.

THE OLD ORDER CHANGETH.

THE old order in this world changeth. Upon the Mountains of the Lord are the feet of them who bring the Glad Tidings, whose coming the weary world has needed ever since the day when it went away from the Divine Heritage down into Egypt, to there be sorely oppressed by all the conditions of that land or spiritual state. For the Messengers of the Lord are even now upon the Spiritual Heights publishing the Glad Tidings unto Zion (or those Souls who once knew the messages the Messengers now give), and telling unto all the inhabitants of Jerusalem (the world as a spiritual system) what great things the Lord hath done, and is now doing, in order to accomplish the Redemption of all His children. And the feet of the Messengers are beautiful, because the message which they declare from the Lord is full of light for the understanding, and is a message of true Goodwill unto all men and compassion towards all creatures.

Behold from Mount Gerizim unto Mount Ebal, and even unto Gilgal, is the message being proclaimed that all the true Israel may know Him whom they would serve, and that all those who have not known Him may come to the understanding of His holy purpose, and behold how beautiful it has always been ! Behold how even the Mountains of Lebanon are covered with the sacrifices of His great and unfailing Love! They are encircled with the Cloud of His Presence, and send forth sounds as the voice of many waters and magnetic rays like the lightning illumining the sky ! For the Kingdom of the Divine Love is a Kingdom of Divine tenderness, whose greatness is unspeakable, a tenderness which makes itself manifest towards all the children, even to those who have gone out into the far country of evil and spiritual impoverishment. It is a Kingdom where the Divine Love knows no change, where that Love makes itself manifest in the most wonderful sacrifices for the children, even unto the sacrifice of all that is ever dearest and most precious, as was shown forth in the unspeakable Sin-offering—profound in its meaning for the Soul, though so little understood in its nature.

Behold how the Lord descends upon Mount Horeb that all the House of Israel may behold Him! For it is the Kingdom of the Celestial, where abide the Sons of God, the Kingdom unto which the Sons of God are called, and where the service before the Lord is that of sharing in the Divine Travail on behalf of all the children, the sharers of the sufferings of Christ in His Soul Travail. For Mount Horeb towers above the plains of Sinai, as Lebanon towers above Horeb, and the Dwellers on the Mount are those who know the Lord and make manifest His truth as His Messengers unto all who are able to receive it. For the Celestial Kingdom is one of Light, one on which the Light of the Divine breaketh that it may again be broken unto all who dwell on the planes below. It is the Kingdom whence proceed the Christs of God in whom the Light of the Divine burns, and from whom it goeth forth as the Divine Wisdom to bring light unto all who sit in the darkness where the Divine Love is unknown. And all who have known the wonderful vision of the Lord upon Mount Horeb are the Sons of God, who are now again entering into that Vision of most wonderful Glory, and who are seeking to break it upon the planes of the Earth, that all who are looking for the morning may behold the light. The Cloud upon the Mount is the Presence of the Divine who speaketh with unveiled countenance unto all who dwell upon its heights.

Behold how the Lord has descended upon Mount Sinai, where the Elders of Israel now stand to receive the Blessing of the Lord! For Mount Sinai is the place of the Divine meeting with the Soul whose ways have been purified, and where it receives the Law of the Divine Love known as the Law of the Testimony. And the Law of the Divine Love is that Law of Life whose foundations are Love, whose ways are pure, whose bulwarks are righteousness and peace, and whose honour men behold as something far surpassing the honour of the world, because it regardeth the Divine Name in all things. The Law of the

Divine Love is the law of that life whose love breaks in compassion towards all who suffer and are heavily laden, and seeks to make the suffering and heavy burdens its own; which makes manifest a very real and very great pity unto all the creatures, and which reveals itself in a life of devotion on behalf of their redemption from the sufferings imposed upon them by men and women who in their thoughtlessness and through their wrong training, have the creatures killed to minister to their false tastes and beliefs.

The Law of the Divine Love is now being proclaimed and interpreted through all who have entered upon the Redeemed Life, and are seeking the Divine Love to be realised on this Earth.

J. TODD FERRIER.

THE NEW ORDER.

WITH the passing away of the old order of things through the new introduction of the New Order of life, will gradually disappear many of the terrible evils by which Humanity to-day is sorely afflicted. For the New Order will be one whose life is delivered from the awful material bondage by which the Human Race has been afflicted for untold ages. It will be one in which all that makes for purity and goodness shall have the pre-eminence, and all that enslaves the life of the individual, the community, the nation, or the whole Race, shall be eschewed. It will be an age in which truth and honour shall reign among men and women—the truth of the Divine Purpose concerning all His children, and that honour whose foundations are in love begotten within the life from the consciousness of the Divine Love. It will be one in which every ungentle thought and every ignoble deed will become possible only unto those who desire not the new and better way, and who will not seek unto the realisation of the Divine Love. It will be an age when all who earnestly desire to find that fulness of life presented

by the Redeemed Life and the Estate of Christhood will
not only be able to find what they seek, but to realise it
even unto the most blessed experience of being able to
enter into the joy of having overcome all the
influences of the sense-life, and to rise on to the Spiritual
Heavens to receive illumination from the Divine Kingdom.
It will be an age when all that is truly spiritual shall
triumph over all that is not born from the Divine within
the Soul, so that no longer shall evil prevail against the
best aspirations and purposes of the Soul, but the Soul
find it easier to realise all its most beautiful impulses,
yearnings, and visions of life. It will be an age which will
witness such changes in the custom of Society and habits
of the people that those also who would rise up even out of
their bondage to the sense-life, but find it very hard and
difficult because of the conditions, will have conditions to
aid them towards everything beautiful, good and pure,
instead of conditions acting as impassible barriers to their
true life.

The day is hastening in the which the old order
will not only be no more, and the New Order be with
us ; but also when the full effects of the New Order will be
seen in the family, social and national life. For very real
and very great influences are àt work to impress upon the
minds of men and women nobler thoughts and feelings
whose issue will be in purer and nobler conditions. The
very Heavens have approached nearer to the Earth to
enable all Souls who are upon its planes to work out
their Redemption, in the outworking of which all shall
share in the burden and the glory who are truly anxious
to rise up into the Redeemed life ; for the day of the
Redemption of the Human Race has appeared when all
Nations shall draw closer to one another and cease to learn
the arts of warfare any more ; when the Nations will have
noble ideas of patriotism, because the true patriots of
their land will be noble men and women, lovers of the
Race instead of lovers of personal and national material
glory ; when all societies will be centres of life born of

goodness and love, making themselves manifest in purity, compassion, and pity, so that no evil and injurious thing will be permitted to grow up in their midst, no customs whose ways impose unspeakable hardship and suffering upon anyone, no habits cultivated by the people whose ending is sorrow and Soul darkness, for it will be an age when the Earth will again become the House of the Lord in the sense that the Divine Presence will be known unto many and the Divine Love influence all, so that their habits and customs, feelings and ways, purposes and services of life be pure, good and noble.

The New Order will be one born out of love for the Divine, love making itself manifest unto all Souls and compassion unto all creatures ; love that knows no wearying in its devotion, nor limitations in its services, that counts not the cost of the sacrifice, but only the joy of serving the Divine Love in the service rendered unto His children, and compassion which knows no measure in its outflowing unto all the weak, helpless and fallen amongst the Human children, nor any lack unto the creatures. In that day will no ghastly abattoirs confront the eye where the helpless are made to lay down their lives to minister unto the cruel tastes and desires of the people who should now shelter the poor victims, nor the pitiable sight of the shambles meet our gaze as we walk down the thoroughfares. In that day the fearful and agonising wickedness practised within the Physiological Laboratories shall be swept out of the land as an abomination, and the poor children of the Earth delivered from their terrible conditions.

J. TODD FERRIER.

THE CREATION.

I.

THE GENERATION OF THE EARTH.

In the Arche[1] the Eternal One created the Heavens and the Earth.

The elements of the Earth were yet without form,[2] being within the Great Deep, and void of any separate function and consciousness,[3] and so parts of the Substances out of which all things had their beginning.

And the Spirit of the Eternal One who ever moveth upon the waters[4] of the Great Deep, gathered the elements together and fashioned them into the Earth.

And the coming together of the substances from the Great Deep clothed the Earth with magnetic Light,[5] and separated it from the Darkness within the Great Deep. The Darkness was known as the Night, and the Light upon the Earth as the Day.

And the Eternal One fashioned a Firmament without and a Firmament within. In the Firmament without He divided the Waters into those which were outermost and those which were innermost within that outer Firmament; but in the inner Firmament did He set the Sun and Moon within the Heavens of the Earth, the Sun to illumine the Heavens and the Moon to reflect his light.[6] And He fashioned all the stars[7] within the Earth's Heavens whose shining would tell unto all the Souls upon the Earth the Seasons through which the Earth had passed in its creation.

---

[1] The Heavenly Principle.

[2] They were spiritual substances in a formless state.

[3] Function is the result of consciousness, and consciousness is the result of magnetic polarisation.

[4] The spiritual substances which fill the Great Deep or Space.

[5] Through polarisation of the substances.

[6] The Soul of the Earth known as the Planet-Soul who was a Celestial being, and the Mind which was the magnetic reflector of the Spiritual Light.

[7] The various stages of the Earth's evolution as a Celestial being.

WHEN NEW HEAVENS APPEAR.

NEW Heavens were to be fashioned before the coming of the Lord ; and the earth was to melt with fervent heat.   Thus spake the prophets and seers of ancient times, and for these events have many waited long adown the centuries. Great physical events have been anticipated ; and some have even proclaimed their near approach in different ages. They have looked for a visible appearing of the Lord upon the clouds of the firmament, and so have understood the New Heavens to mean great changes in what is spoken of as the stellar world. They know not any Heavens but what are known to Science, and understand not the nature of Heavens nor their purpose. They have anticipated outward signs and physical wonders, and so have imagined that the Lord tarried, not knowing that Heavens are spiritual states, and that all the phenomena predicted upon the Heavens had a purely spiritual meaning.

But the New Heavens foretold by the prophets and seers were new spiritual conditions which were to environ the world as the outcome of the Redemption accomplished by the Divine Love through the Sin-offering borne by the Christ-Soul. They were the new creations resulting from the blotting-out of the Handwriting upon the magnetic plane, that sad and terrible history written upon that plane by the children of this world when they fell into the states of Soul experience which resulted in the fashioning of the Animal Kingdom known to Science. They were the new spiritual conditions effected upon the magnetic plane, that powerfully reflecting circulus with which the Planet is environed and through which the light from the Heavens of the Sun is broken upon the Earth ; for even the Sun is not what he seemeth to be to the general multitude, nor what he is said to be by Physical Science. And the magnetic plane of the Earth is not what it has been thought. By nature it was entirely spiritual and always able to reflect the glory of the Sun. Its elements were of the very nature of the elements out of which the photosphere of the Sun was formed, and so were beautiful in their ministry unto all the children of the Earth and made manifest the Glory of the Divine Love.   And that wonderful plane whose appearance in its perfect condition was like a sea of crystal wherein were reflected the beautiful spectrum of the Elohim, the seven sacred colours born of the sevenfold Holy Spirit of the Eternal One, the reflection of the Divine Rainbow which the Seer saw around the Throne of the Eternal, contained within itself the elements which constitute true Heavens, and so had its own Heavens wherein the Divine Love was made manifest and the Divine Wisdom interpreted.   But all these elements became changed in their nature and function when the Planet moved away from the Ecliptic or Divine Kingdom wherein it once always moved.   They became so greatly changed that they could no longer receive from the Divine Kingdom the magnetic currents which flowed through that kingdom to sustain the various planetary systems upon it, and, as a result the whole of the magnetic plane became the scene of the most irresponsive elements which gradually lost their own beautiful spiritual magnetic nature and finally became fixed in the Heavens of the Planet.   And when that took place the magnetic plane ceased to respond to any of the attractions from the Divine Kingdom, since only that which is in nature spiritual can respond to the magnetic rays flowing from the Divine Kingdom.   And when the magnetic plane lost its true spiritual power and so failed to respond to and attract the magnetic rays flowing from the Divine Kingdom, it more and more lost the power over all the elements which were within the circulus by which they were regulated in their operations and made to generate orders of life.   The elements known as the metals once belonged to that circulus.   The waters of the great deep were within the circulus, and belonged to what was called the upper and lower firmaments.   The gold and silver, as they are now called, were of the most beautiful elements within the circulus and had a ministry within the magnetic plane correspondingly beautiful.   The less beautiful but powerfully magnetic elements from which some of the quartz mountains were formed, likewise belonged to the circulus, and performed an important service in the distribution of the light broken upon the Planet's magnetic plane from the Divine Kingdom. And the gems with their marvellous colours and inherent distributing power of the magnetic rays, were also within the circulus and were spiritual elements used in the generation and evolution of Souls. But they were all changed in their nature and magnetic conditions, and most of them became non-volatile and fixed. And when the magnetic plane could no longer hold them, they gradually came down to the other planes and became a girdle of adamant around the Planet-Soul, placing her in bondage, depriving her of the beautiful stream from the Divine Kingdom by which her life was nourished, and making her a captive within her own once glorious system. And thus were her glorious Heavens destroyed.

The history of the Earth since that epoch has been one of unspeakable sadness. The mistake made in moving away from the Divine Kingdom had not only grievous issues for the Planet-Soul but likewise for all the children who were upon the various planes ; for the changed magnetic conditions gradually affected them. And though the beautiful ministry of the Christ-Souls helped them to keep upon The Bethlehem or lower Spiritual Heavens generated by the Divine Love to be the home of all who were rising out of the creature Kingdom into the life of the Human Kingdom, yet were they unable to resist the strange influences of the changed magnetic plane, and so lost their own spiritual power as they left The Bethlehem for the magnetic plane where they were dwellers for long ages.

But here we have to speak of the creation of New Heavens, without which the Redemption of the Planet as a spiritual system could not be accomplished. For not only was the magnetic plane destroyed through the loss of all its spiritual magnetism, but The Bethlehem or lower Spiritual Heavens, was destroyed through the influence of the magnetic plane, with the result that no communication could be made to those who had gone down from it on to the magnetic plane. And until the destroyed Heavens of the Planet were either restored or new Heavens were generated from the Divine Kingdom, no spiritual communication could reach the Souls who were old enough in spiritual experience to receive from the Angelic Kingdom. And so for many long ages there was no communication direct to the Soul from the Angelic Kingdom, with the result that the Souls who once knew and understood not only life upon the Angelic Kingdom but even that of the Divine Kingdom, went down into an ever deepening spiritual darkness in which all their inherent light became lost to them because the non-spiritual conditions made its shining impossible. And if so much happened unto them, how much greater was the darkness that overtook those who had not attained even to the realisation within themselves of the light broken from the Angelic Kingdom, for with them the light had been of an objective order though entirely spiritual. They were little children in the great school of life upon the Heavens. They were only in the elementary Kingdom, though some of them had almost passed beyond that stage into the advanced Kingdom where the Human Soul-Estate was to be fully realised in the Angelic Life. When they went down into the darkness they had no inherent light as the outcome of inward realisations, because their spiritual evolution had not carried them far enough to enable them to have attained to such a blessed state ; so they went away into the terrible forms known as the first Saurians and were followed thither by the Christ-Souls.

And when it was perceived by the Divine Love that unless the Planet could have her Heavens restored all the Souls upon her Planes must become lost, the Divine Love commanded the Planet to pause in her course and make her magnetic plane divide and receive such an inrush of magnetic forces from the Divine Kingdom that the Christ-Souls were quickened and attracted again towards the Spiritual Heavens, whilst the Planet-Soul herself was nourished. It was that commanding of the Sun to stand still whose story is still found in the Hebrew Scriptures, a story rejected now by nearly all earnest students because misunderstood and misinterpreted. It was the beginning of the fashioning of the second order of Heavens for the the Planet, the beginning of the present magnetic plane and spiritual circulus by which the light is broken upon the Heavens of the Planet, though it was also almost destroyed when the firmaments were both changed at the periods known in history as the Deluge and the Ice-age.

The New Heavens then begun, though intercepted for long ages, were continued when the Ice-age passed away. They were continued sphere by sphere as the outcome of the Divine Love operating in the Heavens of the Sun and changing for a time the action of the magnetic rays so that what is now known as the Photosphere of the Sun out from which are beheld by the Astronomers to proceed great streams of magnetic currents, became the generator of the Heavens of the Earth. And by means of these beautiful streams of spiritual magnetic forces the New Heavens were generated for the Earth. They were Heavens suited to the Earth's condition then, and such as could be refined more and more as the Souls upon the Earth rose from spiritual states unto higher spiritual states. They were beautiful, though they were not so refined in their essences as the Earth's original Heavens. They rose from sphere to sphere as the Divine Love operated upon them, each sphere providing for the children who rose into it. And had the magnetic plane of the Earth not had impressed upon it the sad and awful history of the descent of the children of this system into the unspeakable conditions which arose as the outcome of the Planet's mistake in moving away from the Divine Kingdom or Ecliptic, and which led to the fashioning of the Animal Kingdom known to Science, the Earth would have been restored to her pristine spiritual glory untold ages ago. But the condition of her magnetic plane and the state of her children prevented the Divine Love from effecting her Redemption to her Ancient State. And it was not until the magnetic plane was purified in its elements that the Redemption became possible. And the purifying of that plane was the work of the Divine Love through Him who has been spoken of as the Christ-Soul, and those who were of the Christhood Order who were given a share in the service of the Divine Love as He bore the heavy burden of the Cross in performing the work of the Sin-offering.

The New Heavens have now been fashioned, for the magnetic plane of the Planet has again been changed so that all those Souls who once knew the Divine Love and the Divine Wisdom may rise up on the Spiritual Heavens to behold the glory of the Divine Love there made manifest, and to hear those things which they must needs know to enable them to rise up into the Estate of Christhood. The New Heavens are with us now for all who are able to live the Redeemed Life. They are sending forth their blessed influence unto all who are truly aspiring to that life. They are influencing unto the ways and life of goodness all who have pure motives. They are now making it become more easy to do good and less difficult to eschew evil. They are changing the old conditions around us so that their presence and power are made manifest. The old order changeth and the New Order is being ushered in because the ever Blessed One whose Name is Love hath fashioned for the Earth New Heavens wherein dwelleth righteousness and peace.   J. TODD FERRIER.

THE CREATION.
II.
THE GENERATION OF LIFE.

When the Firmament was finished wherein the waters above and below were contained, and the inner Firmament was full of the glory of day[1] *so that the outer Firmament was also illumined even until the outermost spheres were reached which were contiguous*

---

[1] *The Heavens within the Planet-Soul illumined from the Divine Sun.*

unto the Night, the land[2] of the outer spheres was commanded to bring forth fruit after the various orders of the spiritual elements out of which it had been generated.

And the land of the outer spheres brought forth abundantly fruit of the fairest kind, flowering trees and plants whose forms and beauty showed forth the Wisdom of the Divine Love.[3]

And when the land had brought forth its fruits, then were also the Seas commanded to bring forth abundantly; and the upper and lower seas brought forth after their kind,[4] creatures of the deep sea and of the air,[5] creatures whose forms were beautiful as they grew up before the Divine and performed their functions within the outer spheres.

Then did the Eternal One behold how good was the life generated upon the Earth, in land and sea and air, and He commanded that the Earth should now bring forth living creatures upon her other spheres also;[6] and the Earth generated the Creature-Souls after the various orders of her Heavens,[7] and made them to pass through the beautiful forms within the spheres of her outer Firmament, until they could dwell within the inner Heavens as the children of the Divine Love.[8]

---

[2] *Not land as understood to-day, which is fixed, but the elements which were known as land.*

[3] *The Vegetable Kingdom as it was originally.*

[4] *The upper and lower seas were the atmosphere and the waters now known as the Seas which also were in the circulus.*

[5] *Creatures like the most beautiful birds and the most beautiful semi-fluidic forms, but then all in a perfect state.*

[6] *The generation of the creature Kingdom.*

[7] *The various Orders of Souls.*

[8] *The various Orders of Souls though all of the Heavens of the Planet, were to pass through the beautiful Vegetable and Creature Kingdoms learning the Divine Wisdom as there found expressed, and thus perform the elementary stages of their evolution before the Divine Love.*

WHEN THE EARTH MELTETH.

WITH the appearing of the New Heavens the Earth was to melt with fervent heat. The old conditions were to dissolve and new conditions were to appear. The very elements were to become changed until the Earth would be as if fashioned anew. Then were to appear the signs of the coming of the Son of Man upon the clouds of the Heavens—the differentiation between what was truly good and what was evil and made for evil, the Divine Judgment upon all evil things and all who loved them as the true way of life.

The melting of the Earth with fervent heat, the dissolving of the Elements, the appearance upon the Earth of new conditions, the coming of the Son of Man upon the clouds of the Heavens, the separation of the good from the evil in the world and the Divine Judgment upon all evil-workers, have been understood and interpreted in an outward, historic manner, rather than as an inward, spiritual experience of the Soul. Everything has had given to it a literal and physical and personal meaning until the true spiritual meaning is lost even to those who profess to read and understand the prophetic teachings and interpret the signs unto the people. The New Heaven and the New Earth are even written and spoken of in a physical sense. And the coming of the Son of Man has been looked for as the appearing of a person—*a man*, rather than the coming of the Divine Love and the ways of life which are born of that Love, into the hearts and lives of all who have desired to be good and beautiful in their ways, but who have been led into the wrong paths through wrong views of life and the terribly wrong and evil conditions amid which they have found themselves. And thus men and women have been led to look outwardly for the signs and portents of the New Heavens and the New Earth with the coming of the Son of Man upon the clouds, rather than inwardly to the sphere of the Soul where all the portents of the coming of the Divine Love must ever be found, portents whose very signs bear the image of that love in greater or less degree, according to the fulness of the Divine Realisation within the Soul. They have expected the Son of Man to come to repeat in outward history what they believe the outward history of the Master's life was when the Christhood and the Redeemed Life were made manifest and interpreted through Him. Nay, they even expect that He will appear amidst all the evil conditions which still prevail, in the character of a judge to give judgments against wrongs and evils and sins, and set up a Divine Kingdom upon these outer planes where He will reign in person for ever; instead of looking for a glorious spiritual manifestation of that beautiful life which He interpreted and the blessed Estate of the Christhood which He made manifest, within the lives of all who believe in the Divine Parousia or coming of the Lord with the consequent natural results in Society. For when the Earth is said to melt with fervent heat as the outcome of the New Heavens, we are to understand spiritual things and not physical, inward realisations with corresponding outward interpretations, and not mere outward phenomena; for the melting is within the life through the fervent heat of the Divine Love as that Love is realised within the Soul as a conscious and blessed possession, a Divine Inheritance infinite'y more valuable to the Soul than the possession of all the world—or the physical system with its sense-powers, riches and joys. It is the melting of all the elements within the Soul's sphere which are opposed to the ways of the Divine Life through the action of the Divine Love, and the refashioning of these elements into pure spiritual substances and things bearing the qualities of the Soul and the image of the Divine ways. It is the melting of all the adverse conditions in the world which militate against the true growth of the spiritual life, and the replacing of them with conditions which will aid all who are seeking to be pure and noble to realise that beautiful Redeemed Life implied in the Redemption. It is the taking away of the old barriers erected between people and people, race and race, nation and nation, and the bringing of them all nearer together in sympathy, compassion and love, until at last they will all come to realise how closely related they are, even as the various members of one great family. It is the passing away under the influences of nobler feelings and more generous sentiments of the merely local and physical and historical ideas of life which have cramped every beautiful and spiritual feeling and purpose, narrowed down the Soul's vision of life and service, and giving entirely wrong directions to the mind in its outlook and purposes, and the restitution of the true spiritual view of all Souls in their relationship one to another as the children of the Heavenly Father, and their place in this world as a Spiritual System.

In the coming of the Lord upon the Clouds of the Heavens the Earth was to be renewed in her life ; her waste places were to produce the helpful things of life for her children ; her wilderness was to blossom like the rose, so that her children would rejoice even unto singing the songs of Zion ; her desert places were to become even as pools of refreshing water for all who had to cross them. What is that renewing of the Earth but the awakening of so many Souls to seek into the Redeemed Life and the beautiful Estate of Christhood wherein the Divine Love becomes realised and the Divine Wisdom known ? What were the waste places of Jerusalem which were to become so changed as to produce everything good and helpful, if they were not the unfruitful conditions amid which the children had to live, conditions where spiritual impoverishment are only too manifest even now ? What was the terrible wilderness wherein the wolf made his den and the lion and cockatrice their lairs, and where Souls were attacked who sought to rise out of the evil conditions to find the path leading out of the wilderness into the City of Zion, that they might there find the Angelic Manna and the Streams of Life? If it was not that awful system of the materialisation of the Divine Mysteries whereby the Divine Love was veiled and misrepresented, the Divine Wisdom turned into mere meaningless forms and shibboleths, by which the Soul was deprived of its true nourishment, and kept weak and dark ? And what meant its blossoming even like the rose if it were not the new life infused into the teachings which had been veiled, the awakening of those Communities who should have known the beautiful meaning of the blossoming rose of Sharon, to realise in some measure that the true spiritual life is a Redeemed Life crowned with the inheritance of the consciousness of the Divine Love and the indwelling Divine Presence—which the blossoming rose of Sharon means ? And what was the desert-place into which even the Christ-Soul went, and where it is said that He fed the hungering multitudes upon " five barley loaves and two small fishes," if it were not that non-spiritual condition of the whole world where the five loaves of daily bread alone could be found—the sense-life in its five-fold aspect ; and the two small fishes of the Divine Love and Divine Wisdom which were so changed in their representation that they had not only lost their true nature and glorious fulness, but had been changed into mean things through misinterpretation and materialisation ? And what may be the meaning of such a desert becoming pools of refreshing waters, if not the changing of the whole spiritual outlook for the Soul, and the wells of living waters springing up within it even unto everlasting life or that Divine State when the Soul is crowned with the Divine ?

J. Todd Ferrier.

THE CREATION.

III.

THE GENERATION OF MANKIND.

The generation of the Creature-Souls within the Heavens[1] of the Planet was followed by the generation of the Human Race. The Eternal One thus spake unto Elohim :—" We will now make mankind to image us in all their ways, so that they will understand the Wisdom of the Divine Love expressed in the Great Deep, in the Heavens of the Divine, and within the Kingdoms of the Earth.[2]

And the Elohim fashioned mankind, after the image of the Divine fashioned they them, and made them to bear their own likeness,[3] even the likeness of the Divine Love, through the inbreathing of the Divine Spirit of Elohim.

And Elohim made mankind to have the power over the Kingdoms of the Earth through their having gained dominion over these kingdoms as they passed through them in their evolution before the Divine, learning the Wisdom expressed in these Kingdoms.[4]

And the Eternal One beheld that what was done by Elohim was very good : So He fashioned for mankind a Garden called by Him the Garden of Eden,[5] that mankind might till it and eat its precious

---

[1] The Heavens of the Earth indicate the true nature of the Soul as a spiritual organism.

[2] To fashion mankind from the simple spiritual organism into the complex being capable of receiving the Divine consciousness and so to understand all the Mysteries of Creation, and thus, as a microcosm of the Divine, to reflect the Divine Love and Wisdom.

[3] To bear the likeness of Elohim is to have all the Divine Tinctures reflected within the System of the Soul.

[4] To have gained power and dominion over the various Kingdoms of the Earth through which the Soul passed in its evolution before the Divine was to have acquired a knowledge of the Divine Wisdom expressed in the life of these Kingdoms.

[5] The Garden of Eden was the Angelic Heavens from whose fruits and by whose ministry all Souls were nourished, and the tilling of which by man meant the cultivation of the Angelic life.

fruits and know. of the Divine Wisdom expressed in the generation of the Soul to bear the likeness of Elohim.

And when all the generations of the Earth [6] *were accomplished, then would be the entering into the Rest of the Eternal One,* [7] *the Sabbath of the Lord God, the Fulfilment of the Sevenfold Spirit of Elohim in the crown of the perfect Life.*

THE OPENING OF THE HEAVENS.

O Infinite and Ever Blessed One, who alone openeth the door of the Heavens of Thy dwelling that all who come unto Thee to know of Thy Love and to see how Thy Wisdom maketh itself manifest, may find the true Path unto Life Eternal; grant unto us that we may find the door open, and enter in to partake of the Marriage Supper of the Lamb. May we know the joy of Thy service, the light of Thy Countenance, the perfect healing of Thy Love, the union which maketh us one with Thee and Thy Saints in the Life Everlasting.

How gracious Thy Love is; how full and beautiful in its healing power! Thou changest the bitter waters of Marah and makest of them an Elim through the healing Branch from the Tree of Life. Through Thy servant Moses Thou causest living waters to flow from the Mount of God, for he toucheth it with the Rod of Thy Power. In answer to the prayers of Thy children amid the wilderness, Thou dost send them their daily portion, even the Hidden Manna of Thy Holy Wisdom, the Heavenly Bread. We would lift up our Souls to Thee in the service of Praise; our lives would make melody continually; our song would be of Thee. Amen and Amen.

---

[6] *When the Human Soul was perfected, and so all Souls.*

[7] *The Divine Rest or Sabbath of the Lord is that state in which the Soul becomes One with the Divine which is spoken of in the West as The Atonement, and in the East as Nirvana.*

THE NEW INTERPRETATION.

CXXXIV.

THE EVOLUTION OF THE SOUL.

THE Evolution of the Soul which was intercepted when the children of this World left The Bethlehem (or that Spiritual State in which they were when they dwelt upon the lower Spiritual Heavens) and went down into the conditions which resulted in the present Animal Kingdom, but which is now once more beginning, will now continue until all the children of the Planet at present in the Human Kingdom reach unto the Angelic Kingdom, and all who are in the Creature Kingdom suffering in their great limitations shall come up into the Human Kingdom, and even all who are yet far down in the lower Animal Kingdom shall rise up into nobler form and ways with better conditions for them to evolve in as they make their way up to the Human Kingdom. For the condition of the Planet is now more favourable unto the evolution of the Soul as a Spiritual entity than it has been since its beautiful magnetic plane was destroyed, through the creation of the New Heavens and the purification of the Astral Kingdom. The fashioning of the New Heavens and the cleansing of the magnetic plane will issue in the uprising of all the Souls who once ministered unto the children of the Planet and aided them in their evolution, to once more seek the realisation of the life which they then knew ; and, through the manifestation of the Redeemed Life by them, shall all the children of the Planet be gathered out of the animal states in which so many of them live, to seek unto the life of purity and goodness. And when they reach the Redeemed Life in which the whole being is made pure from the innermost sphere to the outermost, all the Creature Kingdom will also rise up out of the fearful evils associated with the bondage in which they are now as captives in a land of oppression and woe.

J. TODD FERRIER.

THE NEW INTERPRETATION.

CXXXV.

THE EVOLUTION OF THE SOUL.

WHEN the children of the Planet were dwelling upon the various planes prior to the descent of the Planet into fixed conditions, they were in the several stages of the Soul upon the Human Kingdom. They were scattered over the seven planes according to the various stages of their spiritual growth upon the Human Kingdom ; and they were, therefore, all performing their evolution in different degree through what has been called The Seven Ages of Man. A few had reached the seventh plane, and were almost ready to pass up into the Angelic life through the realisation of the Divine Love —an experience which came to the Soul through a more intense polarisation of all its magnetic forces towards the Divine Love by which the life was brought into a more sensitive spiritual state so that there could be communicated unto the Soul, within its own system, the meaning of the Divine Love upon the Angelic Kingdom. These were the Souls unto whom the writers in the prophetic books referred when they spoke of the beauty of the daughters of Jerusalem ; for they were the crown of the life of the Planet at the time, full of the grace of true spiritual beauty upon the Human Kingdom, beautiful in form, beautiful in mind, beautiful in heart, and so beautiful in all the ways of life. They were the Souls unto whom the Prophets appealed to again adorn themselves with the gracious ornaments and garments that they wore before they went away into captivity ; for the garments were the raiment of pure ways and affections, and the adorments the jewels, precious and beautiful, of all the graces which they had acquired on their way from the childhood of their experience until they had entered into the higher conscious state upon the last sphere of the Human Kingdom. They were the Souls unto whom the Christ referred when He spoke of the disaster which had befallen the once Holy City of Jerusalem when the stranger or evil condition had carried away into captivity all the daughters of music and made of them servants and slaves to do their will, the beautiful Souls who had been made the instruments of every evil thing, the object of the evil forces which had arisen within the City. They were the Souls of whom the Seer wrote that He saw them rise up out of the sea wherein the Beast and Death ruled (the beast of the degraded Sense-life, and the spiritual death resulting from that degradation), and ascend unto the first Heavens where they were nourished through the ministry of all who had risen out of their graves within the City, even the Saints or Christ-Souls who had been buried therein.

And we may see in the great awakening of Souls to seek unto the way of the Spiritual World for the Divine Testimony of the reality of the spiritual nature of the Soul and its persistence through the ever changing conditions of experience, their craving for a manifestation of the reality of the Spiritual World and the true realisation of unselfish and beautiful love in all the ways of life, crowned with a beautiful ministry which they like to think of as truly Angelic, a new meaning, and one burdened with the profoundest significance for the Soul. We may behold in the great Spiritualistic Movement which is only yet in its infancy and has not been yet able to rise fully out of the conditions by which all spiritual things in this present world are influenced, the phenomenal and materialistic spirit, but which will soon take unto itself ways still more truly spiritual as all the Souls upon the seventh plane purify themselves on every sphere of their experience, the re-awakening of the First House on the seventh plane of the Planet's children, and their return from bondage. And we may behold in that movement a very great manifestation of the Soul seeking for the sure and certain testimony of its own distinctive spiritual selfhood—a testimony far surpassing anything that can possibly issue from a mere intellectual and philosophical statement concerning the reality of the Soul or the creedal impositions of priestly hierarchies; a testimony which, though not of the highest spiritual order, because it is yet too nearly allied to the physical or sense-life spheres, is nevertheless one which enables those who require the outward testimony, to receive confirmation of their inmost spiritual hopes and cravings, and, when purely and prayerfully sought and received, becomes a means whereby the spiritual nature is strengthened, hope is kept like a gentle fire burning within the Sanctuary of the Soul, and encouragement is given unto the life to pursue the pure and true path by which alone the Soul can rise up of its own accord in response to the more spiritual magnetic attraction, to receive from the *real Spiritual Heavens—i.e., the Angelic Heavens*—the teachings which are so essential to the true growth of the Soul, unto the likeness of the Divine Love.

The manifestation of the Soul seeking for the testimony of its own nature and persistence, for the comfort which such an assurance gives to life, and, as in the case of many, for very real and true guidance along the paths of life, is the sure testimony of the reawakening of the Souls of many of those children of the Planet who had reached the seventh plane, and the new beginning of the Soul in its evolution towards the perfect Spiritual Human Estate. They are the children of the Eighth House on the outer spheres who had almost reached the Ninth House when they would have passed upwards into the Angelic Heavens to enter upon the realisation within themselves of the Divine Love. And with them may be found the children of the Seventh House who had not advanced so far as to be able to dispense with *the outward visible testimonies*, whose life was still partly lived in the objective sphere, and unto whom visible phenomena were essential. For in the new Spiritualistic Movement may be discerned two distinct orders of Souls, or rather Souls in various degrees of development, those who only seek after the spiritual things to be received by means of communication, and those who are anxious to have visible manifestations.

Unless the new beginning of the evolution of the Soul be environed from the Spiritual Heavens through the loving ministry of all who are able to rise on to these

Heavens to receive true Illumination, its progress will be retarded by those who feel after the visible manifestations, and demand them in the mistaken belief that they are the true evidence of Spiritual Realities, the real testimonies of the Soul's nature, the true way along which the beautiful spiritual yearnings and purposes of the Soul should go, and the path to true spiritual progress in experience.

J. TODD FERRIER.

THE REDEEMED EARTH.

The vision of St. John which he beheld in the Day of the Lord when he was lifted up in the Spirit :—

Behold there appeared New Heavens and a New Earth, when the first Heavens and Earth were passed away ; and in them was found no Sea whose waters were full of the bitterness of Death.

And the Beloved beheld the Holy City, the New Jerusalem, as one who had come down from God arrayed in the wedding garments of all who are the Bride of Christhood.

And there was heard a great voice in the Heavens, saying, " Behold ! The Tabernacle of God is within man, that He may dwell with him and be his God. And God Himself will wipe away all tears from his eyes, so that there will be no more any sorrow, nor crying, nor pain, nor death ; for all these things shall have passed away."

And the Beloved One who sat upon the Throne of the Heavens said unto His Servant, " Behold ! the Lord maketh all things new. He writeth upon the Heavens and upon the Earth those things which are of the Faithful and True One, the Alpha and the Omega, the Arche and the Amen ; for He giveth unto all the Heavens and the Earth of the fulness of the Fountain of the Waters of Life."

CXXXVI.

THE EVOLUTION OF THE SOUL.

THE great Spiritualistic Movement of the present time which is the new beginning of the evolution of the Soul, is not confined to those circles known as Spiritualistic, but has extended also unto other centres wherein its expression is less accentuated though none the less real. It may be witnessed in the great trend of thought towards a more spiritual basis as the foundation of all things, a more spiritual interpretation of the things which hitherto have been regarded as physical, a more spiritual feeling amongst people towards each other, a more spiritual conception of the relation of man to man, a more spiritual view of the relation between the various orders and races of mankind, and a more spiritual outlook upon all the orders within the circle of life. For with the awakening of the Souls who once knew the meaning of spiritual things, who understood the inter-relation of all the orders and races of the Planet's children from the outermost sphere up and inward to the seventh plane, who knew the various orders and races in their various stages of development, and understood the life they had to live and the kind of ministry which they most required, there has taken place a great forward movement to restore the true and pure conditions necessary for the true evolution of the Soul. The spiritual movement now witnessed in the noble endeavours of many to purify the conditions of the national and social life, to remove the stumbling-blocks out of the way of the children of the Heavenly Father, to close up the avenues of evil by which so many are ensnared, to change the conditions amid which they live so that it may be more easy for them to do good and more difficult to do wrong, to turn the thoughts of men and women away from the ways of the mere outward and sense-life into ways which lead to the attainment of true life within the heart and Soul, to change the habits of the people and the customs of society and the whole trend of

the National life into pure and true ways in which compassion will reign, pity be made universally manifest to
man and creature, and the Divine Love shine through the
noble and uplifting and inspiring conduct of all—in that
movement may be found the expression of the awakening
of those Souls who were the ministers unto the Children
of the Planet upon the outer planes.

And there are other aspects of this new beautiful
spiritual movement and service in which may be detected
the Souls who ministered upon the inner planes unto the
Souls whose ministry was upon the outer planes, and unto
those Souls who had risen almost unto the Angelic Kingdom.   For in the ministry wherein the Divine Mysteries
are set forth in various presentations according to the
requirements of those unto whom the ministry is being
performed, and the interpretation of these profound Soul
and Planet histories in all their spiritual and Divine
relationship, there may be beheld the work of those Souls
who came forth from the Kingdom of the Divine Love and
Wisdom, who knew that Love through inward realisation
upon the Spiritual and Celestial Heavens and understood
its beautiful purpose towards all the Children of the
Planet, who understood that Love in its nature and manifestation, and knew it to be ever pure, tender and compassionate, who likewise knew that Wisdom of the Father
as expressed and made manifest upon the Divine Kingdom, because the Light of the Eternal Spirit was within
them.

The new spiritual movement may be now understood
in its most manifold variety, each department being an
essential part of the whole, from the innermost interpretations of the sublime Teachings of the Master to the outer
planes where the way is being prepared for the coming of
the Golden Age when all the children of the Planet shall
be living the Redeemed Life, all the children of Israel be
gathered together into their own land—The Estate of
Christhood, all the children of the Moon find their own
Celestial Home once more, all the children of Venus

return unto their long lost beautiful spiritual spheres, and all the Planets have their Ancient Estates restored unto them.

Then will indeed The Redemption be complete and the Sons of God sing for very joy; then shall the Holy City of Jerusalem know no more any evil, nor the sorrow and darkness born from it; for the Divine Love will be its Everlasting Light, and the Eternal One its abiding Temple.

J. TODD FERRIER.

THE CITY OF CHRISTHOOD.

The Vision given to the Beloved One when He was lifted upon the Mountain of the Lord:—

The Holy City of the Lord[1] descended from God unto the Earth.

Within her burned the Seven Sacred Fires of Elohim, clothing her in the Glory of God.

Her light was as a Jasper-stone whose facets are clear as crystal, and was therefore most precious.

Around her a wall was raised, exceeding high, and she had Twelve Gates, and at each Gate an Angel whose name was that of the House of Israel; three Gates looked towards the East and three towards the West, three towards the North and three towards the South.

And the wall of the City was built upon twelve foundations named after the Lamb of God, and they were the Apostles of the Lord[2].

And the City lieth as a square, whose length and breadth and height are equal, the measurement being that of a full-grown man—i.e., of an Angel[3].

---

[1] *The Soul in the state of Celestial Christhood.*

[2] *The twelve foundations are the twelve states through which the Soul passes in its true evolution as it is being built up into a Celestial System, and these states are as twelve Apostles proclaiming the coming of the Christhood.*

[3] *The City was the measure of a full-grown Soul, and a full-grown Soul is an Angel of the Lord.*

And the walls[4] of the City were of Jasper; but the City itself was built of pure gold [5], transparent as glass.

And the foundations[6] of the wall of the City were garnished with every kind of precious stone—Jasper, Sapphire, Chalcedony, Emerald, Sardonyx, Sardius, Chrysolyte, Beryl, Topaz, Chrysoprasus, Jacinth, and Amethyst.

And the twelve Gates were as twelve Pearls, each Gate being one perfect Pearl.[7] And the City had no more any earthly Temples, because the Eternal One was the Overshadowing Presence and Temple, and the Lamb was its worship.[8]

And the City required no more another Sun to lighten it, nor Moon to shine at night[9]; for the Glory of God lightened it through the worship of the Lamb.

And the Nations of them who are of the Redeemed Ones shall walk in the light of it; and the Kings of the East[10] shall bring the Glory of the Lord unto it.

Its Gates shall not be shut at all by day, and there is no night in it.

---

[4] *The Walls are the fourfold life built upon the Divine foundations or spiritual states, whose great height implies the Celestial Estates of the City; for they are built of Jasper, pure spiritual being.*

[5] *The City encompassed from the Divine is built upon the Divine Love—the pure Seed of the spiritual alchemist.*

[6] *The twelve precious stones were the various states in their reflective condition. Each stone representing a state wherein the Light of the Elohim was broken and reflected, each tint having a significance in indicating the progress of the Soul in its evolution.*

[7] *The twelve Gates were the twelve labours which have to be accomplished by the Soul now in its fallen condition, and the Pearl the emblem of conquest.*

[8] *The outward forms of Religion grow less and less until they cease to have any place in that spiritual system where the Divine Love is the Light and Love of the Soul.*

[9] *i.e. It required no outward lights or knowledges born from the plane of the mind.*

[10] *The Celestial Souls who were the Kings who came unto the land of the Christhood, and who Glory only in the Divine Life and Worship, which is the Glory also of the Lord.*

THE HERALD OF THE CROSS.

Vol v. New Series. February, 1909. No. 2.

THE TREE OF LIFE.

And the Angel showed unto me a river of pure clear Water of Life, which reflected the Light of Heaven like a perfect crystal as it proceeded from the Throne of God and of the Lamb.

In the midst of the stream of it, and upon each side, there grew the Tree of Life whose fruits were twelve, each in its season ; and whose leaves were for the healing of the people.

And wheresoever the river floweth there shall be no more anything accursed : but the Throne of God and of the Lamb shall be there, and all His servants shall enter into His service.

And they shall behold His Face, and the sign of His name shall be upon their foreheads.

There shall be no night there in which the light of the candle is needed ; for wheresoever the river floweth there shall be the Light of Life which proceedeth from the Lord as their Sun : and they shall reign evermore with Him.

And the Angel said unto me, " These Sayings are from the Faithful and True One who hath sent His Angel to speak of them unto His servants."

" Behold ! He cometh."

ST. JOHN.

SHALL EVIL INDEED TRIUMPH?

"Behold, I create good and not evil, saith the Lord!"

THE Licensing Bill is said to be dead, and that with it
have fallen many hopes of fair women and brave
men. Many hearts beat happily at the prospect of one of
the appalling evils in our midst having its power to work
mischief greatly lessened, and the paths made clearer for
the realisation of that blessed day in which the terrible
Drink Curse would be swept from the land. They rejoiced
in the great endeavour to break the power of the unspeakable evil, and beheld in it the prophecy of yet greater
things towards the final overthrow of all the false and
evil forces associated with the Drink Curse.

But for the moment the enemy of sobriety, purity and
nobler living has triumphed. The awful evil has made
manifest its powers to prevent the coming of good. It
has defied the approaching dawn of a more beautiful age
for the lives of all who suffer from its destroying influences through having its dark and terrible forces
marshalled in secret to oppose the oncoming light whose
shining will make manifest unto all who are seeking
righteousness and goodness and purity, the unspeakable
nature of its work upon the individual, the Society and
the Nation, and cause it and its evil works to melt away
before its illumining rays and purifying power. The
Drink Trade has raised its voice in great sayings full of
the subtlety born of its own evil, and claimed for itself the
position of being a minister of good unto the race. It
has breathed forth threatenings against those whom it
could not otherwise hope to influence; and in its cunning
and false pretentions, its arrogance and mock compassion,
pity and religious feeling, has spoken blasphemously
against the works of the Most High. It has laid claim to
be an essential part of the fabric of the State, though all
its work is that of undermining the life of the people
within every sphere by its insiduous, alluring and miraging
system. It has laid claim to contribute largely to the
well-being of the people, to be a nourisher and healer of
their lives, even whilst it smites all who are deceived by

its allurements and covers the land with its slain ; for even as it poses before the whole world as the truest friend of man, its whole purpose is to enrich itself at his expense, as it robs its prey of all true wealth, nobility of spirit, purity of desire, and peacefulness of disposition. It has even professed to be anxious to raise altars of spiritual service where the Soul might find true nourishment and refreshing, whilst it has covered the land with the altars of its abomination upon which thousands and tens of thousands of helpless victims have been laid low as sacrifices unto its power.

Was there any marvel that it opposed the noble endeavour to undo something of the evil it had wrought ? Need we wonder at the awakening of all its latent forces for mischief and the marshalling of these against all who put forth effort, who have seen its wickedness and have given themselves in service to deliver the nation from its fearful thraldom ? To behold it in all its hideousness and witness its ghastly work is to know that its name is DIABOLUS, the dark and fearful Soul-destroyer, the enemy of every good and pure way, the defamer of every thing noble, the prostituter of every spiritual power within man and therefore the opposer of everything truly noble and divine. Like the beast from the abyss, whose agent it is, the whole Traffic in the Drink Trade warreth against the Saints of the Most High.

But the victory is not always with the powers which appear greatest ; nor the battle given to those who seem strongest, and whose armies are most scattered over the plain. And so with this gigantic evil in its coming overthrow. For there are armies contending against it on behalf of the children of the Heavenly Father which the Trade beholds not and which it reckons not of. There are unseen Hosts at work, though the lowly workers in the outer spheres may not yet have beheld and recognised them, whose work will soon be made manifest in a glorious victory for purity through the abolition of all the fearful conditions out of which the evils in the world are generated. Behold! all ye who are able to see beyond the objective world,

how the Hosts of the Lord cover the planes of the Heavens?
Ye lowly workers in the midst of the evil conditions,
endeavouring to drive back the flood of impurity which
the awful Drink Curse has made to sweep over the land,
open your spiritual eyes and behold who it is who is with
you in this great work! Like the servant of the prophet
we wonder who is fit for these things in face of so great
and powerful and boastful an enemy because our eyes are
holden that we see not the Hosts of the Heavens all
around us. But the morning breaketh. Dawn has come,
the sun soon shall show itself, and no more go down into
the darkness of such a night of spiritual impotence and
ignorance. Before the light the darkness born of the
whole Drink Traffic will flee away, and its curse be no
more known in our midst.   J. TODD FERRIER.

THE VOICE OF ONE CRYING.

*The Angel of the Lord came unto me in the night-
time when the whole City lay asleep, saying unto me,*

*" Arise, and go forth into the desert, and there
await the Word of the Lord which shall come unto
thee." And I arose and went as I was directed into the
desert, and there abode until the Angel of the Lord
should call me forth again.*

*And when the days were fulfilled in which the
Word of the Lord came unto me again to bid me go
and stand before the City and proclaim the message of
the Lord, I was carried away from the desert and was
informed of the Spirit of the Lord concerning those
things appertaining to the Holy City of the Lord and
all the House of Israel who were within the City of
Jerusalem, and also concerning the House of Judah.*

*And when the Spirit of the Lord taught me
concerning the history of the House of Israel and the
captivity of the House of Judah and the destruction of
the City of Jerusalem with all her children within her*

gates, and the desecration of the Holy House built upon Zion and Moriah, then knew I how terrible was the calamity which had befallen all the Souls within the City.

And the Angel of the Lord spake unto me saying, go and stand before the people, crying unto them to seek unto the Lord and Him only, and know the Redemption which He hath wrought out for them by the power of His Love, how He hath made bare His power in the eyes of all who are able to behold it, and to know that it is even He, the Redeemer, the Holy One of Israel.

And I went as He commanded me and called unto all who came before me, the word which the Lord had given unto me to speak, how the City of Jerusalem had fallen a prey to her enemies, and all her children had been carried away captives ; how Judah had fallen, and the whole House of Israel had gone down into Assyria where the oppressors afflicted them, and where the sacred vessels of the Holy House of the Lord were desecrated and put to uses in the service of idols ; and also how the Lord Himself had delivered them all in His Love and opened up the way for their return unto their own land to rebuild the ancient city of Jerusalem, and the Sacred House of the Lord upon Zion and Moriah.

And many who heard the message of the Lord which He gave unto me to speak, returned unto their Ancient Estate in their own land and began to build the walls of the City, and restore the Sacred House of the Lord upon Zion and Moriah that its beautiful service before the Lord might be again established.

And the walls of the City rose day by day as the children of Israel, who were within her gates, laboured to perform the word of the Lord which He had given me to speak unto them.

THE HEALING OF THE PEOPLE.

" In that day shall there be upon the bells of the horses, Holiness unto the Lord."

WHEN the Bells upon the Horses give forth sounds full of truth, echoes of the harmonies of the Heavens, true interpretations of the music of the spheres, then shall the healing of the people be accomplished. For the Horses are the minds of the people, and the Bells upon them are the visions of life which when pure and beautiful, fill the whole world with harmony through their messages of healing. When the Bells upon the Horses have written upon them in letters of Gold, " Holiness unto the Lord," then will the various orders of mankind know that they are indeed all one great family in various stages of Soul-growth, each distinct people representing some distinct stage of growth, each distinct form of Religious manifestation representing the state of spiritual attainment at which each had ceased in their Soul evolution when the whole Human Race went down into those conditions of life now expressed by the present Animal Kingdom. For the Human Race is one organic whole, and should have grown up into a perfect spiritual organism, each unit being a true member and filling his and her own place. And the great spiritual organism known now as Humanity is even as one family before the Divine ; and its Redemption from the terrible evil which overtook it, has been and now is the object of the most beautiful solicitation on the part of the Divine Love. For the perfect life unto which all the Great Religions have pointed is that life which is the fulfilment of the Divine Purpose towards the Human Race—a purpose burdened with the most beautiful realisations of the Divine Love. And so, when the Bells upon the Horses once more bespeak the pure and true life, the noble unselfish service of each order of Souls unto every other order, the beautiful universal spiritual love which is always the accompaniment of inward spiritual realisations and which knows no distinction of Race or people, then will the Divine Purpose find fulfilment as all Souls in their various orders pass up into the glorious realisations.   J. TODD FERRIER.

THE RESTORATION OF ISRAEL.

" O Lord God of Israel, why is this come to pass that there should be one Tribe lacking in Israel to-day ? "

" And I heard the number of them who were sealed, one hundred and forty and four thousand of all the Tribes of the children of Israel."

WHEN the Bells upon the Horses have engraven upon them " Holiness unto the Lord " then will be the Advent of the Lord into the midst of the people. In that day He shall reign upon the Earth ; and the Earth shall be the Lord's, and the fulness thereof, the whole world and they who dwell therein. For in that day there shall no longer be any tribe lacking in Israel. The land no more shall mourn for the captivity of Judah nor weep over the House of Israel ; for the Planet-Soul and all her children shall be as those who are redeemed, and the Christhood Order shall be once more restored unto their priestly office before the Lord, and their service unto the children within the House of Jacob.

The Bells upon the Horses of the House of Israel are the thoughts and purposes of the mind of all those who were of the Christhood Order, who once knew the meaning of Holiness unto the Lord before Ephraim went away after idols and forsook the way of the Lord (the spiritual mind betrayed to seek for its true life amid the outward and materialised spheres). For when all who once knew the sacred meaning of Christhood again behold that vision with their minds and seek unto its full realisations, then will the world behold what that Christhood was which the ever blessed Master made manifest through Jesus, what He meant when He called all who were able to follow Him to become even as He was ; what He intended when He spoke of that oneness with the Father into which He had entered, and to the realisation of which He urged His followers to seek through the bearing of the Cross. And when the world beholds that vision made manifest in the ways and services of all who once knew the Master and the meaning of Christhood ; when it witnesses the meaning of the Redeemed Life unto which He calls all Souls and comes to know it to be one of true purity, goodness and compassion, one in which no evil thing finds any place, one in which only love reigns in beautiful manifestation unto all Souls and all creatures, then shall it come to understand the meaning of the ministry of the Master and the Redemption of which He spake, and, at last, to follow on to know that beautiful life.

When the Bells upon the Horses of the whole House of Israel shall have engraven upon them Holiness unto the Lord so that all the messages which they ring forth are those of goodness and truth, the Glad Tidings of love for all Souls and compassion unto all creatures, the Heavenly Message of Peace upon the Earth through the accomplishment of the Goodwill of God unto all Souls, then also will the Bells upon the Horses of the House of David have engraven upon them the Redeemed Life. For the House of David in which a fountain has been opened up for all sin and uncleanness, is the Soul as it passes through the House of Purification by means of which it realises the Redemption, and is prepared for the service and life of its Lord ; and when the Christhood is beginning to realise itself within the Soul so that the life of the Soul yearns to flow out in what has been spoken of as streams of living waters, the outflowing of goodness and love, then does the state known as the House of David or Purification become a reality in its experience with all its great and profound grief because of the past history written upon the mind ; and when the Soul loves goodness and truth and endeavours to make these manifest in all the spheres of experience, then it not only rings out Messages of Glad Tidings for the whold world, but it makes the Bells upon the Horses of the House of David or state of Purification ring out goodness and love, compassion and healing unto all lives. When the mind has truly attained all that is implied in the expression, " The House of David," then will it be as one of the Redeemed who have passed through the great Tribulation and made white the garments of life in the Blood of the Lamb—the Divine Love flowing into and through the Soul. And when all those who once knew the sacred and holy Estate known as

Christhood have passed through the House of David—
i.e., realised their Redemption—then will the whole world
ring with the glad messages of the Redeemed Life,
messages of healing for the Souls of all creatures, messages resonant with a great and glad hope for all the
children of this world who are in bondage to the sense-
life, and who know not the blessedness of that life which
is born of the Divine Love within the Soul.

J. TODD FERRIER.

LET THE DESOLATE REJOICE!

*The Lord reigneth! Let the Heavens rejoice,
and let the Earth be glad, and all the inhabitants
thereof.*

*Let the desolate no more mourn over the desolation
of Zion, nor cry aloud that the Lord hath forsaken
them; for behold He cometh to restore unto Zion her
ancient heritage, to build again her walls as in the
former times, and fill her Sanctuary with Praise.*

*For the desolation of Zion will be no more when
the Lord returns unto her; her songs will no longer
be those of sorrow in a strange land, and of wailing
because she is fallen; for the Lord will comfort her
through His Presence, even until all her sorrow fleeth
away, and her tears are dried, and her songs become
full of Praise and Gladness.*

*Let all who have been bereft, sorrow no more that
they are as those who are orphaned, and weep no more
in their loneliness because they have been as those who
are forsaken; for the Lord will be a Father unto His
children in their distress that they may know the
loneliness of orphanhood no more, nor be as those
forsaken.*

THE RESTORATION OF JERUSALEM.

*"Break forth into joy, and sing together ye waste places of Jerusalem!
For the Lord hath comforted His people, and is even now working Redemption
for Jerusalem."*

WHEN the Bells upon the Horses have engraven
upon them Holiness unto the Lord, so that they
ring out only messages concerning the way of His holy
Love and Wisdom, and seek only to make those messages
to be realised in the life of the people, then will the true
Songs of Zion once more be sung, the true worship of
Israel be restored, and the temple of the Lord be rebuilt
within the Ancient City of Jerusalem; then will be the
true ingathering of all the children of Israel, and the
restoration of the children of Judah unto their own land,
and the rebuilding of the ancient city even until its later
glory excels the former glory which it enjoyed. Then
will be restored the Temple service of Israel, and the holy
oblation and sacrifice offered unto the Divine Love.

When the Bells upon the Horses or the thoughts within
the minds of all who desire to know and love the Lord,
ring out glad messages of love and peace unto all Souls,
and compassion and pity unto all creatures, then shall
Jerusalem resound with the pure mirth of unalloyed joy;
for the children within her gates shall all be free from
bond-service to the sense-life. They shall no more know
the oppression with which they are now oppressed by all
those elemental conditions born of impure and unlovely
thoughts and ways; for their ways will be those of
children who have been redeemed, and their thoughts full
of tender love and peace unto all. No longer shall the
stranger tread the streets of the City, nor the Courts of the
Sanctuary be desecrated by his oblations; for only the
children of the Lord shall walk in them, and His true
priests serve within His Courts, when all the elements are
so changed within that they will no longer make evil, nor
cause heavy afflictions to fall upon life. For the stranger
who treads down the sacred things within the Sanctuary,
and pollutes even the courts of the Lord, filling the streets
of the city with its desecrations and its slain, is no other

than the whole system so well known in these days through its manifold manifestations of the materialisation of everything pure and beautiful which is of the very nature of the Soul and the Divine. For that awful system is indeed in opposition to anything spiritual, foreign to the Divine purpose concerning this world and the Soul, a stranger to the original conditions of the Planet and the Divine intention concerning the life of man. It is a system which has made of Jerusalem a desolation, and of her children victims of oppression. It has oppressed the Soul by its cruel bondage, and desecrated its Sanctuary by filling it with false and graven images. It has caused, at times, the true oblations and sacrifices of the Soul unto the Divine Love to cease, whilst it has polluted the land with its false altars of devotion and impure sacrifices for worship. It is that awful system by which everything relating to the nature, history and purpose of the Soul, has been changed from being purely and essentially spiritual, to have only outward and material meanings, until even the Soul is looked upon as something generated in material ways whose life can only be unfolded by means of a material environment and such experiences as now befall all Souls who dwell upon the planes of the Earth.

But when the Bells upon the Horses of the whole House of Israel—the thoughts and purposes of the minds of all who are longing for the Redeemed Life and the blessed Realisations of the Christhood Estate, the true Israel or Cross-bearers—then will the whole system of the materialism of everything Spiritual, Soullic and Divine, pass away. The new interpretation will supersede all the present literal and material interpretations which are given unto the histories associated with the Soul and the manifestation of the Divine Love towards it. The beautiful life made manifest by the Master will no longer be simply associated with the outward and personal and so the mere physical life of Jesus, but with Him who was making manifest through Jesus the meaning of a Redeemed Life and the nature of a Christhood, even the Christ-Soul who was overshadowed by the Adonai. No longer will the

wonderful and beautiful and profound teachings supposed
to have been spoken by the Master, have assigned to them
only outward and historical meanings, but be beheld by
the Soul in their true and full spiritual significance as
stories belonging to the realm of the Divine and the
Kingdom of the Soul. No longer will the interpretation
given to the Divine Love and Wisdom prevail against the
Lord and His Anointed One, but pass away before the
outbreathing of that wonderful Love which the Divine
Father breathed into all those who once knew Him, unto
all of whom the Holy Paraclete was know long ages ago,
and who were to come into the consciousness of His
indwelling Presence. For when the Bells upon the Horses
of the whole House of the Cross ring out the message of
the Divine Love, and make that message concrete in the
Redeemed Life and the inward illumination born from the
indwelling Presence, then will the whole system of the
present materialised religions fade away, and the true
Divine Kingdom be understood, seen and felt. Then will
the Golden Age come when all will enter into true life,
and the world be full of joy and beautiful life and service unhampered, unhindered, uninjured and unhurt by
evil. For the Redemption of all Souls will have come,
and the whole world will once more be young with the
vigour of spiritual life.   J. TODD FERRIER.

JOY IN DELIVERANCE.

*Cry aloud, O Earth! Shout for very joy, O ye
dwellers within Jerusalem! For the Lord who is thy
Redeemer, the Holy One of Israel, is great in the
midst of thee.*

*He hath broken the power of the oppressor and
loosened the chains wherewith he bound thee. He
hath comforted thee in the midst of thine enemies, and
hath made manifest His Loving-kindness towards thee
as in the ancient days.*

*Therefore, rejoice O captive daughter of Zion, for
great is the Holy One in the midst of thee.*

AN ANCIENT PROPHECY.

Sing aloud, O thou who art accounted as the barren ones of the Earth, and as those who have not travailed to bring forth; for thou shalt bring unto the birth more children for the Lord than those who have been married unto the ways of the world.

Therefore thou mayest enlarge thy tent and stretch out thy curtains, lengthening the cords and strengthening the staves of thine habitation; for thou shalt break forth on the right hand and on the left until the children inhabit the land where the Gentiles dwelt, and cause the desolated cities to be inhabited.

Fear not; neither be dismayed because of all that thou hast been made to pass through since the day when the enemy deceived and smote thee and made of thee a reproach, filling thy life with shame and thy heart with sorrow and anguish; for the Lord who was also thy Maker, the Holy One of Israel, hath redeemed thee.

With great Loving-kindness hath He always regarded thee though thou didst feel as one rejected and forsaken even by Him who only sought thy redemption and who could not hurt or grieve His children. Even when the Mountains were removed and the Hills brought low, did His Loving-kindness not depart, nor was the covenant of His peace broken by Him.

O thou who hast been so sorely afflicted, tempesttossed, and uncomforted, behold, I will relay thy stones of fair colours and thy foundations of Sapphires; and of thy windows will I make Agates, and of thy gates Carbuncles, and all thy borders shall be laid with precious stones.

THE GARDEN OF EDEN.

I.

" And the Elohim planted in the East of man a Garden, called Eden, and therein They put every kind of tree bearing precious fruits of which man was to partake and be nourished thereby."

WHEN the Bells upon the Horses of the House of the Cross, the true Israel, ring forth the Divine Love so that all the world may come to know the meaning of that Love in its nature and beautiful ministry unto all Souls, then will the wilderness of Judah become a fruitful garden, and her desert places blossom as the rose. Her lost beautiful inheritance will once more be restored to her, and all her children again dwell within the gates of the once Angelic House known as the Garden of Eden. For the Garden of Eden is the Angelic state within the Soul from which proceed all the sacred influences begotten in the lives of those who know the Divine Love; and when the Divine Love flows through all Souls then will the Garden of Eden be restored unto them. Yea, even those who have not yet fully realised the beautiful meaning of that Love, but whose faces are turned Eastwards whence the Light cometh (the Divine Kingdom whence all Light proceedeth), shall enter into the blessed joy of of that state as they press forwards into the Angelic Life. Indeed, even the Creature-souls shall come to feel the blessed influences of that beautiful realisation by the Soul; for as they were within the gates of Eden before the Soul fell away from the knowledge and realisation of the Divine Love, so shall they again share all the blessed influences of the Redeemed Earth and so be encompassed by the Edenic conditions born from the love within the Soul.

The Garden of Eden was full of the Presence of the Divine. God walked with Man; Man communed with God and served before Him. All life was hallowed; even all the creatures dwelt in safety. All things were harmonious; antagonism was unknown; the creatures were all peaceful. There was no strife of any kind in Eden; every sphere of life was harmonious and beautiful; every experience was helpful to the true growth and culture of the Soul. The Garden was full of every kind of beautiful life-giving fruit suited to all Souls, from the Creature Soul up to him unto whom the Divine Presence was known. For the fruit trees were the Angelic influences, love and Wisdom, the Heavenly conditions sphering the Soul, the Divine Wisdom broken in various forms of spiritual knowledge suited unto all those who had reached that state in their evolution in which they were able to receive instruction from the Angelic Heavens ; and the Divine Love flowing out unto all as the River of Life, nourishing the fruit trees with its life-giving waters, and flowing through all the land which the Garden encompassed, Eastwards and Westwards, Northwards and Southwards, even as the outflow of the Divine Love and Wisdom signified in the Runic Cross, the Cross of the Divine Fulness. For in the Edenic state the River of the Divine Love encompasses the four-fold Kingdom of the Soul and of the Planet, from the elementary Human Kingdom to that Soul-fulness expressed by the terms Angelic, Celestial and Divine. It flowed Eastwards towards the Divine Kingdom indicating how the Soul may even be borne upon its stream to that sublime state ; it flowed Westwards unto the Celestial Sphere of the Soul indicating that the Soul may rise up on to those exalted spheres by means of its life-giving power ; it flowed Northwards to the Angelic Kingdom within the Soul where the Divine Life in Angelic forms is known and entered into by all who ascend from the lower Human Kingdom ; and it flowed Southwards through the Human Kingdom where the Soul's early ages are spent, and where it learns those things which are essential to its ascension into the Angelic Kingdom or state of Angelic experience.

The Garden of Eden was a beautiful and sacred reality once upon this Planet. The Planet-Soul was even as the Garden containing the fourfold River of Life, and in the midst the Tree of Life or the Divine Nature.

And when the Bells upon the Horses of all the Souls of those who once knew the beautiful experiences of Eden

ring out only thoughts and purposes pure and Angelic,
and their lives become the expression and interpretation
of these thoughts and purposes, then will the Edenic state
be restored within the Soul and within the Kingdoms of
the Planet, and the whole Earth be full of the Glory of
the Divine Love.

J. TODD FERRIER.

THE GARDEN OF EDEN.

II.

*" Thou hast been in Eden the Garden of God : every precious gem was thine
there . . . Thou wast perfect in the ways of thy life from the time of thy
creation till iniquity was found in thee."*

WHEN the Bells upon the Horses of the Whole House
of the Cross ring out messages of pure and true love
unto all Souls so that all Souls come to know and experience
that love born from the Divine within the Soul, then will
all the gates into the Edenic life be once more open.
From no direction will the gates be shut within its four
square walls ; for the Garden will have no longer the
afflictions which are born of the Night. Its gates will not
be shut at all by day ; and its day will be perpetual, for in
the Edenic state there is no night. No longer will the
Cherubim have to guard the way to the Tree of Life lest
fallen Humanity should put forth its hands to partake of
it and make of it the instrument whereby to become
Immortal amid the destroyed and corrupted elements unto
which the once beautiful Eden was reduced ; for all Souls
will seek only to know the Lord and the wonderful life
unto which He calls them, and they will approach the Tree
of Life in the midst of the Garden to eat of its fruits only
that they may rise up into the conscious life of the
Divine Love and Wisdom. No longer will the Tree of the
knowledge of Good and Evil usurp the place of the Tree
of Life ; for the sense-life by means of which all evil has
overtaken the Soul will no longer prevail over the life when
the Bells upon the Horses ring out messages of pure and
true love unto all Souls. The evil influence of that Tree
will no longer enter the precincts of Eden to embitter its

life, mar its beauty, and tarnish its glory. The Tree of knowledge by means of the sense-life will have passed away ; and the tempter who used it as the instrument by which to bring down the Soul, will have been overthrown. For the serpent who was the betrayer and deceiver of the Soul, was no other than the false Kingdom which had been generated within the Heavens of the Planet, and now known as the Astral Kingdom, the world of Illusion, the Maya through whose instrumentality all true spiritual images were inverted and perverted, the land of spiritual mirage by means of which the Soul was deceived, and allured away from all that was pure and beautiful, to experiences unspeakable in their degradation, sorrow and anguish. And when the Bells upon the Horses are sounding out the Glad Tidings of the Redemption of the Soul through the Divine Love, and all the children of the Earth enter into the blessed experience of that Love and the Redeemed Life unto which it always leads the Soul, then will the mirage of things spiritual and divine cease, the Astral Kingdom be overthrown, and Maya overcome. The seed of the Woman—the powers of the Soul—shall have crushed the head of the serpent, and the Soul shall once more enter into the heritage which was lost when she was driven forth from Eden and all its beautiful life and service through the Illusion and Betrayal.

When the Bells upon the Horses of the House of the Cross (the true Israel) sound forth once more the messages of the Divine Healing of the Nations, the Restoration of all Israel unto their ancient heritage, the Redemption of the whole world unto the life of beautiful purity, love and compassion, and the deliverance of all the Creature-souls from bondage and oppression, then will Eden be once more established in the midst of the people and within their homes and hearts, and the blessed influences of the Divine reign.

J. TODD FERRIER.

THE GARDEN OF EDEN.

And the Elohim, when they had made man, planted a Garden Eastwards within him, and called it Eden.

And within the Garden did the Elohim cause to grow every kind of precious tree whose form was beautiful to behold, and whose fruit was good to eat.

And in the midst of the Garden there grew up the Tree of Life that all who desired to rise on to the Kingdom of the Elohim, might partake of it and have the Life Eternal.

And a river entered into Eden and flowed through it, and parted into four heads. And these became the four spheres of man's life within the Garden.

The name of the first or outermost sphere was Pison. It was the land where much knowledge had to be acquired, and was known to man as the Gold of Havilah. The knowledge was good, and precious even as Bdellium and the Onyx stone.

The name of the second sphere was Gihon. It encompassed all the land of Ethiopia. It was the land where the knowledge gained when in Havilah was used to enrich the life.

The name of the third sphere was Hiddekel. It was the land encompassed by Assyria on its Eastern side.

And the name of the fourth sphere was Euphrates.

And the Elohim spake unto man from the innermost sphere, saying, " Behold, the garden in which thou dwellest is thine to cultivate, to partake of all the fruits, and to grow up before the Elohim into the likeness of them, and into the image of God."

THE PERFECT WAY.[1]

THE presentation given in "the Perfect Way or the Finding of Christ," is one full of the profoundest meanings for Humanity. It is the presentation of the history of the Soul as a spiritual organism in its evolution from an unconscious state of being up through all the grades of consciousness which lie between a single organism and that perfect state known as Christhood. It is the endeavour to present to the mind a history whose entire experiences are wholly spiritual, and to present it in terms which the mind of all who are truly seeking for a spiritual interpretation of the nature and history of the Soul might be able to apprehend. It is the presentation of the history of the Soul in a manner suited to the special needs of the mind confronted by the terrible doctrine of evolution propounded by material Science and a semi-material Philosophy, showing how the Soul is not a mere physical organism, but a truly spiritual being making manifest its life through the various vehicles through which it functions as it rises to and passes from state to state. It is the history of the Soul, not upon the physical planes as these planes are now understood and as they are at present constituted, but upon the planet when all its planes were in a perfect condition, and what is now understood by the term *matter* was in a pure spiritual state. For all the elements of the Planet were greatly changed from their original condition when what is known as "The Fall" took place, so that to-day they are in an imperfect state and often in a corruptible condition, and life born from them is liable to pass into that sad condition, even the highly evolved organism of the human body through which the Soul now functions—an experience which would not be possible in a perfect condition of the elements, an experi-

---

1 The Perfect Way or the Finding of Christ, by the late Dr. Anna (Bonus) Kingsford and Edward Maitland, B.A.

Fourth Edition. Edited by Samuel Hopgood Hart, from whose pen there is an excellent Preface. 6s. net, postage 4d., Foreign 8d.

To be obtained from The Order of the Cross, Paington.

ence which this Planet knew not in its perfect state, and which it is no more to know when its Redemption is fully accomplished.

The story presented comprises, not the physical evolutionary history during which the Soul passed through the present Animal Kingdom, but the history of its evolution upon wholly spiritual planes when there was no evil in this world; when what is understood as Nature (the Mineral, Vegetable and Creature Kingdoms) was in perfect harmony and the Planet itself was as yet unfallen, when all its elements were pure spiritual substances and those in the outermost sphere were yet responsive to the magnetic attraction of the Divine Kingdom, so that there was nothing corrupt or impure or hurtful, but everything was good and helpful to the true unfoldment of the Soul: and it is also the history of all those Souls who, having passed upward in their evolution from simple spiritual organisms into the exalted state wherein the Soul becomes a microcosm of the Divine so that within itself are reflected the Life, Love and Wisdom of the Divine, have become the repositories of the Divine Love and Divine Wisdom and so are able to recover the inner meanings of the entire history of the Soul, the Planet and the Celestial Spheres. And the story of what is known as "The Fall," whilst in "The Perfect Way" related to the awakening of the Soul unto that state wherein evil becomes known through experience, and so is spoken of as actually a fall upwards, is really the story of the awakening of the Soul unto spiritual consciousness after the long ages of darkness resulting from its unspeakable history within the Animal Kingdom; and in that sense it is a fall upwards, because it is "The Awakening of the Soul." And, as set forth in the Perfect Way, the recovery unto it of all the most sacred and beautiful meanings implied in the sacred signs and symbols contained within all the Great Religions, bears eloquent testimony unto the history of the Soul, and reveals the profound experiences through which it must have passed prior to its descent into conditions wherein its Divine Light was extinguished and its true life lost. For, in the language of the Perfect Way, " Only that which the Soul knoweth may be given unto it ; " and the Soul could only have known all the meanings of these sacred signs and beautiful symbols when it was in a higher and purer state than it now is, since comparatively few seem to know them when even now they are set forth and interpreted unto them, though they do cling to the signs and symbols as if drawn by some strange magnetic influence to them. And the Recovery of these beautiful and sacred meanings by the writers of the Perfect Way bears a testimony of the most palpable and profound significance to the past history of their own Souls, and of all those Souls who are able to enter into the purpose and meaning of the presenttation of the Soul's history given through them from the Divine Kingdom.

The writers of the Perfect Way were undoubtedly of that Christhood Order whose members became the teachers and helpers of the children of this Planet when all its planes were spiritual and all its children pure, and when the Soul was performing its evolution under the purest and most beautiful conditions ; who followed the fallen children down into the Animal Kingdom ; who helped them there to rise again through providing all the gentle and beautiful forms of the perfect herbivorous creatures ; who were the first to rise again on to the true Human Kingdom and once more prepare the way for all who were able to come up on to that Kingdom ; and who, through all the long ages of the preparation for the Soul again entering upon its true evolution, have been its helpers, rising at times as high as the Spiritual Heavens so as to be able, to receive some measure of Illumination from the Divine Kingdom—Illuminations which may be discerned within the Great Religions—and thus becoming the spiritual Prophets, Seers and Teachers in all lands and all ages.

The Perfect Way was given to the world to destroy the materialistic systems, Scientific, Philosophic and Religious, through presenting the true nature of the Soul and its wonderful spiritual history, its true requirements and marvellous possibilities, and so recalling all who are able to enter into the beautiful life of the Redemption and the glorious Realisations of Christhood. And that it is now accomplishing that holy purpose will be obvious unto all who are able to understand.

J. TODD FERRIER.

WHY I CONDEMN VIVISECTION.[1]

BY ROBERT H. PERKS, M.D., F.R.C.S.

I CONDEMN Vivisection because :—

It is unscientific in its methods, and consequently the knowledge gained by its practice is self-contradictory and misleading, and when applied for the relief of human disease has usually proved useless, and often harmful. It also tends to cause neglect of the true scientific methods of clinical and pathological research.

It ignores the only true method for the conquest and prevention of disease, viz., the observance of the natural (Divine) laws of man's being.

It is productive of a vast amount of severe suffering to animals without any corresponding advantage or benefit to them.

Its tendency is to debase the moral and spiritual standard of those who practise or who witness it, and to foster a selfish, cruel and callous spirit, and is thus a grave menace to society.

It is a direct infraction of the moral law—the doing of evil in the (false) hope that some good may result.

It is a cowardly and selfish attempt of men, careless of the sufferings of others, to gain knowledge either for their own ends or that it may be serviceable in healing the self-generated diseases of mankind.

Its spirit is the inversion and anthithesis of the spirit of the Divine Love, which makes itself manifest in compassion and self-sacrifice ; whose way is, as The Christ declared, the only one by which man can reach the true goal of his being—the perfect life of the Divine Father.

---

1 Extracts from Why I condemn Vivisection, by Robert H. Perks, M.D., F.R.C.S. (See advertisement pages.)

WHAT IS VIVISECTION?

VIVISECTION, literally the "cutting of the living," is the term used to designate experiments upon animals for the purpose of physiological and pathological research, and includes not only those involving actual cutting, but also those in which the subjects are, to use plain language, starved, baked, frozen, drowned, etc., or inoculated with various diseases, to the same end.

These cruelties—detailed accounts of which are freely and fully published in the various journals devoted to such records, not only without shame but with appreciation—are inflicted upon thousands of warm-blooded sentient creatures annually in the countries of our Western civilization. Only in a very small proportion of these operations is consciousness abolished by the use of efficient anaesthetics such as choloroform and ether; and even when used the convenience of the *operator* and not the benefit of the *victim* is considered, and the anaesthesia is brief and only partial in character; or the victim is "quieted" by the administration of drugs such as morphia, chloral, curare and others—in no sense true anaesthetics—by which it is rendered more or less muscularly inert, *but with sensibility still intact.* In a large number of cases, necessarily including those in which exposed vital organs are under observation for days, weeks, or even months—and in all cases of inoculation of disease, in which the consequent sufferings are often very severe and prolonged—anaesthetics are of course out of the question.

A very brief acquaintance with the literature of the subject is sufficient to convince anyone—even if he be of the most ordinary intelligence—that a vast aggregate of severe and protracted animal suffering, often amounting to "torture of the most atrocious description the mind of man can conceive" (to quote the words of the archvivisector, Claude Bernard,) is caused by this practice, a fact freely admitted by those who uphold it. And this takes place in the laboratories of those nations who pride themselves on being the most progressive, highly civilized and "Christian."

(To be continued.)

THE MESSENGERS.[1]

BEFORE the great and notable day of the Lord there
were to appear the Divine Messengers who would
herald His approach.   They were to declare the day of
the Lord and proclaim the message of His Gospel.   Thus
were they to prepare the way of the Lord, and to make
straight His path.   The valleys were to be raised, the
crooked ways were to be put straight, the rough places
were to be made into a plain, and all the hills and mountains were to be made clear : for the valleys are the low
lying spiritual conditions ; the crooked way is the path
along which the Soul has been taught to walk which is
neither straight nor narrow, but broad and circuitous ; the
rough places are the very hard environments into which
the Soul is born and amid which it finds it most difficult
to pursue the right way ; and the hills and mountains are
the spiritual uplands and Divine Heights which have been
observed through the low lying conditions.

That the Day of the Lord is either with us or approaching the greater number of thoughtful spiritual men and
women seem to believe.   The Churches are looking for the
second Advent and the reign of the Christ, whilst those
who are without the circles of western religious belief and
who follow the philosophic systems of the East are looking for a new Avatâr in the reappearance of Krishna or
Buddha.   And, on the one hand the signs along the outward and historical planes and amongst the Nations which
men have been taught to believe would accompany the
second Advent, are eagerly watched and noted and written
of as the sure signs of the coming of the Son of Man ;
and, on the other hand, the Celestial cycles and Planetary
conjunctions are watched and dwelt upon as having very
special significance, and likely to issue in a new and
great manifestation from the Divine Kingdom.

But whilst all these signs and wonders in the Heavens
and on the Earth may be full of very real significance for
all Souls, because full of a profound meaning for the
Planet, and whilst they may be accepted as indicating

great changes of a spiritual order even to the reappearing
of the Son of Man or the taking place of a New Avatâr,
yet the real signs and wonders preceding the second
coming or new Advent, are entirely spiritual—*i.e.*, they
are not merely stellar or things of a material order, but
are of spiritual origin, influence and purport. So that the
true signs of the new Avatâr or the reappearing of the
Christ, are not to be sought for in the mere phenomena,
but in the great spiritual causes and influences and effects.
And these latter signs and wonders may be discerned by
all whose spiritual eyes are open to behold the meaning of
the New Avatâr in the reappearing of the Son of Man,
not as a man to be reverenced and worshipped as the man
Jesus has been by the whole Western World and the man
Gautama has been by millions in the East but in the
restoration of all who once understood the Mysteries in
their inner spiritual and Divine significations, to that
spiritual state in which the Divine Wisdom will not be a
mere knowledge gained through the study of any philosophic system, but an inward knowledge born within the
Soul from the Light of the Divine Spirit. *For the Day of
the Lord is now. The new Avatâr is taking place. The
Son of Man is now reappearing.* But it is not a personal
appearing, not one manifestation through a person, but the
rehabilitation of the Christhood Order, not as a community
of Souls, but as Souls scattered all over the world rising
up into that beautiful life for which the terms Buddha and
Jesus stood, and arriving at the spiritual realisation which
is implied in the terms Krishna and Christ, the first
representing the beautiful Redeemed Life, and the second
signifying the attainment by the Soul of that wonderful
experience when the Divine Love is so fully realised that
the Soul grows like the Divine, and so arrives at the
consciousness of the meaning of all spiritual and Divine
things.

Have any of the Messengers been with us in these
later days? We think they have. And what was the
purport of their message? This very same glorious

truth, *that the Lord whose coming they were to foretell was not a man, but the restoration of the Soul, even unto the Christhood Estate, the coming of the Lord to the Soul, or the consciousness of the Divine Presence within it.* They spake not of the special coming of any man as the embodiment of the Lord, but of His beautiful coming into the life of every one who was able to receive Him. And, they prepared the way through giving to the Soul a nobler conception of its nature, origin and destiny ; its wonderful history before it became the victim of all the materialising forces which arose within the Heavens of the Planet by which all spiritual and Divine things were changed into mere outward and material histories ; and the true meaning of a Christhood as a restored Vision to the Soul so that it might come once more to understand the beautiful exalted state in which it once was prior to its descent into the darkness produced through the materialisation of all its wonderful history and the Divine Mysteries which once it knew. And they pointed out the true way by which to return again unto that exalted and much to be desired Estate, wherein the Divine Love is realised within the Soul through its Oneness with the Divine, and the Divine Wisdom known through the indwelling Presence of the Divine Love. They had to exalt the valleys by giving a nobler conception of life and ministry to the Soul. They had to make the crooked way straight through pointing out again as the Master had done during His beautiful Christhood, that the path along which the Soul must now travel to retrace its steps from the awful influences of the materialisation of all its own history and the Divine Mysteries is that of the Redeemed Life—a life in which every kind of impurity is put away and only the Divine Life sought after, where love and compassion and pity ever reign. They had to make the rough places into a plain so that even the feeble might be able to walk along the path into the estate of the Redeemed Life, and so on to the Christhood. And then they had to make clear the Hills and Mountains of the Lord, the spiritual uplands and Divine Heights which many Souls once knew because they had climbed them, and which all

Souls are to know and climb. Only then was the Glory of the Lord to be revealed, even unto the seeing of it by all flesh, the feeling of the glorious and wonderful influences born of the coming of the Lord into every life able to receive Him.

That the messages given by those who were sent as Messengers to proclaim the way of the new Advent, the new Avatâr, the reappearing of the Son of Man, are not only being heard and received, but that they are also effecting the purpose for which they were given will be obvious unto all who can discern " the signs of the times."

Unto all who are watching for His appearing will the Lord now come upon the Clouds of the Heavens within the Soul.[1]   J. TODD FERRIER.

SHOW US THY GLORY.

Oh, Thou in whom are all the Spirits of the Lord and the Glorious Rainbow which is around the throne of the Eternal One, make thyself manifest unto all Thy children who now yearn to know Thee as the Holy presence within the Sanctuary of the Soul! Show Thyself unto us in the hour of worship within the Sanctuary where Thy Holy Presence is, as we bow before Thee only and seek only the service of Thy praise. Grant unto us that we may behold Thy glory even as those behold who are Thy servants within the Temple of Zion, the Holy House of the Lord. We would know and behold Thee in the Beauty of Holiness, and serve before Thee evermore as those whom Thou hast redeemed by the Blood of the Lamb and clothed with the White Raiment of Thy Saints. Thou alone art our Saviour and our Lord: we would bless Thee continually. Amen and Amen.

---

1 We recommend our readers to study the writings given through the late Dr. Anna (Bonus) Kingsford and Edward Maitland, B.A., in relation to this very profound and important question. The writings will be found advertised on the cover of this Journal.

THE MESSAGE OF GLAD TIDINGS.

" Sing ye Heavens! And be joyful O Earth! "

" How beautiful are the feet of him who beareth Glad Tidings, who standeth upon the Mountains of the Lord and proclaimeth His Salvation unto all people! "

" The Watchmen behold together the coming of the Lord, and the bringing back of Zion."

THE appearance of the Messengers of the Lord was to be accompanied by messages of Glad Tidings unto all peoples. They were to proclaim the approach of the Lord, the healing of the people, the restoration of all the Children of Israel, the deliverance of Judah from the heel of the oppressor, the restoration of the Ancient City of Jerusalem, and the rebuilding of its walls and bulwarks, the rebuilding of the sacred House of the Lord upon the Mounts Moriah and Zion, and the restoration of the Temple service.

THE HEALING OF THE PEOPLE.

That these messages are now being proclaimed, and that the healing of the people, the restoration of all the children of Israel, the deliverance of Judah and her children from bondage, the restoration of the Ancient City of Jerusalem and the rebuilding of its walls and bulwarks, the re-establishing of the sacred House of the Lord with its beautiful priestly service upon Mounts Moriah and Zion, will be obvious unto all who know the meaning of these things, whose faces are set Zionwards, who love the true Temple-service and are looking for the appearing of the Lord there. For these are great spiritual facts and not mere outward material events. , They are facts relating to the Soul and are not simply of the nature of physical phenomena. They are facts which may only be spiritually discerned, and only by those who love spiritual things. They are not such things upon the physical planes as many to-day think and anticipate, but are histories to be experienced within the Souls of all the children of the Heavenly Father who are upon this world, and even by the world itself. For the healing of the Nations is not simply the healing of all their physical ailments most of which are self-created, but the healing of the

minds of all peoples through beautiful spiritual influences
which will also bring about the healing of all the diseases
born of the wrong and false ways of life which now they
follow. They will be healed from within when they find
and follow the true ways of life; ways of true purity and
compassion and love; ways born of pure thoughts and
noble purposes, good desires and gentle feelings, love unto
all Souls and pity unto all the creatures. Then shall be
their true healing by the leaves from the Tree of Life—
the growth of true and pure spiritual desire, feeling and
love within the Soul, and the interpretation and manifestation of these in all the ways of life. And thus will the
healing be fourfold, and so permanent—the Soul through
its restoration to true spiritual conditions, purposes and
visions; the Heart to pure spiritual affections; the Mind
to noble thoughts and pure generous ambitions; and the
Body to true feelings and desires.

That the people are now in the process of being
gradually healed may be known even unto those who have
not thought spiritually of these things. Here a little and
there a little the healing is being accomplished. All the
true reform movements are working unto this blessed end.
They are changing the conditions which will aid all who
desire true healing to follow nobler ways in life. And the
true spiritual movements which seek only to establish
purity, righteousness and love in the lives of the people
are all helping to exalt the valleys or low spiritual conditions, and so to make straight the path along which the
Soul must needs walk in order to arrive at true healing.

THE RETURN OF ISRAEL.

And the return and restoration of Israel is likewise a
spiritual fact which is now being accomplished. Many
interpret that return and restoration as the return of the
Jews to their own land, with the rebuilding of the little
town of Jerusalem and the Jewish Temple; and there are
even societies formed to give practical effect to these interpretations. What is now known as the great Zionist
movement has been born of such interpretations. Great
endeavours are being made to open up the way for the

re-habilitation of the Jewish people in their ancient land, and so those who believe the references in the ancient Scriptures to refer to outward history, and who have been taught to regard the whole Jewish Nation as comprising what were known as the Houses of Israel and Judah, have imagined that these outward events were sure and certain testimony to the approaching return of the Master. They have given to prophecies full of the profoundest spiritual import mere physical and local meanings, and have again related the Master to a mere National movement.

But the return and restoration has naught to do with the Jewish Nation returning to Palestine, nor with any mere National movement, but is the return and restoration of the Soul unto its spiritual inheritance. For the term Israel means the Soul who has borne the Cross of the Divine Love, one who upon the Heavens has prevailed against all difficulties so as to have become able to share in the consciousness of the Divine nature and be a partaker of the burden of the Divine Love in its ministry unto all Souls. And the return of Israel is the restoration within those Souls of the beautiful consciousness of the Divine Love, the return into their ancient inheritance of the consciousness within them of the Divine Presence, and to the possession of the land they once occupied in the Kingdom which the Heavenly Father gave unto them in the ancient times, even the land of the Christhood Estate. And when all Israel is saved so that there is not only no longer any Tribe lacking but not even a member of all the Tribes, then will the whole House of Israel have returned unto their own land and been restored to their ancient inheritance.

THE DELIVERANCE OF JUDAH.

And what is true regarding the House of Israel is likewise true concerning the deliverance of Judah from the heel of the oppressor. For Judah was not one of the Jewish Tribes, but the Planet-Soul who went away into a most cruel bondage when the materialising of all her beautiful spiritual substances took place. The Captivity of Judah in the land of the oppressor has been long and

terrible; for the oppressor is no other than those conditions of a non-spiritual order which overtook her when
she moved away from the Divine Kingdom; and her
deliverance from the oppressor is the restoration unto
her of true spiritual conditions through which she will be
able to again return unto the land which once she enjoyed
when she was a Celestial being moving on the Divine
Kingdom or Ecliptic in perfect harmony with the Divine
Kingdom, all her children being then spiritual, seeking
only spiritual things and knowing no evil nor the sorrow
and anguish born from it. And the holy City of Jerusalem was not any little dwelling place within her spiritual
borders, but her own full Kingdom known as the Planet
or Earth whose beautiful planes were all in perfect order
and moved in response to the Divine attraction, and were
the beautiful Terraces of Jerusalem. For the holy City
was the Planet as a spiritual system. Her walls were
righteousness and her bulwarks goodness and truth.
Her towers were spiritual powers and her palaces the
manifold spiritual states of all who dwelt within her
borders. She was glorious for situation because she
encompassed with her walls Mount Zion or the Christhood Order, and even Mount Moriah where Abraham was
said to have offered Isaac—the Mount of the Divine Love
whereon the Christ-Soul was consecrated unto the Lord
for the Divine service. For Mount Zion was the Christhood whose members formed the Divine Temple or
spiritual condition of true priestly service, the ministers of
the Lord unto the people in things pertaining unto the
life of the Soul; and Mount Moriah was the Divine
Presence within the City, the consciousness of that
Presence within the Planet-Soul and all the members of
the Christhood Order, the Mount whereon the sacrifice of
the Soul always takes place. And when the whole House
of Israel returns unto the life of the Cross then will Mount
Zion with its beautiful Temple-service be once more restored upon Mount Moriah; and when the whole House
of Judah is delivered from her bondage and each Tribe
returns unto its own land or spiritual estate, then will
Jerusalem be restored to her former glory, and all her

walls and gates, her bulwarks and her palaces, be rebuilt.

Such glorious things were spoken of both Zion and Jerusalem by the Hebrew Prophets who foresaw the coming of the Lord; and such are the Glad Tidings which the Messengers whose feet are beautiful (the Illumined Understanding) as they stand upon the Mountains (the spiritual and Divine Heights) and proclaim the coming of the Lord and the Redemption of all the Heavenly Father's children, are heralding to the whole world.

J. TODD FERRIER.

THE BOW OF THE LORD.

In the silence of the night when I was lifted up in the spirit so that I rose out from the Earth whose darkness lay before me, there appeared in the Heavens the Bow of the Lord.

It stretched from Horizon to Horizon like a girdle round the Heavens, and seemed to encompass the Earth; and its presence shed a peace so hallowed that it was like the Presence of the Divine within the Sanctuary which the Soul feels when it seeks to worship.

It was like the Rainbow in its colours, but perfect as the spectrum of the Elohim, the Sacred Tinctures of the Sevenfold Spirit of the Ever Blessed One through whom all Souls are quickened and illumined, and by whose operative presence within the Soul the Sevenfold Life becomes realised.

The vision of the Bow filled me with the sense of the Divine Goodness, His great tenderness unto all Souls and His abiding Presence within all those who are able to receive Him.

THE HERALD OF THE CROSS.

Vol v.   New Series.   March, 1909.   No. 3.

THE RETURN OF PERSEPHONE.

In the hour of the Manifestation, the Lord laid down His life.

He went away from this world to accomplish the Great Work of the Redemption of Spirit from matter, through the Redemption of the Soul from the elemental world and its dominion over her.

For the Redemption of the Soul from the dominion of the elemental powers was accomplished through the Lord descending into those elements to purify them, so that the Soul might be able to ascend into her own Kingdom once more and know the powers bestowed by the Highest, which are the powers of Christ.

For the elemental world became so changed in its nature that it took the Soul away into cruel bondage and made of her life a way of pain and sorrow, and of her path a road full of tribulation and anguish.

And the Soul was carried down into the darkness born of the changed elemental kingdom, until her light was extinguished and her vision obscured.

But now is the hour of her deliverance from the darkness, and the restoration of her Vision; for, because her Lord hath purified the elemental kingdom, she is able again to rise and behold the Vision of her Lord.

And through a purified Understanding, Persephone is led up by Hermes even into the glorious Heavens of the Divine.

THE ERA OF MANIFESTATION.

" The days of the Covenant of Manifestation are passing away: the Gospel of Interpretation cometh."
" There shall nothing new be told; but that which is ancient shall be interpreted."—CLOTHED WITH THE SUN.

THE Days of the Manifestation are passing away, the Age of Interpretation cometh. The hour of the extreme passion of the Lord is now finished, and the morning of His Resurrection is at hand. For three long days and nights has the Christ lain in the tomb—the three great cycles through which the Earth has passed since the Christhood was made manifest; but now is the early dawn of the new day in the which Christ shall arise. He shall come forth from the grave wherein He was put when His beautiful Christhood was destroyed by all those who crucified Him, and shall manifest Himself unto all who once knew Him; for the grave wherein they buried Him was the Astral Kingdom, the grave which belonged to the mind dominated by everything sensuous. It was the grave wherein no man had lain in the sense that it had never been used before in the same way, though the lives of all the children of the Heavenly Father upon this world had lain in the grave of the Astral Kingdom for untold ages. But when the Christhood was laid there, the Christ-Soul began His Passion, His Great Work of destroying the works of the devil, His redeeming ministry by which He was to overthrow the evil states upon that Kingdom through descending into the Hells, that He might disperse all the terrible conditions which had been set up through the loss unto the Soul of the conscious-ness of the Divine Presence and the uplifting and sus-taining power of the Divine Love and Wisdom. No other had ever lain in it in the way which He did; for it was the burial of the Living and not that of the dead. It was the putting away of the Lord as one who was dead, not the interment of one in whom no life was found.

And the embalming was the embalming of a living Soul which could not know death because it was not born of bloods, nor of the will of man, nor from the flesh, but of

God, when it is said that those nearest to the Master embalmed Him. For the embalming was entirely of a spiritual character, and not mere outward acts and material history. It had nothing to do with the embalming of the body of Jesus for burial, but the embalming within the hearts of all who had beheld the sublime manifestation given by the Master of the Christhood Vision, the Divine preservation of that Vision unto those Souls who had beheld it even unto the entering into the meaning of its life, so that in the days of the Regeneration of the Son of Man they should be the first to awaken unto the meaning of that important event, become the apostles of the Lord, and be able to give unto the whole world the restored Christhood both as regards its meaning for the Soul and its significance unto the whole Human Race. It was the beautiful embalming within the Soul itself of a Vision which had become most sacred and precious unto all who had beheld and understood it, so that when the Days of the Regeneration came that vision might also be recovered by the Soul when the past opened out before it.

The Days of the Manifestation which are now passing away were the days of the era known as the Christian, though it has never been more than nominally so in its adherence to and following of the Christ. The era has been one long failure in the attempts which have been put forth to interpret the meaning of the Christhood for the Soul and the tragic Sin-offering for the world. The Manifestation was the making manifest by the Master as Jesus the meaning of the Redeemed Life unto which he called men and women, and the nature and significance of the state of Christhood for all who were ready to enter upon the life unto which He called the Soul. It was the Manifestation of the meaning of the Divine Purpose concerning the life to be lived by all the Heavenly Father's children, the true exposition of the life of purity upon every plane, the true interpretation in action of the Divine Love broken in a most real compassion unto all Souls whatever their state, and genuine pity towards all creatures ; whilst it was likewise the manifestation of all

that was implied in a Christhood, the revelation unto the
Soul able to receive so great a truth of the Divine Inheri-
tance or possession implied in the knowledge of the
Divine Wisdom when all things are understood by the
Soul, the interpretation of the meaning of the Divine
Immanence within the Soul as a consciousness of the
Divine Presence. And in this way it was a manifestation of the Divine Love and Wisdom, the meaning of that
Love and Wisdom, the life unto which the Realisation of
that Love led and the knowledge which the Wisdom gave,
and the only true and sure path along which the Soul
must walk if it would enter into the Realisation of a true
Redemption from the power of every kind of evil thing·
and so know the Redeemed Life, and thus prepare itself
to enter upon that yet harder path whose goal is Christhood.

But owing to the burial of the Christhood through the
destruction of the beautiful picture of the Estate as interpreted by the Master, the Manifestation became lost to
the Soul. The writers of the Four Records verily
accomplished the crucifixion and death of the Christhood
when they presented the picture which is found in the
Records with its colours all local and so mixed as to con-
fuse the reader and hide from the Soul the meaning of
both the Redeemed Life and the Estate of Christhood.
For the Christhood in the Records is not one wherein the
life is absolutely pure (though it is claimed for the Master
that He was pure), since it implies that the Christ was " a
wine-bibber " even whilst He taught self-denial and purity ;
that He took such food as implied the taking of the lives
of sentient creatures even whilst He proclaimed Himself
to be the exponent and interpreter of the Divine Pity ;
that He sought to establish an earthly kingdom in the
name of the Divine and gave His immediate disciples
commands concerning it, even whilst He constantly
declared that *His Kingdom was not of this world*, and
that *the Kingdom of God was within Man ;* that He
taught His disciples to call no one Lord and Master save
God only, and yet laid claim to be their Master and Lord;

that He laid great stress upon true humility as a grace which they must all cultivate so that none might seek to be first amongst them, but always to be as the true children of the Heavenly Father and servants of their Lord, even whilst He singled out one of their number to be the chief corner stone upon which the earthly kingdom was to be built, and as the only disciple who was able to discern who and what the Christ was.

It was the betrayal of the Master's Manifestation by Judas Iscariot—the Astral Kingdom; the false representation of what He said and did, of what He was in His life as Jesus and in His sublime Teachings as the Christ. And the whole history of Christianity—Ecclesiastical, Scholastic and Christological—bears astounding testimony to this truth. J. TODD FERRIER.

THE DIVINE DESCENT.

The Lord hath made Himself manifest once more as in the Ancient days when the Glory of His Presence covered the Sanctuary;

For He hath descended in the Cloud to take up His abode in the Sanctuary in Zion that He may make Himself manifest in Israel, and likewise unto the whole House of Judah.

The Lord hath made bare His arm in the eyes of all peoples, since He hath shown unto them how glorious is His dwelling-place, and how holy is His Temple;

For He hath declared through his Prophets how great is His purpose and how wonderful are His ways towards the children of His Love; and how He hath spoken through His Messengers concerning the Return of the Soul unto her own Kingdom, and into her most ancient Inheritance when she was the possessor of the knowledge of the Divine Love and the light of the Divine Wisdom, and when the Sacred Lamp within her Sanctuary was kindled from the Sacred Flame of the Eternal and Ever Blessed Spirit.

THE HOUR OF THE INTERPRETATION.

" All that is true is Spiritual. . . . . If it be true, and yet seem to you to have a material signification, know that you have not solved it. . . . . Seek its interpretation. That which is true is for Spirit alone."—CLOTHED WITH THE SUN.

IN the passing away of the days of the Manifestation, the hour of the Interpretation cometh. For whilst the Manifestation which should have been perpetuated all through the Christian era through all who followed after the finding of the Christ, has been one of unspeakable failure because of the conduct of those who fell under the dominion of the Astral Kingdom and misinterpreted the whole meaning and purpose of the life of the Master, and so presented a picture of the Redeemed Life as expressed in Jesus, and of the Christhood revealed in the Sayings and Teachings of the Christ, which was a perversion of the life lived and the Teachings given ; yet that era was meant to be one of Manifestation in which the real nature of the Christhood would have come to be understood, and the Redeemed Life apprehended and entered upon as that path of Purity which led to the realisation of the Redemption, and prepared the Soul to enter into the meaning and experience of the Christhood Estate. It has been indeed anything but the Manifestation of Christhood, though the whole Western World has pro-fessed to believe in it and follow its ways; for the West has been verily the land of the setting Sun, the land wherein the Christhood sank beneath the Spiritual Horizon after having been eclipsed even to the darkening of all its beautiful and wonderful light. *For the Western World has built up an outward and visible Kingdom in the name of the Master, rather than the Divine Kingdom within the Soul.* It has taught the children of the Heavenly Father to seek for the Redemption of the Soul in other ways than those of purity of life upon every sphere of experience. It has all through the era so presented the Christhood unto the Soul that the beautiful meaning and purpose of it could not be distinguished; so that the Christhood made manifest came to have a significance attached to it which was foreign to the entire spirit of any such state, and the manifestor of the Christhood came to occupy the place of the Divine Love Himself in the minds and hearts of all who earnestly sought to enter upon the true path which led unto the realisation of the Redeemed Life and the consciousness of the Divine Presence within the Soul. For the man Jesus was deified, and the human vision was presented as the fit and true object to worship until it took the place of the Ever Blessed and Eternal One.

But the hour of Interpretation has come when the true meaning of the Manifestation shall be given, the nature of the Estate of Christhood interpreted unto all who are able to understand so profound a truth as it implies, and the true Redemption expounded and illustrated in the Redeemed Life of all who are able to enter into the blessed realisation. The grapes from the true Vine have been crushed in the winepress of the whole Western World, and the hour of the Vintage has come ; for the Love of the Divine which the World was unable to understand unto the receiving of its most wonderful and most beautiful Manifestation, has been poured out with a fulness men wot not of for the purification of the whole of that Kingdom through whose evil conditions the tragic crucifixion and burial of the Christhood took place, and upon which the awful Sin-offering had to be accomplished.

The hour of the Interpretation of that sublime though terrible Mystery has now come.

J. TODD FERRIER.

THE OPENING OF THE PRISON-HOUSES.

In the day when the keepers of the prison-houses shall quake for very fear because of all that the Lord hath done for His children in the accomplishment of their Redemption, know that the end of the evil times draweth near:

For the keepers of the prison-houses are those elements within the mind which are at enmity with the Soul, which hold it in bondage to the things of sense, and fill it with reproach and anguish.

The prison-houses shall all be shaken to their foundations even as when the Earth quaketh and trembleth, and the structures raised by men are brought low;

For the prison-houses are the elements within the system of man which are at variance and enmity with the Soul, which make of man's life upon the outer spheres a house of bondage and oppression, and which detain the Soul and prevent her from rising up into the land of pure light and liberty.

The guards who chain the captive Peter[1] to them and make him sleep between them in the prison-house, shall awaken to find that the chains wherewith they bound their captive have been broken and the captive set free even whilst the prison gates were closed;

For the Angel of the Lord shall descend even to enter the prison-house where the Understanding has been held in bondage with chains, and guarded by the outward authorities, and set it free that it may go forth out from all the bondage and oppression of the prison-house to proclaim the glad tidings of deliverance to all within the House of Mary.[2]

---

[1] Peter meaning the Understanding.
[2] The House of the Soul. (Vide, Acts of the Apostles.)

THE CRUCIFIXION OF CHRIST.

"And they led Him away to be crucified."

"And they crucified Him between two thieves, one on the right hand and the other on the left."

"They crucify afresh the Lord of Glory."

THE way unto the Redeemed Life is now open as it has not been for many ages. Not since the days of the Master through whom the Christhood was made manifest, has the path been so clear along which the life must needs walk in order to reach by inward realisation the Redeemed Life and the state of spiritual Christhood. Not since the blessed Master lived His Christhood have the spiritual influences been so great as they now are. Nay, to-day they are greater because of all the wonderful work which He left this Earth to accomplish—that is, left His Christhood Estate to enter upon His Priestly Office of purging away all the fearful history written against Humanity on the Astral Kingdom. For when He was dwelling on the Earth as the Christ, living the Redeemed Life and revealing unto all who were then able to receive so great a Mystery as the meaning of the Christhood, *the Handwritings upon the middle wall or partition* were still against the Soul so that the Soul found the way upwards to the spiritual life very difficult, and, indeed, impossible for anyone who had not previously known the path. Because the Astral Kingdom was in the condition found described in the Apocalyptic Vision by St. John where it is spoken of as the Beast who made war with the Saints of the Most High and threw them down. It was in a state that was also described by the Seer as the Pit wherein the Beast had his dwelling. For in the Vision the Astral Kingdom is personified and spoken of not only as the power "that maketh war with the Saints," but as the enemy of the Divine ; and its personification has misled the minds of the people to regard the thing signified as a great, and, in a sense, Divine personal enemy of the Ever Blessed One, who has been known as Satan, the Devil, Beelzebub, the Archenemy and the Archfiend, one whose power has been considered almost equal to that of the Eternal.

It is recorded that the work which the Sublime Master came into this world to accomplish was its Redemption through the overthrow of Satan and the destruction of all his works. And to accomplish so great a work it was not only necessary for Him to live the Redeemed Life in the World, and to make manifest His oneness with the Heavenly Father through the manifestation of the Christ-hood, but that it was likewise necessary that He should die as a Christ upon the Cross in order that the Ranson of all Souls might be accomplished. And the entire doctrine held by the Western World which has believed nominally in the personal Christ and, until very recent years, in the personal Devil, is built up upon the teaching given by the Master concerning the Redemption, but through having been applied personally, locally, and historically as relating to the personal life, the true and innermost meanings implied have all been lost to the Church. The death upon the Cross has been understood as relating to the Crucifixion of the personal Jesus by the Romans and Jews, instead of the very real and tragic death of the Christ-hood of the Christ-Soul who made it manifest through Jesus, taking up the Divine Cross of unspeakable love and bearing it in descending from His once most glorious Christhood into the very depths of that impure Kingdom known as the Astral, there to enter into conflict with the powers which it represented against the Soul, and overthrow them through changing all the conditions upon that Kingdom, blotting out the evil images upon it through attracting them magnetically unto Himself and changing their nature so that they should no longer have power to prevent the Soul from rising up out of that Kingdom on to the Spiritual Heavens.

The work of the Christ was not finished upon the Roman Cross ; it has been continued all through the ages known as the Christian Era. It began, not upon the Roman Cross when the Master was the victim of the unspeakable hatred of the Jewish leaders and the weak-ness and callousness of the Roman Judge, but when He passed away from His glorious Christhood to take up the priestly work in blotting out all the graven images of a magnetic nature which were written upon the walls of that Kingdom whence all the evil which has befallen this distraught Planet, has proceeded ; and it has continued down through the Christian Era even unto these days wherein it has been accomplished, so that all Souls may now enter into a condition which makes the Redeemed Life possible for all, and an easily attained state by those who through all these ages have been in spirit even as the saints of God, seeking the purified life. It was not finished when the Master was supposed to have left this world to appear in the Divine Presence with His life-work completed, to plead that work as the ground of the Soul's acceptance by the Divine Love and the forgiveness of all its sin ; but it has been continued since He passed on to the Astral Kingdom, and, though now accomplished, it will only be fully finished when the Redeemed Life is attained and the Christhood realised by all those Souls who once were of the Christhood order. The Crucifixion indeed was real, and the Cross so heavy to bear that he almost sank beneath its load from sheer spiritual exhaustion, and would have done so had not the Divine Love sustained Him in the hour of His dire extremity ; but the reality was not in the outward and historic event, but in the inward. It was the Crucifixion of the Soul, the dying of His Christhood, *the bearing of the Divine Cross upon His Soul in accomplishing the Great Work upon the Astral Kingdom.*

Upon the man Jesus that Cross could not be laid because he was the vehicle of the Christhood[1]; but it was laid upon one who is spoken of in the history found in the Records where the crucifixion is portrayed, as one Joseph of Arithmathea—the Ioseph of the Divine Heights, the Divine Crossbearer ; IΩΣΗΦ, the Cross, the Divine Love, and Priestly Office. The very language is significant both of His Nature and Office. There was in very deed a Joseph at the birth of the Christhood of the Master upon the Earth-planes and a Joseph at the close of the manifestation of

His beautiful exposition of the Divine meaning and purpose concerning the Soul; but they were not on the physical planes at either the beginning or close, but on the spiritual. And they were the same. At the beginning Joseph was the generator of the spiritual state known as Jesus—the perfect embodiment of the Redeemed Life; and at the close Joseph of Arithmathea became the bearer of the Christ's Cross which could not be borne by him who came to be called Jesus. And he bore it even unto the place called Golgotha—the house of death. For the Ioseph of the Crucifixion was He who dwelt upon the Divine Heights, the Spheres of the Gods, as the term implies; and when He poured out His life even unto Death, He descended from those Heights of Divive Realisation to bear the awful burden imposed on Him by the past history of the Soul. He stooped to the needs of all Souls, even to those who were afar off upon the Sea wherein spiritual death reigned, and all who were in the uttermost parts of the Earth. He descended from the glorious Heights of the Gods where the Ineffable Light is Eternal, to even know the terrible darkness arising out of the depths of the spiritual state known as the Magdalene. For it was such a stooping to our fallen estate as no one could have ever imagined unless it had been given him to know it from that Kingdom whence all things are truly known; It was such a *Humiliation* as the sleeping Church has not even dreamt of in its slumbers, nor her scholars beheld couched in the language in which that Humiliation has been spoken of. It was such a Humiliation as not even the most intimate of the Master's Disciples associated with His profound and most sorrowful Sayings.

Truly it was a Humiliation worthy of the Gods, worthy of that Divine Love within the Christ-Soul, to stoop in the process of the Redemption to the needs of all who were in the outer darkness! Who will measure that Love or guage its sorrow and anguish? Who is sufficient to understand its awful suffering, and the agony endured? Who could portray the unspeakable pain which He suffered in His Travail of Soul as He bore the burden of the Cross, blotted out the Handwritings written upon the Astral Kingdom by the Soul when it fell into evil, overthrew the elemental forces whose presence were inimical unto the true life of the Soul, and accomplished for all Souls what could not otherwise have been accomplished, namely, the opening up of the way by which even the least in spiritual strength and experience might be able to rise up out of evil and receive Angelic ministry from the Divine Love to enable the Soul to grow in Goodness, Purity and Love before Him.[1]

J. TODD FERRIER.

WHO HATH UNDERSTANDING?

" *Who hath believed our report? Unto whom hath the Arm of the Lord been revealed?* "

" *Who hath heard with the hearing ear and the understanding heart what great things the Lord hath accomplished for us and for the whole House of Israel?*"

" *Why is it that the hearts of the people wax gross, and that their ears are heavy and dull to hear?* "

" *Ears have they, but they hear not; eyes have they, yet they see not; neither is there understanding within their hearts.*"

But let him who hath an ear to hear, the power to see, and the desire to perceive, hear what the Spirit saith unto all Souls.

---

[1] *In the Records it is stated that Jesus sank beneath the Cross, and that they laid it on one Simon a Cyrenean. In this way was the wonderful significance hidden and lost of the meaning of the action of the Divine Love.*

THE CRUCIFIXION.

THE Crucifixion of the Christ was the misrepresentation of what the Redeemed Life meant, and the
obliteration from the Christhood Vision of the real nature
and significance of the Christhood made manifest through
the Master.   The life which He lived, the profound
nature of His Sayings, the wonderful spiritual histories
of the Soul and the world contained in the stories and
parables and some of the incidents associated with
miraculous events, the true path of life unto which He
called the Soul, the pure ways which He made known as
those by which alone the Soul could arrive at the experience of the Redeemed Life and come at last to know
the joy of the Divine Love within the Soul and experience the blessed consciousness of the Divine Presence
within its Sanctuary, the very meaning of the nature and
function of the Holy Paraclete, the Resurrection of the
Christhood, the glorious Ascension, the Parousia of the
Lord, and the Restoration of Israel in the Regeneration
of the Son of Man—all these wonderful and blessed
things did they who wrote the Four Records fail to
understand in their spiritual significance, and so they
gave to them outward and physical-history meanings and
thus almost destroyed all of them for the Soul. Not
discerning spiritual things themselves, they changed
what was purely spiritual in its relationships and
meanings into material things, and thus led the Soul to
seek for the meaning of all of them along paths where
they were not to be found. Themselves missing the
beautiful and profound spiritual importance of them for
the Soul, and being unable to discern that they had no
relation whatever to things apprehended by the outward
senses, they took the wonderful and profound histories to
have only personal and outward application, and so
presented them in the Records in such a way that none
could discern their hidden and Divine meanings.

The Crucifixion was therefore a very real and tragic
one, and one which has had very real and tragic results
for all who have been misled by the false presentations of

the Mysteries embodied in the Teachings of the Master now found in the Records, as the whole history of the outward Kingdom established in the name of the Master testifies unto all who read it with an open and unprejudiced understanding. For the History of that Kingdom has been one of strife almost from its foundation, one which has shown the whole influence of the outward Kingdom to have been to narrow the Vision of the Soul and cramp its life to such an extent that the Soul has not been able to discover the fallacies of those who founded the outward Kingdom, nor the terrible falsehoods foisted upon them through the materialisation of the Mysteries and the misrepresentation and misinterpretation of the Christhood and the true Redeemed Life.

J. TODD FERRIER.

THE RESURRECTION MORNING.

On the first day of the week[1] cometh Mary the Magdalene[2] unto the Sepulchre[3] while it was yet dark,[4] and findeth the stone[5] rolled away from the Sepulchre wherein the Lord was laid.

And Mary stood without the Sepulchre,[6] weeping that she could not find her Lord.

And as she wept she beheld two Angels, one at the head and the other at the feet where the Lord had lain.[7]

---

[1] *The first day of the week was the early dawn of a new age—the age in which we are now living, and which began in the year* 1881.

[2] *Mary the Magdalene was not only the State unto which all Souls had gone down, but referred very specially to the Christ-Soul in His return.*

[3] *The Sepulchre was the Astral Kingdom wherein the Christ-Soul lay through the long night of the history of the Sin-offering.*

[4] *It was yet dark (spiritually) when the Christ-Soul awoke and rose from the tomb wherein He had been laid.*

[5] *The stone which was rolled away was the opening up of the way into the Spiritual Heavens.*

[6] *The failure of the Soul in its return to recognise the meaning and vision of the Divine Love and Wisdom.*

[7] *The two Angels were the Divine Love and Wisdom, the one guarding the head or life, and the other the feet or way—Gabriel and Raphael.*

And they spake unto her, saying, " Woman,[8] why weepest thou ? Whom seekest thou ? "

And unto them she said, " They have taken away my Lord, and I know not where to find Him." [9]

But they said unto her, " He is not here : He is risen from the dead, and He will make Himself manifest unto you."

And when they had so spoken, Mary turned away from the sepulchre and beheld the Lord before her vision, yet knew not that it was He.[10] But when He made Himself once more manifest, then was she glad and filled with great ioy.[11]

THE SOUL BEHOLDING HER LORD.
(A PRAYER).

O Most Holy and Ever Blessed One ! How full of Love Thou art ! How wonderful in all Thy gracious ways unto all Thy Children ! Thou takest away the darkness to bestow the Light of Thy Holy Presence. Thou dost speak unto the Soul in the language of old times when she knew Thee within the Sanctuary, and beheld Thy glorious image there ; for Thou in the greatness of Thy Love hath descended unto her low Estate to accomplish for her great things, even the Redemption of her Life.

We would bless Thee with all our Heart, and make of our lives songs of Praise, and of our powers the instruments wherewith to serve Thee and all Thy Children. Amen and Amen.

---

[8] *The term which originally implied the Intuition by which the Divine Vision is beheld.*

[9] *The acknowledged darkness in which the Intuition would be in on the morning of the return.*

[10] *The darkness within was so great that the Intuition did not know the true Vision.*

[11] *The joy born within the Soul when the true Vision broke upon her and she knew once more the Lord, knew the meaning of the Christhood and the perfect Vision of the Divine.*

THE DESCENT INTO HELL.

" He descended into Hell."—THE APOSTLES' CREED.

" A Body hast thou prepared for me; as a slave, mine ears are bored."—
PSALMIST.

" By which also He went down into the prison-houses of the bound."—
PETER.

WHEN the Master began the work of Redemption upon the Astral Kingdom, He descended from the Estate of Christhood to that represented by the Magdalene—a state in which no beautiful Spiritual light shines, one where the life is lived in a way that denotes "the outer darkness," one bereft of all true spiritual desire, and in which the Divine Name is unhonoured. He was born through parents in whom naught spiritual could be found, whose every impulse and desire were after the things of the body. He was born into an environment the very antithesis of the one by which He was surrounded when He came into the world to make the Christhood manifest. He was environed in an atmosphere full of the noisesome pestilence which characterised the Roman Court life of the Nero period, and so became the victim of all the terrible evils of those times. He came to know the unspeakable things which then were wrought. He passed through many awful experiences ere He reached Maturity and awoke to the meaning of the terrible conditions amid which He had been born. And when His Soul awoke from the stupor resulting from the Astral Kingdom descending upon Him and He began to realise what it had cost Him to lay aside His beautiful Christhood, the anguish which broke upon His Soul was such that even those around Him were confounded, so great and sore was it. He had gone down into the fearful pit full of miry clay and venomous things in human form, to become for a brief season even as those who dwelt there in order that He might know the reason why it was so difficult for those who once went down into it to rise up again, and that He might blot out all those images upon the Astral Kingdom through whose presence such a life was perpetuated.

IT WAS HIS DESCENT INTO HELL. And it was a

real descent; not an imaginary or hypothetical one such
as the Churches have professed to believe in and have
tried to explain, but without a true concensus of opinion
or satisfactory interpretation. For none of the views
held and expounded make the descent other than a
spacial descent of the personal Master, which could
scarcely be spoken of as a descent of the Christ-Soul,
any more than the appearance of the Master in the midst
of a company of impure men and women could be said to
be a real descent from Christhood into impurity. *Hell is
a state, and to descend into it is to descend into those conditions which make the state.* And so, for the Christ to
have descended into Hell, must have meant that He took
unto Himself those conditions which would constitute
that state. He must have taken upon Himself a body
through which he would be able to make such a descent;
for such an experience could only be entered into through
a vehicle whose impulses and desires were such as to
constitute the state known as Hell. And that He did take.
upon Himself such a body even the Psalmist foresaw
when he penned these words when writing concerning
the Sin-offering, "*Behold I was shapen in iniquity, and in
sin did my mother conceive.*" For the entire Psalm in its
original form related to the Sin-offering and the Restoration of the Soul to the Christhood Estate, and portrays
the evil done and the anguish of Soul imposed by it. It
speaks of the fearful dread of the Soul lest He should
lose altogether the power to receive the Divine Spirit,
and pleads that evil may not prevail against Him. Nay,
the agony within the Soul is so great that He seeks to be
delivered from the burden, so fearful is it, so overwhelming to the whole being, and prays that at last the
Divine Love may justify Him and make clear the
judgment which led him to undertake such a terrible
burden. And, when speaking of the wrong doing which
would form that burden, He clearly expressed His own
abhorance of it, and how. He should feel that it was
wrong committed against the Divine Love only. And
towards the close of the Psalm which contains this

astounding and sadly tragic description of what the Christ-Soul would pass through when He descended into Hell, He prayed that He might not only be restored and again be able to proclaim the Divine Love and Wisdom unto Souls, but that He might be saved from the great transgression, which was to deny the Divine Name.

Who has heard the language of that Psalm without feeling its profound pathos, without hearing its unspeakably sad and pathetic notes reverberating all around them, without a deep consciousness of the fact that He to whom it referred could indeed have been no ordinary human Soul? Who has heard it in the spirit without a growing conviction that the Soul who could go down into such depths of evil and feel the awful burden of its wrong, and sorrow and agonise over the evil with an anguish words fail to describe, and who asked the Divine Love to at last justify Him and make clear that His judgment was good, was no mere man?

Verily, the Sin-offering portrayed in the Psalm was so real, that the burden of it is even visible throughout the Psalm; and the throbbing of the Soul in His anguish, and the indescribable agony endured may even be heard!

The descent of the Sublime Master from His beautiful Christhood into the state of Hell, was so real that, as He approached the close of the Manifestation of the beautiful Estate of Christhood, the Vision of what was coming into His experience arose before Him and filled His whole being with such horror that He even then cried out in unspeakable agony of Soul to be delivered from it all.

SUCH WAS HIS GETHSEMANE BEFORE HIS CRUCIFIXION.

J. TODD FERRIER.

---

[1] Let readers prayerfully peruse the LI. Psalm in the light of this interpretation. They will find a truer rendering of it in Vol. IV., p. 250, of THE HERALD OF THE CROSS.

REASONS ASSIGNED FOR VIVISECTION.

(*Continued.*)

THE chief reason given for acquiescence in, and con-
donation of these barbarities, and one which is
usually thoughtlessly accepted without further enquiry as
being adequate, is that such methods of research are
necessary and indeed indispensable in order to gain knowledge for the successful treatment of disease when a very
little investigation would have revealed the fact that there
is anything but unaminity of opinion on this point
amongst those who ought to know, for we have the
recorded testimony of many of the most eminent members of the medical profession to the effect that no knowledge of real and lasting value has been gained thereby,
but, on the contrary, that such "knowledge" has been
eminently unsatisfactory, contradictory, and misleading,
and has often seriously hindered the real advance of
medical science. (See appendix I.)

And here it is well to call attention to the fact that
although vivisectors in this country are loud in proclaiming that their researches have for their sole aim the
alleviation of human disease, and are undertaken in a
purely altruistic and humanitarian spirit—knowing full
well that it is only in this (false) belief that even a selfish
public tolerates the gross cruelties involved in them—yet
their brethren of the Continent are usually found to disa-
vow any such humanitarian objects with cynical frank-
ness; Professors Richet and Hermann are perhaps their
foremost representatives, who by virtue of their position
must be assumed to be well acquainted with the motives
which actuate their colleagues, and this is what they say
on this point:

"I do not believe that a *single experimenter says* to himself
when he gives curare to a rabbit or cuts the spinal cord of a dog,
'*Here is an experiment which will relieve or cure the disease of
some men.*' *No, he does not think of that.* He says to himself,
'I will clear up an obscure point.   I will seek out a new fact.'"
—CHARLES RICHET, M.D., Professor of Physiology, Paris, in
Revue des deux Mondes, Feb. 15, 1883.

Extracts from "Why I Condemn Vivisection," by Robert H.
Perks, M.D., F.R.C.S. (Eng.)   *Vide* see advertisement pages.

"The advancement of our knowledge, and *not utility to medicine*, is the true and straightforward object of all vivisection. *No true investigator in his researches thinks of their practical utilization.* Science can afford to despise this justification with which vivisection has been defended in England."—Dr. L. HERMANN, Professor of Physiology, Zurich, *Die Vivisections-frage*, Leipsic, 1877. (Italics mine).

Anything offering a more complete illustration of what vivisection really means than do these testimonies of its chief friends it would be difficult to imagine, nor can a greater condemnation of it than that contained in these utterances be well conceived.

I have said that vivisection is often condoned thoughtlessly, because if the actual practice could be revealed, brought home, as it were, in all its naked hideousness to persons not yet hardened by familiarity, they would recoil in horror from it.

Let us suppose a sick man consenting to an animal being brought to his bedside and subjected to prolonged torture and mutilation in the hope that he might *possibly* gain thereby relief of his disorder ; would not his neighbours, as their hearts were torn by the cries of the victim, denounce him with one accord as a heartless wretch unworthy of the name of man? I have sufficient faith in the better feelings of humanity to believe that this would be so.

Yet such is the present apathy and lack of imagination, to use no harsher terms, that in the absence of practical realization people tacitly become the aiders and abettors of numberless deeds of darkness of this nature perpetrated ostensibly on their behalf and in their interests.

It is not my purpose within the limits of this pamphlet to discuss the questions, as to the exact amount of pain inflicted in certain cases, or the value of the results alleged to have been gained by the practice of vivisection. The primary consideration which confronts us is this—Is it *right* or is it *wrong*? Is its practice a violation of the moral law, and of the Eternal and Divine laws of Justice and Love? If it be, as I believe it to be, such a violation, then the former questions are relatively unimportant ; for no pleading of "good intentions," no amount of "good results," no minimising of the amount of pain inflicted, can justify it. Such a plea might, with equal want of logic, be advanced to establish the contention that the good results accruing from the benevolent distribution of stolen property by a thief can justify his crime.

On this point I qoute Herr D. L. Ortt :—

"In our decision on the morality of a question, we may not ask whether it will be useful or prejudicial. We admit in other cases that a human life is not to be esteemed the highest and most important of all things. We esteem it brave and noble that a man should offer up his life for an ideal. We admire the heroes who died for their fatherland, or from loyalty to a cause or person : we extol the martys who died for their creed and thereby we proclaim that we esteem ideals higher than a human life. . . . We should hold it cowardice if any one, to rescue his life, had renounced loyalty to his prince, his fatherland, or his creed. Is it not then cowardice that out of fear to lose our miserable life we should forsake loyalty to our highest feeling of humanity and allow innocent creatures to suffer in order to prolong somewhat our days on earth, or to improve a little the condition of our health ?

"Let each one answer this question for himself.

"For my part, when I first faced the question of whether vivisection was or was not lawful, of whether animals might be sacrificed, when this would indeed bring good to many men, or, indeed, to a great number of animals, there flashed into my mind suddenly the thought of how Jesus would have regarded the question. Would He ever have plunged the vivisecting knife into the body of an animal to further science or the prosperity of mankind ? And when I considered in this light my choice was made. Then I knew vivisection to be an evil, howsoever one may seek to justify it.

I think it is not difficult to see that vivisection, in its nature, is essentially anti-human as well as being opposed to the Divine Will ; for its true roots lie deep in cynical egoism and callous selfishness, the prolific soil from which spring the worst crimes.

When vivisection was first introduced into England on an extended scale in the middle of the last century, the medical profession (like the persons in the case we have supposed) recoiled in horror from the attempt to advance knowledge by such means, and their leading organs, including the *Lancet* and the *British Medical Journal,* condemned the practice in no measured terms. (See appendix III). What a confirmation is their changed attitude towards it to-day, of the fact that long and familiar association with evil surely clouds the understanding and debases the moral standard! Truly one cannot touch pitch and escape defilement!

Robert H. Perks, M.D., F.R.C.S.

To be continued.

THE CREATURES' DELIVERANCE.

The Manifestation of the Lord which is now breaking upon the Soul, will cause His Light to be beheld in the dark places of the Earth;

For it shall be that, when He appeareth, those things which are of the darkness, and the evil born from the darkness, and all the anguish born of the evil, shall flee away.

Through the Unfoldment unto the Soul of the meaning of His Glory, and the Interpretation unto the Understanding of the nature of His Love, will the prison-houses of the stricken Earth be opened that the oppressed may go free;

For, through the Vision of the Glory of the Lord within the Soul, and the knowledge of the meaning of His Love within the Heart, shall all Souls arrive at the life of Compassion, and make it manifest in their pity unto all Creatures.

Through the Glory of the Lord within the Soul shall the groaning of the prisoners who are made captive within the houses where deeds of evil are wrought in the name of Good, cease;

For those who now oppress the creatures shall be ashamed of all their works when they know what it meaneth to afflict and oppress the weak and defenceless.

THE RESURRECTION.
(THE RESURRECTION OF JESUS.)

" Thou wilt not leave my Soul in Hell, neither wilt thou suffer Thy Holy One to know corruption."—ACTS.

THE Resurrection which is now affirmed to be the very ground of all real belief in the Divine Nature of the Master, but which so many find themselves unable to accept as an historical fact, was a very true history though not written on the material planes. It is quite true that it came to be related to the man Jesus who was represented as having died, been buried, descended into Hell to preach unto the spirits bound in the prison-houses, and then to have risen again from the tomb on the third day ; but it is also true that the man Jesus through whom the Christhood was made manifest, did not die when the Jews crucified Him, but that He revived and rose to life again in the midst of His most intimate friends, because the elements of physical death were not found in Him. For in a perfect body there are no elements of physical death ; and though the body may be laid aside when the Soul has to pass into other conditions of environment, yet, it is put off as the garment is laid aside which covered it. And the body of Jesus was perfect in that all its elements were pure and were responsive to the central will, and, therefore, were not in a state to know corruption in any degree.

And so when it is affirmed that He revived and rose again in what has been understood as the Resurrection, a great truth is set forth, though it is not of the nature which the Western World has believed. For the writers of the Records not understanding what was meant by the presentation of the Resurrection found in the Sayings of the Master as these were presented in the Logia of St. John, nor knowing the great truth that the body of the Master, being so pure, could not know corruption, confounded the revival of the body of the Master with the great truth set forth in the doctrine of the Resurrection. And they so environed that great truth in material pictures and local history, lighting these up with the glamour of astounding physical events through a Divine intervention, that the meaning of the Resurrection had no longer any Spiritual and Divine Significance beyond the supposed interposition, nor any direct and individual meaning for the Soul. For it was a *physical Resurrection that was presented*, and made the foundation of the doctrine which has been instrumental in blinding the spiritual eyes of many to the great and all important and sublime truth implied in the real Resurrection which the Master taught to His most intimate followers. For the doctrine of the Resurrection of a body which has once seen death to all its elements, has not only been a dominant note of the teachings of the Church all through the era of its history, but it has led the Soul to think of physical resuscitation to the body which has known death as the only true Resurrection, and thus has taken away from the Soul all that the Resurrection meant for it. For the true meaning of the beautiful Teachings concerning the Resurrection which were given by the Master, related to the restoration of the Soul, the raising of it up out of the grave of spiritual death wherein it had lain buried since the day when it allowed itself to be crucified between the two thieves of gross superstition and the materialisation of all the beautiful sacred histories relating to the Divine Love, the Divine Purpose towards the whole of His children, and to the Soul itself.

J. TODD FERRIER.

THE RESURRECTION.

(THE RESURRECTION OF THE SOUL.)

" Verily, Verily, I say unto you, The hour is coming, and now is, when the dead shall hear the voice of the Son of God ; and they who hear shall live."

" Marvel not at this ; for the hour is coming in the which all who are in their graves shall hear His Voice."—St. JOHN.

THE doctrine of the Resurrection upon which the Church built its belief in the resuscitation of the body whose elements had all known death, was one which concerned the Soul alone. It had no relation whatever to anything material, but wholly to a great and blessed spiritual experience. It referred to the awakening of the Soul to the reality of its own spiritual nature and its coming forth from the tomb of a non-spiritual state wherein is no knowledge of the Divine Love and Wisdom, into the realisation of a new and more glorious life wherein the consciousness of the Divine Presence within its Sanctuary is realised, and the Divine Love and Wisdom known. It spoke of the Divine Love towards the Soul ; of the Angelic ministry from the Divine Love unto the Soul even whilst it lay asleep within the tomb of the sense-life wherein it had been placed through the evil conditions amid which it found itself when its inherent spiritual light was extinguished and it was crucified between the two thieves of superstition and materialism. It spoke of how the tomb had even been sealed by those in outward authority, and guarded by them lest the Soul should escape ; and it showed how the Angel of the Lord would roll away the stone, and command the Soul to come forth into life again. It presented the Soul as having been taken away from the home in which the Divine Love had placed it, even from the home of Joseph of Arimathea—the Ioseph who was always with the Christ-Soul during the Manifestation ; the Divine Love known as the Adonai upon the Divine Kingdom whose dwelling was in the Divine Heights, as the term Arithmathea implies ; the Sign of the Cross, because He alone could Redeem ; the Bearer of the Cross, because He alone could carry it—for, prior to what is now known as "The Fall," the Soul dwelt within the Home of the Divine Love, knowing not evil but only the service of a perfect love. It showed the state into which the Soul had gone down when it represented it as lying within the tomb wherein man had never lain, shut up and guarded by the authorities who at the time were in power, meaning by that that it was no mere earthly grave whose door was sealed and guarded, but the spiritual state which had overtaken the Soul when its beautiful spiritual life was cut off through its betrayal and crucifixion by the outward powers or material influences which ruled everywhere. It showed how terrible was the darkness which had overtaken the Soul when it represented it as in the state of Mary the Magdalene on the morning of the Resurrection, mourning over all the unspeakable loss that had come to her when they took away her Lord and she knew not where to find Him; for it was the state of the Soul that was there portrayed and not any outward history, the very terms implying the meaning—Maria, the Soul who has known the Divine Love and Wisdom; and Magdalene, the one who has known the darkness where the light of the Divine shines out. And on the Resurrection morning the Soul was yet in such spiritual darkness and overwhelming sorrow that she knew not her Lord when He spake unto her, knew not His Visage or the Ever Blessed Vision within her own Sanctuary, knew not His voice when He spoke, until He made Himself known in a form familiar unto her, and revealed Himself again as her Lord.

The Resurrection of the Soul will thus be seen to have a very real meaning for all who are ready to arise out of the grave of the Sense-life; out of the bondage imposed by the outward authorities or dominant and dominating material forces whether individual or collective, whether Social, Scholastic or Ecclesiastical; out of the darkness imposed within the tomb where the Divine Love is unknown, to seek the Lord of all Life even unto the finding of Him.

J. TODD FERRIER.

THE EARTHLY AND THE HEAVENLY.

But some there are who ask how the dead are raised up, and with what kind of body they come forth.

Thou foolish one, unless what thou sowest be such as will rise up into life, it must needs see corruption and know only mortality.

The glory of earthly things is not as the glory of heavenly things; for the one passeth away with the changing fashions of the things which are mortal, but the other continueth, growing ever more and more until the perfect day.

The things which are mortal cannot know immortality, nor corruptible things incorruption; for that which is of the Earth is earthy, and that which is of Heaven is heavenly.

And as the things of the Earth yet know decay and corruption, they cannot have immortality; but the the things of Heaven know no decay, having within them the life which is Immortal and Eternal.

The first things of the Earth were spiritual and were not unnatural, and the natural man was then a living Soul; but now those things accounted natural are not spiritual, and the present natural man discerneth not the things of God.

For the things of God none knoweth, save the Spirit of God who is in man; and none other may interpret them unto him but the Heavenly Counsellor. For who knoweth the things of God save the Spirit of the Lord? And who could instruct man save the Lord whose Spirit is within him?

But the earthy man whose eyes are beholden that he cannot see other than earthly things, discerneth not the things of the Spirit.

THE RESURRECTION.
(THE RESURRECTION MORNING).

"On the first day of the week cometh Mary the Magdalene unto the Sepulchre while it was yet dark, and findeth the stone rolled away."

"But Mary stood without, weeping. And as she wept, behold the Angel appeared unto her, and said, why weepest thou ? Behold, He is not here, but is risen, and shall make Himself manifest unto you."

"And when she turned away from the Sepulchre, she beheld the Lord whom she had loved."

THE Resurrection of the Soul whose story was materialised and made to refer to the resuscitation of Jesus, has now come. It has broken upon the world in the most unexpected way. The Christ Soul has again arisen from the tomb wherein they laid Him, and has even appeared unto many ; and all who have heard the voice of the Son of Man, have come forth from their graves into newness of life. For the Angel of the Lord hath descended from the Heavens of the Divine Love and hath rolled away the stone which the authorities had placed at the door of the tomb and sealed with their signature. And now the Christ-Soul who went down even unto the depths of Hell that He might give forth of His great Love for the Children of the Father, the Love wherewith the Father had loved Him even before the foundation of this present cosmos, having triumphed over the powers which prevailed against the Lord and His Anointed Ones, and broken the bands wherewith the enemy bound the Soul, hath arisen and come forth from the tomb wherein they laid Him. For the true life which He lived and the true Teachings which He gave unto His most intimate followers, have been recovered, and are now being presented to the world so that all who hear and understand may also arise out of their spiritual captivity and sense-life bondage, and go up into the Holy City of the Redeemed Life crowned with the beautiful Estate of Christhood—the true Crown of Life wherein the Divine Love is realised within the Soul, and the Divine Wisdom is become a glorious possession.

The Resurrection of the Christ-Soul and the awakening of the Christhood, has taken even the watchers beside

the tomb with surprise. The early visitors who had
forgotten all that the Master had said unto them
concerning the things which would happen, were as-
tounded, when they themselves went to the tomb, to meet
the Angel of the Lord who informed them that He had
risen ; for the tomb was the Astral Kingdom which also
contained the Middle Wall or Partition whereon were the
Handwritings which were against the Soul's upward
progress, and even Hell itself. And the early watchers
were all those Souls who had to share in the burden of
the Sin-offering upon the Astral Kingdom, who loved the
Christhood Estate interpreted by the Master and made
manifest unto them, *who sought through all the long
night of the silence of the Christ-Soul to find the true
path leading unto the blessed experience of the inward
realisation of the Divine Love and Wisdom,* the Saints
of God in every land who travailed in great pain to
realise and make manifest the glorious life. Unto them
hath the Angel of the Lord spoken, saying, "Whom
seekest Thou? Behold! He is not here, but is risen.
He shall make Himself manifest in Galilee, as He
said "—*i.e.,* within the purified mind.

Whom seekest thou? The living Lord? Behold!
He is not in the tomb where they laid Him. The
conditions of the Astral Kingdom could not contain
Him. The limitations of things sensuous could not keep
Him confined within their tomb, even though the
authorities had set their seal upon the stone which
guarded the door. Behold! He is not here where men
laid Him when they put away His beautiful Vision and
shut it up within the tomb of their materialised
environments and interpretations. He whom ye seek,
all ye who truly seek the life presented by the Master, shall
surely show Himself unto you. For the Christ-Soul was
the Divine Love made manifest and the Divine Wisdom
interpreted unto all who were able and willing to behold
and receive the Divine Life ; and that Love and that
Wisdom of the Heavenly Father which are ever the same
in their nature and purpose, are again being made

manifest so that all who are able to discern and enter into the blessed life which they give, may behold them, and come unto the glorious realisation of their meaning within the Soul.

Behold! He is risen indeed and hath appeared unto Simon Peter, Mary the Magdalene, and many of His brethren! He is not here, He is not there, in this city or in that desert-place, or where the tombs built by men are found, and where the dead dwell ; *but He is within the City of the Soul, amid the Galilean Hills, by the shores of the Galilean Sea, on the Highway to the Village of Emmaus.* For the Kingdom of God is *within the Soul ;* the Christhood Vision is to be beheld amid the uplands of a purified mind (the Galilean Hills) by the shore of the Sea of the Spiritual Vision where the very Heavens are reflected (Galilee), on the way to the realisation of the Christhood (Emmaus), and even in the Garden where the Soul has known its Gethsemane. For unto the weeping and devoted Soul who has known the awful state re-presented by the Magdalene, the Vision grows clear when the gentle voice of the Divine Love speaks. Within the Soul who has been like Simon Peter, full of the Divinest and Noblest impulses, the true discerner of the nature and meaning of the Christ Manifestation, yet subject to those material conditions which have always betrayed the Soul since it first left the Divine shelter, the Vision comes full of healing and spiritual strength. And so unto all the brethren of the Christhood, all who are truly endeavouring to live the Redeemed Life and to walk in the path which leadeth unto the glorious Inheritance of the Saints, the Christhood Estate, the Vision is given according as the Soul is able to receive and see. Yea, even unto doubting Thomas whose spiritual trust does not pass beyond the limits of outward and sensuous testimony, the Vision may appear when the Soul retires into its Sanctuary, having first shut the gates of the sense-life lest the external elements or authorities might disturb the mind and so prevent the Vision from being beheld unto a true apprehension of its meaning.

The Lord is risen indeed ! All that the Christ foretold has come to pass. The Vine has borne its fruit, the
vintage has been gathered, the Winepress has been made
full and the grapes trodden. The Divine Love has
Travailed all the way from Bozrah to Edom, and in
returning has had his garments red dyed in the work of
treading the Winepress alone : for the way from Bozrah
unto Edom was the lonely path of the desert from the
Christhood Estate unto the land or estate in which the
Divine Love is unknown. The Christhood of the Divine
Soul who made manifest the Christhood through Jesus,
was laid aside when He descended into the states where
the very fires of Hell burned; where the fruits of the
Divine Love which filled Him in His Christhood were
crushed in the Winevat of the world of evil, and His once
beautiful garments were all stained. But the Winepress
having been trodden, and the return unto Bozrah made,
the Angel of the Lord who rolled away the stone from
the door of the tomb, now proclaims that the Lord is
risen indeed ; for the Christ-Soul has awakened, and
many who slept have arisen with Him and have entered
into the City of the Christhood Estate.

It is the Resurrection morning. The new Day has
indeed broken, and a great hope has come unto many
Souls through the glorious Vision of the risen Christhood
wherein the Divine Love is once more known and
realised and the Divine Vision is beheld within the
Sanctuary of the Soul. The very Heavens are telling of
the wonders wrought by the Divine Love ; and those who
are listening of the dwellers upon the Earth, not only
hear the messages, but are filled with wonder, praise,
and the fear of the Lord. Phenomena of the most
astounding nature are beheld by all who have watched
for the Resurrection morn to break ; but the Phenomena
are not in physical wonders and unnatural material and
ostentatious displays, but in the great awakening of Souls
to seek for the Christ-life and Christ-Spirit.

J. TODD FERRIER,

THE HERALD OF THE CROSS.

Vol v.   New Series.   April, 1909.   No. 4.

A DAY OF GLADNESS.

Let the Heavens rejoice, and let the Earth again be glad !

Let the Seas tell it forth in their roaring, and the Winds bear the message far and wide !

Let the Hills which catch the rays of the Morning Glory, make it manifest ; and the deep Valleys wherein no light has broken, at last behold the Glory of it !

Let the Mountains flow down before its coming, and show unto all Souls the wonders of the Day ; and let the Depths sound forth the glorious harmonies begotten of the hour !

And let all Souls know what it meaneth for the Lord to come into His own ; to establish His Kingdom in Israel and make manifest His Righteousness in Judah ; to build again His Tabernacle in Zion and His Altar upon Mount Moriah; to redeem Jerusalem from her enemies and restore all her Gates and Palaces.

For the Day of the Lord is upon us when the Earth shall return again from her Captivity and be healed of her mistake, and when the Double Portion of the Divine Blessing shall be given unto her from the Divine Love Who is healing her.

THE PSYCHIC VISION.
WHAT IT IS,
AND
HOW TO REALISE IT.

THE subject is one which is full of a strange fascinating power to many, one touching on the mysterious

awe and even fear on the part of some Souls; one which draws the lover of true spiritual things ever further and further along the path towards the Realisation of the Divine in his holy quest to see and possess the Holy Grail. It may not always be understood in its nature. Indeed, it would seem to be little understood, judging from the use to which the expression is put, the character of many of the visions to which it is applied, the general and often vague meaning attached to it. It has come to be associated with experiences which are not necessarily psychic, which may be entered into by those who are not upon the plane of life whereon the true Psychic Vision is beheld, which relate to much which has no connection whatever with the true Psychic Vision, and which not only tends to obscure the meaning of that Vision, but to lead the Soul away from the only path by which it can attain unto the Blessed Realisation.

I.

WHAT THE VISION IS.

That this is not a wrong view of much that passes under the name of the Psychic Vision will be best seen as we approach the question of what the Psychic Vision is, and in endeavouring to answer the question we have to keep before our minds the true and derivative meaning of the term Psychic, and then to discover from the very meaning of the term the nature of the Vision.

The word Ψυχη, being the Greek term for the Soul, has relation only to the Soul. And the Psychic Vision is the vision of the Soul, so that a true Psychic is one who sees from the Soul the meaning of things wholly spiritual and Divine. And the Vision of the Soul as to its nature, intensity, exaltation, and fulness will depend on the state in which the Soul is at the time. The Soul sees only from within. It is not like a spectator standing upon the outermost sphere, but one who is within all the spheres, and who sees from the very innermost centre through all the spheres. Her vision must always be in harmony with her own nature; that is, it must be truly spiritual. Even when she looks outwards through all the spheres of her operations and through which so much of her experience of life upon the world comes, she must needs always view everything in the light of her own nature; that is, she must view all things in their spiritual relationships. For the Soul is a pure spiritual organism, containing within herself potentialities marked with the image of the Divine, an organism whose nature and constitution are not to be known and understood except by the Soul herself, and that only after she has reached the fulness of her evolution, which is the Estate of Christhood. When she is drawn away from her own true Kingdom, which is the Spiritual, by the conditions amid which she finds herself as she vehicles through the human form, and discovers that her own beautiful desires and purposes are influenced and even changed by the conditions, then her life is burdened with sorrow, and her vision of spiritual things is dimmed. For the Soul finds no joy in following the ways of the sense-life as these are generally lived, but finds her joy alone in pure spiritual aspiration and culture, in reaching outward only to bring all the powers upon her various spheres into true harmony with her own beautiful longings and visions, and in ever striving to rise higher and higher towards the fulness of her own life, to climb more and more the steep ascent along the path to the Divine, to reach the summit of "the Hills of the Lord" (or spiritual uplands) which lie in the path, and even to scale the heights of the Spiritual World known as "the Mountains of the Lord" (these being wonderful spiritual interior states) whereon the Divine Visions are beheld. It is her joy to serve her Lord alone; that is, to serve only the Divine in all her experience on the various spheres of her operation, and to seek unto the fulfilment of her own true life in the realisation of Christhood.

This basic thought of the true nature of the Soul as to her elements, function and purpose, and her inherent Divine potentialities—a thought whose clear apprehension is most necessary in these days—will enable us to better understand what the Psychic Vision is as to its nature. It will enable us to differentiate between what are objective and semi-objective phenomena beheld upon the outermost planes, and the phenomena within the innermost sphere of the Soul herself which speak to her of the Divine Love and Wisdom, and interpret these according as she is able to receive. It will enable us to better understand much of the phenomena which is spoken of as Psychic, though it may have little, or not any, relation to the experiences of the Soul upon the various spheres wherein she moves and operates ; and likewise to enter more fully into the meaning of those wonderful spiritual visions which have been the heritage of nearly all the great true mystics in all ages and in all lands, and very specially to recognise the nature and purpose of many of the wonderful Visions and Illuminations found in the sacred Records of the Ancient Religions as well as those given within the Christian Scriptures.

MAN AS A SPIRITUAL SYSTEM.

Perhaps were we to pass into the innermost sphere of the Soul as a spiritual system, by commencing with the outermost sphere, it would help some to more clearly apprehend the great difference between the general phenomena spoken of as Psychic and those phenomena which are truly Psychic. For it should always be borne in mind that man is fourfold in his nature. He is in himself a little system, a Microcosm of the Macrocosm, possessing his own various spheres of operation from the outermost to the innermost. And upon the outermost sphere there are times when the signs of his operations would not lead an observer to suppose (if he knew not otherwise) that man is not a mere creature upon the physical planes of the world, so much and so deeply is he at times immersed in purely material things and interests. The Vision by which he is most arrested upon these outer spheres is that of the sense-life in its manifold presentations. For the lower mind, like the eye, beholds only the things of the sense-life. Its vision is along the plane of the senses. It sees and measures and calculates upon that plane. It deals with material things only, unless the mind and life have been purified and consecrated to the highest vision, life and service. The physical eye sees the objective world, and the lower mind beholds the apparent relationship of the things seen. Even when they transcend the very outermost objective world to behold (upon what may be spoken of as the supersensuous world,) the reflections of the objective spheres, it is only the things which pertain to the sense-life that they behold and relate, though unfortunately they often mistake these supersensuous visions for true visions of another and higher sphere. The lower mind can only behold earthly things even as the eye can only see the objective world, until that mind is so purified that it is in the condition to become a vehicle for the visions beheld by the Mind of the Soul which is the understanding, when it also will seek to see the spiritual relationship of everything. And unless that mind be purified, and all the spheres of its operation, and trained by a purified and enlightened understanding to behold the spiritual significance of things, and to see that their true relationships are all spiritual, then its vision will only be of the Earth, and so earthly; and the true relationships and the profound spiritual significance of everything will be unknown to the individual.

THE SPHERES OF THE MIND.

From the outermost spheres we now come to those which we may speak of as the intermediary spheres in which the higher mind or true intellect, or reason, operates. It is the spiritual mind, or mind of the Soul, which by nature, or rather in its purified and truly equilibriated state, should and would reflect only truly spiritual and Divine things. It is that girdle of the Soul which has been spoken of as having once been bright within, but

which is now dark, and which remains dark until Phoibos
strikes the girdle and it again becomes illumined ; for the
mind of the Soul is the reflector of the Soul, the spiritual
magnetic plane of the Soul upon which the heavenly
images once were thrown through which and by means of
which the Soul of old times was educated in spiritual and
Divine things.   And that mind was once in the state in
which it could receive from the Spiritual Heavens profound and beautiful teachings about the Soul's own history,
the history of this world with all its wonderful planes and
spheres and kingdoms, and the knowledge of the Divine
Love and Wisdom, and reflect these beautiful things into
the Soul.   *Then it was all light within.*   It was illumined
from the Divine Presence within the innermost Sanctuary
of its own system.   Its heavens were lit up with the glory
broken upon the mind from the Divine.   But when the
Mind lost its equilibrium and became inverted in its
powers through descending from the kingdom and spheres
of its life and functions, it also lost the power to reflect
spiritual and Divine things, and took unto itself a new
power upon the spheres unto which it had descended,
namely, the power to reflect material images.   *Then it
became dark within and without* : for it lost the power to
receive spiritual and Divine images or thought-forms so
that its light had to be received from without through
images and thought-forms in the objective and semi-
objective world.   But even though these latter gave unto it
light at times upon the path by which alone it could return
unto its own true kingdom and perform once more its true
function, yet was it dark both within and without for
untold ages amid the conditions in which it found itself
through the influences of all the objective world upon it ;
for the beautiful meanings of the images and thought-
forms of Spiritual and Divine things were all changed.
The inner significance of them was lost.   They became
materialised until even the objective forms took the place
of those inner beautiful truths of which they spake.   On
the one hand they were made the instruments of the most
terrible superstitions which we may find associated with

all the Religions in the old world ; and on the other hand
they became the foundation of an intellectual science
known by the term Occultism, which, whilst it avoided
the lower sphere of superstition, made of the beautiful
images and thought-forms nothing more than the language of an intellectual science into the knowledge of
which men and women had to be initiated ; and they
were permitted to enter into that knowledge only by
means of various rites and ceremonies which grew up
around the science, and which at times imposed upon the
Initiates ordeals of the most trying and even terrible
character.   And thus on the one hand those beautiful
things which had been wholly sacred to the Soul, and
Spiritual and Divine in their true significance, became only
objective forms and instruments of a most wonderful
superstitious   reverence,   and   were   associated   with
the   outward   histories   and teachings   of those   who
became known as the Messengers ; and, on the other
hand, they were turned into an intellectual system, a
philosophic knowledge, whose vision was only along the
plane of the inverted mind, a system of thought which,
however beautiful in its thought-forms with their inner
significance, gradually became less and less spiritual.

Thus was the mind plunged into deeper darkness
concerning the true light by which every Soul must be
enlightened ere it can understand and realise truly
Spiritual and Divine things.   And thus also was the
Vision born of the Divine Presence within the Sanctuary
of the Soul lost.   For it was the province of the mind
to behold that Vision, receive the glory of it, and then to
reflect that glory, so that the entire spiritual system
became illumined with the spiritual light as it was broken
upon the lower mind, and manifested upon every sphere.

And so we may understand how it is that the visions
which are so often of a merely material order, whether
merely sensuous or of a supersensuous kind, are taken to
indicate Spiritual and even Divine things ; how such
things have come to be associated with what is understood
to be the Psychic Vision, and to be taken for it ; and, also,

how those who are able to function upon what are known
as the Occult and Astral planes, and see images upon
these planes, have come to be spoken of as true Psychics,
men and women unto whom the Heavens are opened.

THE SOUL'S TRUE SPHERE.

And now we will look at the innermost sphere of the
Soul's operation, *the within of the man* who knows Spiritual
and Divine things.   As the outward vision beholds only
the things upon the outermost sphere, and the mind sees
only along the plane of the objective and semi-objective
worlds and beholds only their relation to one another and
the world upon the material side (until the mind becomes
so purified that it takes the images thrown upon it from
the inner spheres and looks upon everything as one who
would know the true meaning and relation of everything
to the great spiritual organic whole) ; and as the higher
mind or reason which once truly saw upon the spheres of
the Soul herself, and was able to receive constantly the
light of the Divine as that light was broken upon it, and
to reflect the glory of it through all the spheres of the
Soul's system (but which is now very largely occupied on
the one hand with an objective and often superstitious
religious manifestation, and on the other hand with the
endeavour to discover the inner meanings of the manifold
images and thought-forms which the Occultists of old
time brought down from their spiritual significance); so
the Soul only understands upon her own Kingdom, which
is necessarily a spiritual kingdom, and one in harmony
with her own nature and to which all her elements are
able to magnetically respond.   And when she has visions
of the spiritual things whose meanings are all interior,
and of the Divine Love and the Divine Wisdom under
the images and forms in which she is able to receive these,
she always sees upon her own special sphere.   Her vision
is not objective, but within.   And as she grows in the
path towards the Divine, so do her visions grow purer,
clearer, and greater, until at last she is even able to look
with unveiled face upon the beautiful visions which come
to her from the Spiritual Heavens, the Celestial World,

and the Kingdom of the Divine. And when she is able to so see and understand, then is she in a state to rise on to the various Heavens and receive from the Angelic and Divine Spheres.

Thus do we behold the profound meaning lying couched in the terms the Psychic Soul and the Psychic Vision.

II.

HOW TO ARRIVE AT IT.

We have now to consider what perhaps is after all the most important part of our subject, to inquire how best to reach up to so high an experience and to visions so sublime. And in doing so, let us not forget that these beautiful experiences are not only natural to the Soul, but are her heritage; and that every Soul may again arrive at the condition in her experience when the Psychic Vision will be a reality unto her, and her constant joy.

Now the Psychic Vision being wholly spiritual and dependent upon the true equilibrium of the mind, and the true equilibrium of the mind being dependent upon the magnetic conditions in the outer spheres of operation, it is most essential that these spheres have their magnetic conditions so purified and adjusted that their *polarity will be Soul-ward.* But that means that the whole life will be brought into a state of harmony with the Soul; that the sense-life will be so purified that it no longer dominates the life; that the lower mind becomes the vehicle only of pure and noble purpose, desire and feeling; that the heart knows no dominant affection born from the sense-life; and that the higher mind seeks to be illumined from the light begotten from the Divine Presence within the Sanctuary. And to so purify the entire life is to lift it up into the conditions where the material life does not dominate, but where the whole purpose of life is spiritual— a task which is most beautiful and fruitful in its issues, but most difficult and even arduous in the labours required for its accomplishment. For it means the chastening of the whole man; the elimination from his system of every-thing of an evil and impure order; the casting out from the heart of every false, impure and unspiritual affection, that it may become the throne of only such loves as will aid the Soul in its upwardness and its Realisation of the Divine Life, Love and Wisdom ; the driving out from the mind of every element of the world-spirit, the desire to be as the world-spirit, the mere money-making thoughts and purposes, the mere pleasure-loving desires and feelings, the empty ambitions by which those are swayed whom the world-spirit dominates, the love of power and place and estate which are other than those which are God-given ; and then the cleansing ot all the bodily feelings, tastes and desires, until the body is a purified house, and one fit to be the dwelling of a beautiful spiritual being, possessing potentialities by which even the Kingdom of the Divine may be reached. Such a process means at first great endeavour and strong self-denying purpose. It means that all impure living upon every sphere will be eschewed, and that every endeavour will be made to tread the narrow way which, though so straitened, leads unto the blessed Realisation. It means that the body hence-forth will be nourished and built up of elements which are pure in themselves, and which contribute to the attain-ment of the true spiritual life ; that no such elements as are contained within the general diet of men and women shall be introduced in the mistaken belief that they are necessary, or that they are true and pure elements such as the body should have supplied to it. It means that no creature shall have to suffer pain and loss even to the laying down of its life to supply food or clothing, or in *any way* to minister unto the body ; for with a purified mind and heart the very thought of Abattoirs and Shambles and Physiological Laboratories will be not only repugnant and repulsive, but also a terrible burden of sorrow and even shame that such a state of things exists and is perpetuated in our midst. For no pure body could be built up on the flesh of the creatures ; no pure mind could be cultured upon the thoughts whose very images are the inversion of every tender, humane and pure thing ; no true heart could be nourished by a love bereft of true compassion and pity; the various spheres of the Soul's operation could not be chastened divinely and be spiritually illumined and uplifted even to the spiritual state wherein the true Psychic Vision becomes a reality, where such things are done and approved of or condoned with, since they generate evil in manifold forms, impose untold and even unspeakable sufferings upon both the creatures afflicted and Souls who are affected by the conditions set up by them, and so darken all the life and make it impossible for the light given unto the Soul from the Divine to shine through the system. These terrible and impure things are the cause of the gross spiritual darkness which lieth upon the people; and the putting of them away on the part of many has largely contributed to the wonderful spiritual light breaking upon the world, which is so obvious in these days unto all who are in a state to truly discern and understand. For the new light is the harbinger of still greater things as Souls rise up out of these terrible evils and the bondage to the sense-life in which they are held.

Such then is the way unto the Realisation of the true Psychic Vision, the path along which the Soul must journey if her vision is to be true and its glory reflected through all the spheres of her experience. And if the Soul follow that path, purifying every sphere of her system from the within unto the outermost, then the day will come when the glory of the Divine Love and Wisdom shall illumine her, clothing her with light as with a garment, and causing the glory to break forth upon every sphere, plane and kingdom of her experience. She shall then see as the Seers of ancient days saw, and know as the Prophets whom the Divine Love and Wisdom informed, knew; for she shall be uplifted in her life above all conditions which eclipse the Vision of her Lord, above the planes of materialism, above the supersensuous Astral plane, above the magnetic Occult Kingdom, away from the mere objective, semi-objective and intellectual worlds, unto the Angelic Kingdom, where only purified lives can enter, and upward still upward even until the Vision upon the Divine Kingdom is Realised.

J. TODD FERRIER,

A VISION OF THE SOUL.

In the Night of the Soul when the whole World lay asleep, knowing not that the Day of the Lord was near and that His approach unto its Gates was at hand, I saw the Heavens bowing themselves before Him and proclaiming His Praise.

I beheld the descent of two of the heavenly systems as if they were approaching the Earth, and I knew that they were the harbingers of Glad Tidings unto Men.

In the fulness of their glory they were wonderful to behold, so radiant were they ; and in their fashion they were glorious.

I saw the Constellation Cancer descending through the Celestial Heavens and my Soul was filled with the sense of great Awe, though I knew that the descent was a sign of the coming of the Lord for the healing of His Children.

Then I also saw the wonderful descent of the Constellation Scorpio full of the most glorious light, and great in power to heal and overcome.

And as I gazed upon the heavenly signs, sore amazed at the wonderful Vision, my heart was uplifted and filled with great joy until it cried out in its gladness, " It is the Lord descending," for I knew that the long looked for Day of the Lord had come when He would again make Himself manifest for the gathering together of Israel and the healing of all peoples.

Cancer in the Celestial Heavens and the system of the Soul, represents the approach of the Divine for the purpose of Healing ; and Scorpio in the Celestial Heavens and the system of the Soul, speaks of the Soul regaining her ancient spiritual power, through the approach of the Divine Love and Wisdom to her as she recovers the consciousness of the Divine Presence.

THE COMING ANTI-VIVISECTION CONGRESS.[1]

ALL the friends of the Creatures whose love has sought to manifest itself in true compassion and pity, and who have arduously striven to deliver the Creatures who suffer unspeakably in the Physiological Laboratories at the hands of a misguided and ill-informed Science, are soon to take counsel together concerning their further efforts against the crying and monstrous evil. They are coming from the North and the South, the East and the West to hold conferences with a view "to promote the movement for the abolition of Vivisection, and to advocate a consistent opposition to all forms of cruelty to animals."

The Congress is to be held in London during the early days of July under the auspices of almost every truly Humane Society, led by the chief Anti-Vivisection Societies of the country ; and so full and varied will the programme be that almost every possible aspect of the question will be dealt with, so that the Congress should attract to itself all who are sincerely endeavouring to accomplish the deliverance of the creatures from the cruelties perpetrated upon them, and command their most earnest, sympathetic and practical support.

There are to be conferences of the workers in the various Societies, and subjects will be presented in a way that will open up in discussion the whole field of Vivisection as to its nature, claims and purposes ; and in this way will all the delegates who come from the many countries of the world to represent them, have presented to them the very latest information concerning the practice and results of Vivisection ; and so through them again will the various communities and peoples and nations whom they represent have shown to them what Vivisection means for the creatures, the operators, and the entire human race. Then, in addition, there is to be a public meeting ; an anti-vivisection exhibition which is sure to be

---

[1] *International Congress, London, July 6th—10th, full particulars of which may be had from the Hon. General Secretary, Miss Lind af Hageby, 224, Lauderdale Mansions, Maida Vale, London, W.*

illuminative concerning the deeds done in the Physiological Laboratories, and the implements by which they
are wrought ; an anti-vivisection play which will not fail to
show up the awful system of the torturing of the Creatures
in the name of an enlightened and Christian conscience ;
and then there will be a procession of thousands of
friends and sympathizers through the leading thoroughfares as an appeal to that general public whose apathy
and, alas! utter indifference to the sufferings of the
animals has permitted to grow up in our midst the most
appalling form of the Inquisition ever invented. For had
the British public been truly awake to the most terrible
evils of a system which one is forced to speak of as of the
evil one, a veritable wolf in sheep's clothing, they would
never have permitted it to become established in our
midst, to strike deep its roots into the very life of the
people, to send out its hideous tentacles in all directions
through the establishment of Laboratories for experimentation in every possible centre and draw into them to
crush out in sufferings whose anguish and agonies cannot
be expressed in any language, all the beautiful life of the
creatures on whom it could lay its unholy and unfeeling
hands.

Let us all hope and pray that the coming Congress
may be the instrument by means of which a more healthy
public opinion concerning the practice of vivisection may
be generated, and that, as the result of the endeavours of
all the noble Souls who love true compassion and pity, the
deliverance of the Creatures from the hands of cruel men
may be accomplished.

J. TODD FERRIER.

A VISION OF THE SOUL.

In the Day of the Lord when the two Constellations Cancer and Scorpio descended in the Heavens, proclaiming the Healing and Power of the Divine imparted unto all Souls through the coming again of His Holy Presence to abide within the Sanctuary, I was lifted up by the Spirit and made to see the wonderful Colours of the Holy and Sacred Seven.

To look upon they were indeed glorious, and marvellous in their purity and transparency.

Like great streams of colour full of life-giving energy for all Souls, they flowed through the Heavens, Eastwards and Westwards, Northwards and Southwards, manifesting the Glory of the Divine Love and Wisdom whither they went.

And whithersoever they flowed, all the Heavens became radiant with the Holy Spectrum, and full of the life and power which it was the office of each Sacred Colour to impart.

Unto the Angelic Heavens they spake of the Divine Love and Wisdom as each Soul was able to receive of the Sacred Tinctures, from the least of the Angelic Spheres unto the highest when the Soul is able to receive the Seven Spirits of God and enter the Kingdom of the Divine.

And I saw One in form like unto the Son of the Highest. Around Him were the Seven Sacred Colours, each Tincture in its fulness bespeaking the perfection of His Nature and the fulness of the Divine Love and Wisdom which dwelt in Him:

For the Son of God in the Divine Heavens is evermore the type of the perfected Soul, the Proto-type for all Souls, when the Soul shall have become also the inheritor of the Seven Spirits of God.

THE ASCENSION.

" But if the Gospel be hidden, it is hidden because it was lost :
" For the god of this world blinded the eyes of the children of this world,
lest the Light of the Glory of the Divine Love made manifest in the Christ-
hood, should shine into them "

THE morning of the Ascension was one in which the
Heavens were opened, so that the Angel of the Lord
could be beheld descending to the planes of the Earth bearing a message of Glad Tidings for all peoples. For the Angel
of the Lord who rolled away the stone from the door of
the sepulchre also opened the Heavens for the Soul to
ascend up out of the conditions of the Earth-life into
those of the Angelic life. And when the Soul rose into
the Heavens, then were the watchers glad.

How much has been made of the incidents associated
with the story of the Ascension of the Master out of the
planes of the Earth ! How men and women have dwelt
upon the phenomena described in the Records, and
attached such importance to their validity that they have
affirmed that the phenomena must be accepted as true
upon the outward historic plane, and that only upon that
plane did the event with its attendant phenomena take
place. They accept in their literal form the various
accounts given in the Records, even though these accounts
differ as to the place where the Ascension was supposed
to have taken place. Nay, as in the case of the Resurrection, so likewise is it with the story of the Ascension,
they hang upon the physical phenomena, the reality of
the appearing and passing away of the Master. To them
there is no great and glorious truth underlying these
supposed events ; a truth which has no relation to the
physical phenomena, and which is indeed hidden by the
physical history presentation ; a truth whose value for the
Soul is unspeakably great, and whose loss to the Soul
through the confused, obscured and materialised presentation has been the cause of so much spiritual darkness
throughout the whole of the so-called Christian Era.
They have come at last to view the whole manifestation of
the Christhood as something physical, to give to almost all
the Teachings arising out of the manifestation a material

meaning, and even to make the human body, which was the vehicle of the Christhood, Divine. They have interpreted nearly all the wonderful histories given by the Master, and which had very special reference to the past of the Soul, as mere outward histories with special local significance. Through the loss of the Vision within the Soul through which and by means of which alone may Divine things be discerned, they have brought down every profound and exalted spiritual truth from the Heavens whence their meanings may be understood, to the outward and material planes where their meanings for the Soul have been lost. They have made merely personal and local what was impersonal and universal; changed the meanings of Spiritual and Divine things into mere things of the sense-life, given them an outward and material significance where the meanings were inward, Soullic and Divine; transferred them from the Kingdom of the Father in the Heavens of the Soul herself, and from the plane where she should always function and must function if she would know the Divine Love and Wisdom, unto the outermost spheres of experience where they were made to relate to the experiences common to those spheres, until even the most sublime inward experiences of the Soul were related to changes and events of a physical order.

In this way was the glorious truth implied in the Ascension related to the outward form of the Master rather than to the Ascension of the Soul.

J. Todd Ferrier.

THE ASCENSION.
(THE ASCENSION OF THE MASTER.)

" What will ye think when the Son of Man ascends into the Heavens whence He came ?
" The flesh profiteth nothing : it is the Spirit who quickeneth and whose words are full of Spiritual Power."

THE Resurrection of the Soul was the harbinger of its Ascension into the Spiritual Heavens. When the Soul awoke within the grave of the material world with its dominant forces born of the sense-life, and arose from the tomb wherein it was bound in the grave-clothes with which the world of the mere sense-life adorns the Souls of all whom it betrays and crucifies, it also began its Ascension towards the Spiritual Heavens. For the Ascension which came to be associated with the Master, and which was related only to the outward form rising up out of the Earth into the sky, was the presentation by the Master of how the Soul arose out of the earthy conditions of her environment and ascended through the various spheres even until she reached the Kingdom of the Divine. The story of the Ascension which may be found in the Four Records with that varying presentation which gives to these presentations the mark of inaccuracy, not to say misrepresentation, was the story of the Ascension of the Soul from the planes of the Earth into the various degrees of Spiritual Realisation. It was the presentation to the Soul of the meaning of the Resurrection Life, the vision of all that would follow a true rising up out of the conditions imposed by the sense-life, the experiences which would be entered into as the result of the serious endeavour to break the material bonds which held the Soul in bondage to the things of sense, the heavenly fruits of that true spiritual deliverance and redemption which is the sure issue of the Resurrection of the Soul. For whilst it primarily spoke of the uprising and Ascension of the Christ-Soul after the Sin-offering had been accomplished, it likewise spoke of the experience which came to every Soul when it rose out of matter—that is, out of the impure life which is born within body and mind where the sense-life dominates. The Ascension of the Christ-Soul unto the Father was the realisation once more within Him of the Divine Presence and Vision, the return into that state wherein the Vision of the Ever Blessed One became once more a reality. And it was not such a realisation as is presented in the Records either as to nature, time, or space ; for it was not a physical upliftment in which the form rose up from the planes of the Earth and passed upward into the stellar-world ; nor did it take place in Judea or Galilee as geographical districts, nor in the time known as that of the Apostles. It was entirely a spiritual experience, an inward Divine uplifting, the rising up of the Christ-Soul until He again reached the Divine Kingdom. And it only took place after the Sin-offering had been accomplished in this very age upon which we have entered. For the long dark ages of the Christian Religion, wherein the Christ-hood has been believed in ostensibly by the whole of the Western World, were the ages in which the Sin-offering was accomplished by the Christ-Soul ; and now that He has risen as one who was dead and is alive again and hath ascended unto the Father in that He has once more entered into the consciousness of the Presence of the Divine Love and Wisdom within the sanctuary of His innermost being, the Ascension is now taking place : the Christ-Soul is returning into His beautiful heritage, the consciousness of the indwelling of the Father. For the Ascension soon follows the Resurrection of the Soul. And it takes place in various degrees as the Soul is able to endure the Vision of the Divine and Ever Blessed One.

J. TODD FERRIER.

A VISION OF THE SOUL.

I was in the Spirit in the Day of the Lord and was carried up unto the Heavens of the Divine where I beheld a most wonderful Sign.

It was a Cross composed of a multitude of Stars the base of which rested upon the foundations of the Heavens wherein I beheld it, and which appeared to fill the whole Heavens, so great was it.

As I looked upon it the overwhelming sense of the Divine Presence filled me, for I knew that it was the manifestation of the Divine Nature upon the Kingdom of the Divine Love and Wisdom, the embodiment of the Adonai upon that Kingdom, the Sign of the Cross.

And I lay as one who had the deep consciousness of bearing the burden of Iniquity, Transgression and Sin upon him, beholding the wonderful Sign and feeling the unspeakable goodness of Him concerning whom it spake.

Then I became conscious of the outflowing towards me from the Presence of the Divine Love of the Healing of a great Peace which spake unto me of that Love whose fulness is infinite, whose compassion is unfailing, and by whose very tenderness the Soul is made great.

And, lo! the burden with which my ·Soul was oppressed seemed to become lightened as if its weight were being shared by the Divine Love even until the Iniquity, Transgression and Sin with the sorrow and anguish born from them, were all taken away.

For the wonderful Vision with its even more wonderful Sign was the testimony to the Soul that in the Divine Nature is to be found the fulness of the meaning of the Cross.

THE ASCENSION.
(THE ASCENSION FROM GALILEE.)

" Then the eleven disciples went away into Galilee, into a Mountain where the Master had appointed to meet them ; and when they beheld the Lord, they rose into the Heavens and worshipped."

THE two accounts of the Ascension given by two of the Records, place that wonderful event in both Galilee and Bethany. And the account given in the Acts of the Apostles names the Mount of Olives as the place, even though that latter was supposed to have been written by the same writer who gave Bethany as the scene of the event. That both the accounts cannot be true if the Ascension was an event upon the outer physical planes will only be too obvious to an earnest seeker after the truth ; and that the writer who was considered the most cultured of those who wrote in the early days of the New Religion should have given both Bethany and the Mount of Olives, is certainly not conducive to calling forth the trust of a student in the veracity of the writer and the validity of the story of the Ascension.

Yet that which the writers who wrote the various accounts did not understand, and which they brought down and materialisèd through giving to them local and physical settings so that their meanings became lost, may have within them profound and beautiful teachings for the Soul. The things which now seem so contradictory as statements of material events, may be beheld to contain nothing contradictory when their meanings are known and understood. They will indeed be known to form two parts of one sublime spiritual experience into which the Christ-Soul entered after He rose out of the Sepulchre of the Astral Kingdom—an experience which is repeated in some measure within every Soul who has arisen out of the grave of matter and gone forth to live the Christhood life. For the Mountain of Ascension in Galilee is the uplifted state of the Mind—the mind elevated through spiritual aspiration even until it knows the glory of Lebanon and the dews of Hermon, the glory of the Divine Love and the refreshing of the Divine Spirit. And the Ascension of the Soul from Galilee is the Divine Realisation born within the Soul through the uplifting of the Mind till it could drink in of the Divine Spirit and behold the Glory of the Lord. For the Ascension is an ascension *in state*, not a spacial event. It is *an inward* movement of the Soul within her own Heavens, not an objective motion into the stellar universe. It is the outcome of the Soul first rising to seek unto the Divine Realisation of all her potentialities, and then the uprising of the mind far above all mere earthly potencies, ambitions, visions and purposes to know the glory and joy of the Lord of Life, until at last the Soul is able to ascend even into the Presence of the Divine.

The Ascension will now have a new but a more worthy meaning for all who are able to perceive the beauty of the Spiritual mystery which it implies. And the Ascension of the Christ-Soul will be the more readily entered into in its beautiful and yet pathetic significance, when the meaning of the Sin-offering has been apprehended and understood, and the Resurrection has become known as a great spiritual fact experienced by Him in the return of the Soul from Edom where the Christhood garments have all been red-dyed through treading the winepress of unspeakable sorrow, unto Bozrah where the Christhood once more came unto Him. And the experiences which came to the Christ-Soul in such sublime fulness after His terrible Sin-offering shall come at last to all Souls who seek unto the finding of the Divine. They too shall ascend from the Mountain of Galilee—the uplifted and purified mind—and rise up into the Heavens until they come at last to the Presence of the Divine.

J. TODD FERRIER.

THE ASCENSION.
(FROM BETHANY.)

"And He led them out as far as Bethany, and He lifted up His hands and blessed them ;
"And it came to pass that as He blessed them they were carried up into the Heavens."

THE Ascension from Galilee, as we have seen, was the rising of the Soul into the Presence of the Divine as the outcome of the rising of the mind above the world-influences and finding those spiritual uplands known as the Mountains of Galilee, spiritual states within the mind in which it enters into the consciousness of the Glory of the Lord. The Ascension from Bethany was a yet further uprising of the whole being. For as Galilee represents a purified mind so Bethany represents the Soul in a state of Christhood. And as the Mountains of Bethany speak of spiritual states into which the mind has risen in its endeavours after the Divine Way of Life, so Bethany indicates the beautiful inward realisations of the Soul begotten through the upliftment of the whole being, realisations which speak of the consciousness of the Divine Presence, the Illumination of the Divine Spirit, and the perpetual inflowing of the stream of the Divine Love to the Soul. And so the Ascension from Bethany is the rising of the Soul on to the Divine Kingdom itself. To ascend from a state of Christhood, meaning by that, to rise yet higher into the Divine realisation—is to ascend unto the Kingdom known as the Kingdom of the Father.

It will thus be seen what profound meanings underlie the two accounts of the Ascension when the truth is separated from the dross of material dressing in which they have both been presented. It will be seen that the apparent contradictions are the outcoming of the material-ising of things wholly spiritual and Divine, the giving unto them purely and only personal and local significations. And it will likewise be seen how beautiful indeed were the Teachings given by the Master concerning the Ascension of the Soul, first from Galilee and then from Bethany as the outcome of the Redeemed Life and the Realisation of the Christhood Estate. J. TODD FERRIER.

THE ASCENSION.
(THE MORNING OF ASCENSION.)

" And the dead in Christ shall rise first."

" Them also which sleep in Jesus shall God bring with Him."

" Awake Thou that sleepest, and arise from the dead, and Christ shall give thee light."

NOW is the morning of the Ascension of all those Souls who were to arise first from the grave as the outcome of the second coming of the Master. " The dead in Christ " were to first arise ; to be followed by all " who fell asleep in Jesus." Who were they who are said to have died in Christ ? And of whom was it written that they fell asleep in Jesus?

In the state known as Christ, there is no longer any death. For to be in Christ is to be alive for evermore. It is to have overcome death and all the conditions which give rise to that sad spiritual state. And so when we read that those who died in Christ are first to arise and ascend unto the Lord in the Heavens, and know that any such experience is at once a denial of the state known as Christ since in Christ there is no death, we are compelled to seek for a meaning which is at once in harmony with " life in Christ," and also with the thought that Souls who were once in Christ had died in that state. It is quite true that many understand the expression as implying that those who died in Christ are those who passed over into the spirit world confessing belief in the teachings concerning the Christ which the various Churches in all the ages of the Christian Era have taught, and that because of such a belief they are to be raised from the dead first. And that view also embraces those who are said to have fallen asleep in Jesus, by which is meant that they passed away from the outer spheres confessing their trust in the redeeming power of the man Jesus. But such a view not only contradicts the statement that in Christ there is no longer any dominion of death, that those who are in Christ cannot die since the elements of death are not in them ; but it would exclude from the blessed truth implied all those who passed over prior to the manifestation of the

Christhood, and all peoples and Souls who never heard the Gospel which passes in the Western world as the embodiment and intrepretation of the Life and Teachings of the blessed Master. It would make the rising again from the dead in a state of Soul which would receive the Divine approval, contingent upon a belief in the personal Jesus, and some view of His Life and Teachings such as one of the Churches holds, and thus reduce what was and is one of the most profound spiritual experiences to a mere intellectual and theological process. It would change what is one of the most difficult things to accomplish by the Soul, though it is indeed glorious when accomplished, into something dependent upon religious environment. Nay, even those who hold this view concerning this most beautiful and much to be desired Soul-experience, differ amongst themselves as to the state and how it is to be acquired—that is, they differ as to the meaning of *being in Christ*, and the exact means by which it is to be attained.

But like all other pure and true things, this blessed truth may be understood ; and when it is truly understood, then will the glorious light which it contains for the Soul also be beheld. Its meaning is entirely spiritual, having naught to do with any such meaning as is implied in the resuscitation of bodies which have been laid aside. And the meaning of "having fallen asleep in Jesus," and, "having died in Christ," will be also quite clear to the mind.

The Ascension of all those Souls who once "died in Christ," and those who "fell asleep in Jesus," is the arising once more out of the conditions of the life lived by the children of this world, of all those who once were in that state of spiritual experience represented by the term Jesus, to know that beautiful state of Redeemed Life in which all the spheres are purified through the triumph of goodness and love within the Soul ; and also the arising out of the darkness of a spiritual order which lieth over this world into the glorious Light of the Spiritual Heavens, of all those Souls who once knew the Estate of Christhood but who went away from that blessed realisation during their ministry unto the children of this world, and so passed into conditions so unspiritual that all the light of Christhood within them was extinguished. They went down into spiritual death from a state of Christhood, just as those who fell asleep in Jesus went away from the beautiful Redeemed Life to live like those who knew not either the state of Jesus or that of Christ.

The return of these Souls is now. It is not only the morning of the Resurrection but it is likewise the day of the true Return of Persephone, the entrance of the Soul into the Redeemed Life once more and her ascension, out of the dark caverns or conditions of life in this world into those of beautiful purity, goodness and light. The Heavens are now open, and the angels of God may be beheld ascending and descending upon the Son of Man.

J. TODD FERRIER.

A VISION OF THE SOUL.

I was lifted up out of the conditions upon the Earth and carried upwards until I beheld the Angelic Heavens, which opened unto me.

And as I looked I saw the Heavens of the Divine Love and Wisdom descending to overshadow the Souls of all who were able to receive the Ministry from the Divine Kingdom, and to aid those who were dwellers upon the Earth who sought to rise up out of the conditions which prevailed upon her planes.

The descending Heavens were glorious with the Glory of the Lord whose Radiance was truly marvellous to behold ; and the Glory was reflected in the raiment with which the Angels were clothed.

And I beheld the Heavenly Hosts performing their beautiful ministry before the Lord as they bore down to all the dwellers upon the Earth the Blessing and Healing of the Divine Love.

And many of these ministering ones, besides being Angelic in fashion, bore upon them the Sign of the Cross which was beautiful, and which was made luminous from the Radiance of the Divine. These passed upwards to the Divine Kingdom, and then through the Heavens, bearing within them the Light of the Divine Wisdom, and transmitting unto all Souls upon the Earth who were able to receive the Blessing of the beautiful inward healing which ever floweth from the Divine Love.

And I beheld also a Golden Staircase whose base rested upon the planes of the Angelic World. At the foot of it there was a Luminous Cross indicating the nature of the service performed by those who passed upward upon the Golden Staircase.

The Golden Staircase was flooded with the light proceeding from the Divine Radiance which poured out its fulness from the Heavens of the Divine Love and Wisdom.

And I saw many Souls who had reached the Angelic World, approach the Golden Staircase and ascend it. And as they rose into the Glory of the Divine Radiance, the fashion of their appearance changed from glory to glory until they were even as the Luminous Cross.

Such are those Souls who seek unto the fulness of the Divine Nature, Life and Service.

WHENCE COME DISEASES? [1]

Again, assuming for the moment the truth of the statement that vivisection is absolutely necessary if we would gain the knowledge required for the successful treatment of disease, might we not expect that it would be only undertaken as a dreaded and dreadful *last resource*, when all other means had failed? But the facts show that the very opposite is the case.

The majority of the ills from which we suffer may be arranged as to their causes in three main groups, thus :—

(a) Those due to violation or neglect of hygiene, public or personal, including such as are caused by overcrowding, dangerous trades, food adulteration, etc.

(b) Those due to dietetic errors, viz.: overfeeding and gluttony, the use of flesh foods, alcohol, narcotics, &c.

(c) Those due to the premature exhaustion of vital force or nervous energy ; the result of the haste to be rich, and the too strenuous struggle for purely egoistic ends which characterizes our modern civilization, aided by the depleting effects of the passions—hate, envy, greed, sensuality, etc.—which find full play therein ; or to the conditions of hopeless struggle, worry, and fear which, together, with grinding poverty and semi-starvation, are the lot of the many, and which are very largely due to the action of our ruthless competitive commercial system, accentuated by the injustice of many of our social laws.

In the light afforded by such a classification which shows disease as the result of the violation of law, physical, ethical, or spiritual, is it not certain that if man were to repent him, in the true sense of the word, of these errors, and earnestly set about amending his ways on all · planes of his being, nine-tenths of the diseases which afflict him would speedily disappear and be unknown in the course of a generation or two; by which time the consequent enhancement of physical vigour and stamina

---

1 Extracts from " Why I Condemn Vivisection," by Robert H. Perks, M.D., F.R.C.S. (Eng.) *Vide* advertisement pages.

would most probably have rendered him immune to the remainder.

Why then has this radical and rational method of dealing with disease, or rather its *prevention*, been neglected? (except in very limited and special directions) Because *self* stands in the way; and such reform would necessitate the renunciation of much that man considers desirable. In fact, it would involve *self-sacrifice*, and rather than face this alternative he prefers to retain his luxuries, vices and follies, and to attempt, instead, to wring from the involuntary sufferings *of others* the knowledge that he hopes may save him from the disease and death which are the inevitable results of his transgressions. Truly a vain and cowardly attempt to escape the retributive effects of his own iniquities!

WE REAP THAT WE SOW!

Thus does vivisection reveal itself as the very antithesis of the Law of Love whose Golden Rule " to do unto others as we would that they should do unto us " has ever taken the chief place in the teachings of all God's inspired messengers to man throughout the Ages, and most notably in those of The Christ. This marks it as the negation of good, as essentially evil, and as of the infernal.

It is vain to expect from such a source any saving knowledge or deliverance from disease! Rather will this cruelty, this selfish infliction of unmeasured sufferings upon our sub-human fellow-creatures, yield a terrible harvest of quite another sort.

In fact, are we not already reaping that which we have sown, in the increase of disease and lunacy which is now in evidence, and especially in that fearful and paralysing sense of fear—fear of sickness, of poverty, of death, fear of we know not what impending calamities—that dominates and renders miserable the lives of so many amongst us, and which is a marked mental characteristic of the Age?

And is it not a lamentable fact that, with a few noble exceptions, the attitude of the teachers and members of

our Churches towards this evil is one of indifference or
selfish acquiescence? When will they realize that by
their tacit sanction, and acceptance of the fruits of this
atrocious crime—for it is nothing less—they are actual,
though vicarious, partakers of its guilt; that they crucify
the Lord afresh in the torments they inflict on His
creatures, and by so doing darken the Vision of His
Presence.

Well may they feel that spiritual weakness and
poverty is their portion, when Love, Compassion, and
Pity, the first principles of the Gospel of The Christ,
whose followers and brethren they profess to be, are
supplanted in their midst by a spirit of heartless self-
seeking.

It is indeed high time that Christendom awakened
from its apathetic slumber, and realized the true meaning
of this practice, so that it may be banished from our
midst.

The following from the pen of the late Dr. Anna
Kingsford gives us in eloquent and thrilling words a
presentation of the true nature of vivisection and its
identity in kind and method with the works of the black
magicians of all ages :—

"Side by side with the true priestly magic, there has always
been the unholy art of the wizard, the art of black magic, that of
the man who sought to produce miraculous effects by evil
means. To know, to heal, to work marvels by true magic, it is
necessary to live purely, to abstain from indulgence of the flesh,
and to do the deeds of love. All this did not suit the man of
the world, who desired to attain the same results, but without
the self-sacrifice. He had recourse then to devils, and wrung
from them by evil means miraculous powers. To satisfy and to
propitiate them, he offered living oblations in secret places, and
sacrificed to them the most innocent victims he could procure,
putting them to hideous deaths in order to obtain the knowledge
or power he sought. The same part is played by the vivisector
of to-day. He is, in fact, a practitioner of black magic; he
obtains his knowledge by means of the exact counterparts of the
bloody devil-sacrifices of the wizards, and, like them, he damns
himself in the process. In what shall we say the practices of
the secret devil-worshippers of mediæval times differed from
those which now go on in the underground laboratories of the
Medical School in Paris? (and elsewhere). There, as from time

to time a door swings open below that flight of stone steps leading down into the darkness, you may hear a burst of shrieks and moans such as those which arose from the subterraneous vaults of the sorcerers of the dark ages. It is—as it was then— the wizard at his work, the votary of Satan pursuing his researches, and at the price of torture and of his soul, wresting knowledge from the powers of evil.

"It used to be deemed a damnable sin to practice such black arts as these. But now their professors hold their Sabbat in public, and their enunciations are reported in the journals of the day. It is held to be superstition to believe that in former ages wizards were able by secret tortures and unheard-of atrocities to wrest knowledge from Nature; but now the self-same crimes are openly and universally practiced; and men everywhere trust their efficacy.

" What is needed is the revival of the true magic of the Pure Life, which heals without blood and gives health without vicarious disease. It is black magic, which, in order to cure a patient, first transfers his complaint to an innocent victim. He who accepts health at such a cost shall but save it to lose it." .

THE ETHICS OF VIVISECTORS.

It is an universal experience that familiarity with cruel and bloody scenes, or participation in cruel acts, invariably leads to a deterioration of the moral sense, and exercises a distinctly brutalizing effect on spectators and actors alike; and as evidence that vivisection produces such effects—as might be predicated from its nature—it will be sufficient to quote from the writings of some of the most "celebrated" experimenters. Thus M. de Cyon in a work which he prepared for the guidance of students says that the true vivisector must approach a difficult vivisection with *"joyful ardour and delight"* (*Methodik*, p. 15). Claude Bernard wrote thus :—" He (the vivisector) is no ordinary man. He is a learned man, a man possessed and absorbed by a scientific idea. He does not hear the animal's cries of pain. He is blind to the blood that flows. *He sees nothing but his idea."* (*introduction a l'Etude de la Medicine Experimentale*, p. 180). An awful picture, to quote a recent writer, of a man besotted with a lust of knowledge, just as murderers are sometimes besotted with a lust of gold : the one as pitiless and as regardless of all law as the other.

Again, note the answers given by Dr. Emanuel Klein, one of the most active of vivisectors in England, and who is still working here, to questions put by members of the Royal Commission, 1875. (I give only a few extracts) :—

Asked by the Chairman of the Commission (3539) : "When you say that you only use them (*i.e.*, anæsthetics) for convenience sake, do you mean that you have no regard at all to the sufferings of the animals ? "—"*No regard at all.*"

Asked again (3541) : Then for your own purposes you disregard entirely the question of the suffering of the animal in performing a painful experiment ? "—"*I do.*"

Asked (3546) : "Do you believe that that is a general practice on the Continent to disregard altogether the feelings of the animals ? "—"*I believe so.*"

Asked (3553) : "But you believe that, generally speaking, there is a very different feeling in England ? "—"*Not among the physiologists ; I do not think there is.*"

Asked (3739) : "And you think that the view of scientific men on the Continent is your view, that animal suffering is so entirely unimportant compared with scientific research that it should not be taken into account at all ? "—"*Yes, except for convenience sake.*"

These replies indicate a deplorable callousness to suffering in the speaker himself, and he admits that in his opinion many English vivisectors feel and act as he does.

ROBERT H. PERKS, M.D., F.R.C.S.

A PRAYER FOR ALL CREATURES.

O Ever Blessed One from whom floweth unceasingly Compassion unto all Souls and Pity unto all the Creatures, and who ever desireth that all Thy children should be like Thee in the ways of their life, help Thy servants so to live that in all their ways in life and their service in the world they may interpret aright Thy Holy Purposes and make manifest Thy beautiful Love, and thus help to hasten the day when all Thy Children shall come to know Thee as Thou art, and all the Creatures who now are made to pass through the chambers of horror and anguish be delivered from the oppression with which their lives are burdened and hurt.   *Amen and Amen.*

THE HERALD OF THE CROSS.

Vol v.   New Series.   May, 1909.   No. 5.

TONGUES OF FLAME.

When in the night season as the world lay asleep I felt myself carried, as it were, up out of the planes of the Earth, I was taken unto what seemed to me to be a new yet familiar sphere where many things of remarkable form and colour were shown unto me.

They were all full of the wonderful grace and beauty which (when upon the Angelic Heavens) I had beheld, and were the signs of the Presence of the Divine Love and Wisdom, and the language of symbols unto the Soul.

I beheld resting upon the head of all who were performing the ministry of Interpretation of the Divine Mysteries upon the Heavens, a Tongue of Flame [1] whose movement was ever upwards and spiral,[2] and whose energy appeared to be of the nature of the Eternal One.[3]

I also saw that the Tongues of Flame were parted at their base, to the right and the left, where they rested upon the head.[4]

---

[1] *The symbol of the possession of the Holy Spirit.*

[2] *The whole movement of the Soul in whom is the Holy Spirit is ever upward, and its magnetic movement is like a spiral.*

[3] *The energy of the Holy Spirit is like the Eternal One.*

[4] *The parted Flame symbolises the possession of both the Divine Love and the Divine Wisdom.*

WHITSUNTIDE.

IN the Festivals of the Church that of Whitsunday is laid great stress on as being one of the most important. It follows the Ascension, and is regarded as the fitting crown of the departure of the Master from the Earth to take His place at the right hand of the Divine Majesty on High. It is thought to have been the beginning of the Divine Kingdom which the Master said He had come to raise up; the time of the outpouring of the Eternal Spirit upon all flesh, but very specially upon those who had known the Master; the laying of the foundations of the true Church, and the bestowing upon the immediate disciples of the Master powers of a remarkable and phenomenal kind. The Baptism of the Holy Spirit, as it was called, was said to have been predicted by the Master as the result of His Ascension to the right hand of the Father, and that the disciples were to tarry in Jerusalem until they were so baptised with power.

If the Day of Pentecost as described in the Acts of the Apostles took place, so that the disciples actually then received the Baptism of the Holy Spirit and power from the Divine, then the teaching of the Records is at fault concerning the sayings and doings of the Master. For more than once it is distinctly stated that after the Resurrection the Master breathed upon the disciples, and said unto them, " Receive ye the Holy Ghost," and that before being parted from them on the day of the Ascension, He imparted Divine power unto them and sent them forth to found the Kingdom of His Father amongst all Nations whom they were to baptise into the name of the Father and the Son and the Holy Spirit.

That both of the statements cannot be right will be obvious to the careful reader of the various narratives. If the Holy Spirit was imparted unto the immediate disciples by the Master prior to His supposed Ascension, then there was no need for them to tarry in Jerusalem until the Divine afflatus came upon them. If they received the Holy Breath from the Master, and had the necessary power imparted to them by which to go forth to found the New Kingdom and baptise into it of all the Nations those who accepted their message, then they would not have tarried in a city where all the conditions were against them, where their Master had been cruelly betrayed, condemned and crucified, and where His followers carried their lives in their hands, so to speak. They would naturally have given the city a glad farewell, after all that they had witnessed. And even were it true that in the teaching and baptising of all Nations they were commanded to begin at Jerusalem, they would then have begun their mission by declaring the message which had been given to them, and then have sought to make good their escape. But instead of that they tarried in Jerusalem, met often together to pray for the coming of the power of the Spirit, laid the foundations of an outward Kingdom to be known afterwards as the Church of Christ, and then had the power which was supposed to have been given them in the upper room in quiet fellowship with the Master, duplicated by the astounding phenomena described in the second chapter of the Acts of the Apostles, when the Holy Spirit came upon them in the form of a rushing mighty wind, whose coming was heard in all the room and beheld by all present in the form of tongues of flame.

The Baptism of the Spirit recorded in the Acts of the Apostles by which the great Church Festival of Pentecost or Whitsunday was created, was not an inward realisation in which the Soul became uplifted out of the conditions of the Earth and was able to know from the Divine the inner meanings of the Divine Love and Wisdom. It was rather an outward and most strange ostentatious and phenomenal display in which the recipients spake in strange tongues which they knew not, many things relating to the Master, without knowing whether they were uttering truth or error concerning Him. The coming of the Spirit was there shown to be only a great objective display astonishing every one, from the disciple to the most incredulous listener. The recipients were filled with excitement instead of that deep spiritual calm which is associated with the experience of the realisation of the Spirit. They were led to make incoherent utterances, so far as they themselves were concerned, instead of the realisation of that inward illumination which is the true gift of the Holy Spirit and which enables the Soul to know the things of which the Holy Spirit speaketh. The flame of fire is indeed the token of the presence of the Divine Spirit; but not as an objective sign visible to the eye of any man : the tongue of flame is the inward spiral movement of the innermost being towards the Divine caused by the Divine attractions unto which the Soul responds and rises unto the Kingdom whence the Holy Spirit can be received. And so it could not be said by any man, nor by any one other than those upon the Kingdom whence the Holy Spirit proceedeth.

The Day of Pentecost for the Soul is one of profound calm and inward spiritual light, a day in which all outward things are silent in the Presence of the Divine.

J. TODD FERRIER.

THE SOUL'S ENTREATY.

O Love, Infinite and Eternal, who givest of Thy fulness unto all Thy Children as they are able to receive, whose riches all may inherit and whose Vision all may behold, grant unto us that we may be able to receive of those riches, even grace upon grace, until we attain unto the fulness of the Life unto which Thou in Thy great goodness hast called us. Vouchsafe unto us the blessing of the consciousness of Thy Holy Spirit as Thy Presence abiding within us, that we may ever have the inward Light of Thy Wisdom whose flame is kindled from Thee.

Amen and Amen.

THE BAPTISM OF THE SPIRIT.

THE day of Pentecost was one full of the most marvellous phenomena audible and visible to the outer senses; but the Baptism of the Spirit was a season in which all the outer senses were silent, and only those of the Soul were active. All the phenomena of the account given in the Acts of the Apostles were in direct contrast to the beautiful inward realisations which came to those who were able to receive the Baptism of the Spirit. Indeed the presentation in the Acts of the Apostles was the antithesis of what actually took place. Nay, it was such a materialisation of inward and profound Soul experiences that all who have been misled by that presentation have sought in like manner for the Baptism of the Holy Spirit, and have been led to look for phenomena to indicate that it had taken place, and that where no phenomenal experiences followed the seeking for the Spirit to descend many have been led to think that no Baptism has taken place. It is what the Church has sought in all her history. It is what she has come to believe concerning the operations of the Eternal Spirit. How far from the true path of the Holy Spirit in His beautiful operations in the whole being of the Soul who has been able to receive the Baptism, she cannot be led to see, so holden are the eyes of those who assume to lead and teach the people, who sit in her chief seats of learning, and who are supposed to interpret the Sayings and Life of the Master. For the Church has followed only the way, erroneous and misleading, of the presentation in the Records. Her foundations were phenomenal, and her history has always shown that she sought after the phenomenal. She was cradled in experiences of the most phenomenal character, and she has been phenomenal ever since.

The Baptism of the Spirit cometh not with ostentatious display. It cometh not with observation in an objective sense. It is a purely subjective experience, one seen and felt and realised only by the Soul in whom it takes place. And it is an experience of such an exalted character that only those who have fitted themselves through spiritual aspiration and growth towards the Divine may pass into the exalted state which it represents. It is not given to all who pray for the Spirit, though beautiful spiritual influences will be sure to always follow true prayer. For many pray for things the meaning of which they do not understand, and the Baptism of the Spirit is one. For the Soul can only receive from the Divine Lord according to its ability those wonderful inward realisations implied in the Resurrection Life, the Ascension into Heaven, and the Baptism of the Spirit.

The profound experience known as the Baptism of the Spirit which was said to come to the immediate followers of the Master on the Day of Pentecost, is stated in the Gospel Records as having been passed through whilst the Master was still with them, and that it came to them as the result of the Master breathing upon them. It is so stated more than once in these Records, notwithstanding the fact that it is also clearly set forth that such an experience could not come unto them unless He went away. " If I go not away, the Comforter, who is the Holy Spirit, cannot come unto you ;" thus is the coming of the Spirit written of in one Record ; whilst in another it is written that when the disciples were all gathered together the Master appeared unto them and breathed upon them, saying, " Receive ye the Holy Spirit ;" and then in another of the Records the disciples are counselled by the Master to await the coming of the Spirit upon them with power from on high. And yet one more form of the presentation of the coming of the Holy Spirit is given in the Fourth Record, where it is stated that the Master said unto the disciples that the Paraclete, the Holy Spirit, who proceeded from the Father, and who had once been known unto them ; whom the world could not receive because it knew Him not, but who had been with them from the beginning, would again make

Himself manifest unto them, teach them all things and bring all things to their remembrance.

The various presentations cannot be harmonised. They stand in the Records as the monuments of the work of all those who knew not the Master but who tried to give to the world an account of His supposed Life and Teachings. They are the monuments of the effect upon the mind of the various writers of the Astral Kingdom which has always given to the mind perverted presentations of the most profoundly inward spiritual experiences, since the ages when it was first generated. They are monuments of the delusive character of that Kingdom, which has been well named Maya or the Realm of Illusion ; for to it may be attributed all the terrible perversion of the most sacred and beautiful teachings concerning the Soul and the Divine Love and Wisdom. The misrepresentation of the Life of the Master, the perversion of nearly all the beautiful Teachings He gave concerning the Soul and the ways of the Divine Love, the inversion of nearly every great and glorious spiritual fact through making of things wholly spiritual and Divine, mere outward and local histories upon the physical planes, was accomplished by him who was said to have betrayed the Master, viz., the Astral Kingdom, the real Judas who betrayed the Christ. And the description of the Baptism of the Spirit on the day of Pentecost was the crowning act by which the betrayer who influenced the mind of the writer of the Acts of the Apostles, obscured the beautiful meanings set forth in the Logia spoken by the Master concerning the very nature of the Holy Spirit or Paraclete, and His operation within the Soul, and thus destroyed for the Soul the vision born from the indwelling of the Holy Paraclete, and sent it to seek for the realisation of the beautiful experience known as the Baptism of the Spirit in a direction which took it away from the true path where alone it could be found.

J. TODD FERRIER.

THE MESSENGER.

I saw upon the Angelic Heavens one like unto the Son of Man.

His appearance was beautiful to look upon, and His Countenance was radiant with the light which proceedeth from the Glory of the Lord.

As He moved through the Heavens I beheld a great multitude following Him whithersoever He went. Their faces were like those of the Angels, radiant with the light proceeding from the Glory of the Lord.

These were those who had ascended out of the conditions of the Earth, who had arrived at the true knowledge of who the Son of Man was, and had sought to only follow Him.

And as I looked it was given me to know that it was even He who once was known as Moses in the days when He brake unto the Children of Israel the Heavenly Wisdom which became known as the Manna of Heaven, the Angels' Food, and that which was afterwards known as the Ambrosia of the Gods.

For Moses was not a man, as has been supposed ; but the Son of Man, the ever meek and lowly one, the patient Burden-bearer for the children of the Heavenly Father, the Interpreter of the Divine Love and Manifestor of the Divine Wisdom, the Revealer of the Father upon the Mountains of Sinai and Horeb, the Medium through whom the Living Waters ever flow into the Soul, the Guide through the Wilderness who turneth the bitter waters of Marah into Elim, who feedeth the hungry soul with the Goodness of the Lord, and who healeth all who have been bitten and wounded by the fiery serpents of the sense-life.

THE SACRED FLAME.

The Soul illumined is like a Lamp whose flame is kindled from the Lord.
The Lord Himself is the Light of my Soul; the flame of His Holy
Spirit burneth within me as a shining Light. He kindleth my Lamp so that
the Light of His Presence falleth upon my Path.

WHEN the Soul is truly Baptised from the Divine,
then is the Sanctuary of the Soul lit as a Lamp
which has been kindled from the Lord. For to receive
the Holy Spirit is to become united unto the Divine, to
know the meaning of the Atonement when the whole
being becomes responsive to the Divine so that it is as
the Divine in all its purposes, ways and service, to have
that interior Illumination in which and through which
the Soul knows the innermost meaning of Divine things.
For to possess the Holy Spirit is to possess the Sacred
Flame whose movement is ever upward to the Divine.
It is to have as an inheritance *the Spiral motion* by which
the Soul rises ever higher towards Divine fulness.

The Breathing forth of the Holy Spirit by the Lord
had therefore a meaning whose depth the writers of the
Records little knew. It had a significance burdened
with the most beautiful experiences, wonderful realisations, and momentous services before the Divine, of
which the writers of the Gospel Records wot not. They
received the expression from the Logia written by St.
John, but not understanding its import, they applied it to
a physical act on the part of the Master when they made
Him breathe upon the disciples and say unto them that
as the result they were to receive the Holy Spirit. They
knew not that it was the Holy Breath of the Divine
within the Sanctuary of the Soul who had known the
Holy Paraclete, and who had once more arrived at the
consciousness of His Presence, as the Master had said to
His immediate disciples that they would. They knew
not that it was absolutely an *inward* experience, and had
nothing of the phenomenal nature about it such as they
portrayed. What they read in the Logia of St. John
they related to mere outward experiences on the part of
the disciples, and understood the action of the Divine
Lord within the Soul to have been an act performed by

Jesus.   Thus came it to pass that one of the most sacred, one of the most profound, one of the most blessed experiences into which the Soul passes in her movement towards the Divine, became perverted and materialised through the false presentation which led the Soul to view the Baptism of the Spirit as something received from without her own system and which came to her from external sources, something that approached her objectively and came as it were through the physical atmosphere, a power which had to be looked for outwardly like the powers in the phenomenal world.

In this way was the sublime truth of the Baptism of the Holy Spirit lost.   And through all the ages of the Christian Era the true seekers after the Divine have had to grope in the darkness caused by the inversion of the true meaning of the possession of the Holy Spirit by the Soul.   They have often been led to seek outwardly for that most blessed inheritance even whilst they possessed it within the Sanctuary of their Soul, but knew it not, nor how to arrive at its realisation.   And it has been that outward seeking which has so frequently prevented the Saints in all ages from arriving at the true vision of the meaning of the Christhood and even of the Redeemed Life.   It has been that outward seeking which has prevented them from having the perpetual Light of the Spirit shining within them, so that their hours of true illumination have been fitful and their times of spiritual darkness great.   It was indeed a great triumph for the Astral influences when the beautiful Soul-mysteries were changed in their nature and brought down from the planes of the Heavens to those of the Earth ; for unto the Soul it meant darkness, and spiritual and Divine loss.

J. TODD FERRIER,

THE HOLY PARACLETE.

" But the Holy Paracle'e, who is the Remembrancer from the Father, when He is come again He shall bring all things to your remembrance, whatsoever things were given unto you."
" He shall not speak from Himself; but He shall speak of the Father."

IN all the Records the gift of the Holy Spirit is made dependent upon the Christ. In these Records it is stated that all power from on high is given unto Him. And thus the personal Jesus has come to be associated with the great truth underlying these profound impersonal spiritual statements, with the result that the inner meaning of them is lost to the Soul. How beautiful is the truth implied in the thought that the gift of the Holy Spirit is dependent on the Christ? Yet it is not to be interpreted in any personal way, nor circumscribed by any thought of some special individual, since it refers to the Estate of Christhood within the Soul, a spiritual attainment in which the Soul becomes illumined from the Divine as one anointed from the Lord. Upon the realisation of such an attainment by the Soul is the Baptism of the Spirit dependent. Without the realisation of Christhood there can be no realisation of the Holy Spirit within the Soul. Unto the Soul in the Estate of Christhood are all Heavenly Powers granted. Herein likewise is to be discerned a profound truth. For when the Soul once reaches that stage in its true spiritual evolution towards the Divine which is known as Christhood, it is capable of receiving unto itself, not only the Light of the Holy Spirit but also, the powers of the Highest by which it may rise still upward from sphere to sphere even until it become as the Divine. It is in that sense that Souls who seek to follow the Christ—by which is meant to seek unto the Estate of Christhood—are said to be sharers with Him in the Kingdom of the Father, and reign with Him.

These two great and blessed truths the writers of the Four Records destroyed for the Soul through giving to them a purely personal and individual meaning, when they took the Sayings from the Logia and applied them to Jesus. They misrepresented the beautiful impersonal Sayings given by the Master, and presented His unspeakably beautiful and humble Spirit as claiming to be the sole instrument through whom the gift of the Spirit could be obtained. They made Him who never spoke in any personal way of any powers which He possessed, but who always spoke of these powers as from the Father, claim to have had conveyed to him by the Father all the Heavenly Powers so that He might exercise them as He desired, and convey them upon whom He would. They knew not the esoteric meaning of so many of the Sayings found in the Logia which were related to the term Son of Man, and so gave to them an exoteric and personal meaning and thus destroyed their esoteric and impersonal significance. They took the term Son of Man to refer to the personal Jesus, so that all the beautiful and profound Teachings whose meanings were altogether impersonal, and which spoke of the life implied by the very term Son of Man, and of the nature of the service which that life had to render unto the Divine, came to be associated with the merely personal and outward life.

Thus was the Holy Mystery known as the coming of the Paraclete unto the Soul not only obscured but practically changed into something of an order distinct from the Soul herself when she had performed her evolution and arrived at that experience when the Baptism of the Spirit was not only received by her, but when the Divine Presence within her was consciously known. That which is potentially in all souls by the very nature of their constitution, and was and is inherent in all those who have travelled in their evolution to that stage in which the Soul has received the gift of the Holy Spirit, was made an objective power and one to be received at the hands of the personal Master; whilst He was placed in the invidious position of holding the power and bestowing it upon those who acknowledged Him as the Christ.

The Holy Paraclete is within all Souls potentially, and is inherent in the Souls of all who have arrived at the Baptism of the Spirit.

J. TODD FERRIER.

THE MESSENGER'S WORK.

When I was lifted up above the conditions prevailing upon the Earth and saw the coming of the Messenger, and heard the Hosts of the Heavens proclaiming His approach to the planes of the Earth, it was given me to understand the purpose of His mission.

I saw upon the Heavens innumerable thought-forms all relating to the work which He had to accomplish, truths relating to the Divine Love and Wisdom all awaiting the coming Hour of Interpretation when they should be again given unto the Soul.

These truths were all in the language of signs and symbols, and spake of the Divine Love and His beautiful purpose concerning all Souls.

As I looked upon these, and their beautiful meanings opened out like the most delicate and precious flowers unfolding, I beheld the work of the Messenger to be that of giving the new language unto the Soul by which her ancient heritage might be restored unto her, and all the wonderful signs and symbols which were given in ancient days rescued from the unspiritual and material meanings now associated with them.

GRAVE MORAL EVILS.*

SUCH damnatory testimonies might be largely multiplied, but these will suffice to illustrate my point, and
fully justify the late Mr. Henry Lee, F.R.C.S. (Consulting
Surgeon to St. George's Hospital, London, and Lecturer
on Pathology and Surgery to the Royal College of
Surgeons, England) in his opinion that—

"The hands of the vivisector, *by the repeated use of morally
unlawful things, gradually become hardened, and a kind of
creeping paralysis finally extends to the vital parts.* We have it
on evidence before the Royal Commission that, while interested
in his experiments, he thinks nothing of the animals' sufferings,
but, which is of far more importance, common experience shows
that as a rule he is quite indifferent to the mental and sometimes bodily sufferings which the records of his experiments
produces upon a large section of the public."

In the light afforded by these extracts, it is manifest
that the growing practice in our Medical Schools of
demonstrating the elementary facts of physiology by
experiments on living animals, before classes of young
and impressionable male and female (!) students, cannot
be otherwise than productive of grave moral evils, and
this amongst precisely that section of the rising generation (the medical) whose ethical and altruistic ideals
should be of the highest, if they would prove themselves
worthy of their profession and of the confidence reposed
in them by their fellows. The opinions of many well-
known physicians testify to the reality of this danger.
From these I select the following :—

"I would shrink with horror from accustoming large classes
of young men to the sight or animals under vivisection. I
believe many of them would be become cruel and hardened,
and would go away and repeat those experiments recklessly.
Science would gain nothing, and *the world would have let loose
upon it a set of young devils.*"

DR. S. HAUGHTON, *of Dublin, in evidence
before the Royal Commission, 1876.*

* "Why I condemn Vivisection," by Robert H. Perks, M.D.,
F.R.C.S. *Vide* advertisement pages.

"Watch the students at a vivisection. It is the blood and suffering, not the science, that rivets their breathless attention."

> Prof. Bigelow, *late Professor of Surgery in Harvard University, in paper read before the Massachusetts Medical Society.*

"In the hands of the teacher it may be rankly abused; of scientific pursuits it is *the one most liable to error*; it suggests no end to itself, but seems to grow by what it feeds on, becoming by repetition and contest more and more extended and multiplied; . . . and for all such reasons . . . *is calculated to lead to what would be designated intellectual and moral evil.*"

> Sir B. W. Richardson, *Biological Experimentation*, p. 138.

And as long as seventy years ago the celebrated Dr. Abernethy, the contemporary of the noted vivisector, Majendie, said : "Vivisection has the *direct effect of deteriorating the moral sense:* and once the moral sense is destroyed, it is impossible to foresee the consequences."

An Unscientific "Science."

Further, the attempt to gain knowledge respecting the processes of human physiology and pathology by the vivisection of the lower animals is radically *unscientific.* In respect to the former, because the abnormal conditions —pain, shock or anæsthesia—under which the experiment is conducted necessarily vitiate any conclusions which may be drawn from it, as Sir B. W. Richardson observes in the work just quoted above—"It is utterly impossible to observe natural function *under the shadow of pain* either in man or animal"; and as regards the latter branch of investigation, it is well-known that the reaction of the lower animals to injury, induced disease, and drugs, differs greatly both in kind and degree from that of man to the same agents, so much so that it is notorious that in all such investigations, the results have been confusing and contradictory (and therefore worthless) in the highest degree; in plain words have served to darken knowledge rather than to reveal it.

Claude Bernard, master vivisector as he was, voiced his opinion on this point in one of his lectures, by advising his students, whilst pursuing the study of human disease, to forget all they had ever learned from vivi-section. And many vivisectors, both in the past and to-day, have used this very fact, *i.e.*, the impossibility of obtaining reliable knowledge of human diseases, etc., through experiments on the lower animals, as the ground of their advocacy of, or apologies for, human vivisection, many cases of which have come to light in recent years ; some indeed have been published by their authors with a degree of shamelessness and cynicism rarely surpassed. (See appendix IV.)

And it was precisely this reason which was urged by the supporters of a Bill for the Utilization of Criminals by Vivisection, introduced into the State Legislature of Ohio, in recent years (and which was only rejected by a small majority).

The section of the public who have hitherto treated this subject with selfish apathy would do well to lay to heart the truth *that human vivisection is the logical and inevitable outcome of animal vivisection ;* it may, when higher considerations fail, by its suggestion of danger to their own precious persons, serve to arouse such from their attitude of acquiescence in this crime.

Lastly, we have learned that as regards the higher animals there is no abrupt line of demarcation between the physical structure, the physiological functions, the reasoning powers, of the various genera, and that in these they differ not in *kind* but in *degree* only of de-velopment and specialization, and that man is but the "elder brother" of them all.

To admit (as I think a careful study of biology compels us to do) that the animals are in this sense akin to ourselves, differing only in degree of development, is to admit that we have responsibilities and duties towards them as lesser children of the same Supreme Father, which cannot lightly be neglected, evaded or set at naught, and which unmistakeably indicate that the true relation of man towards them so far from being that of the hard taskmaster and ruthless exploiter for any and every selfish purpose, should be that of guardian and friend (as far as their natures will permit) and as their helper, striving to develop their intelligence to its utmost capacity. So doing he fulfils the Divine law of Love to the neighbour, whilst ennobling his own nature; and reaps a rich reward in the affection and fidelity to his "little brothers."

A RIGHTEOUS VIEW.

To be competent to decide rightly respecting this matter of vivisection, it is not necessary that we be experts in medical or other science, or able to judge accurately the value or otherwise of knowledge said to have been gained through it, our decision must be based on the due consideration of the *ethical* and *spiritual*, rather than the merely utilitarian bearings of the subject, and here the layman stands on an equality with the expert. As the late Mr. Ed. Maitland well put it :—
" The appeal is from the specialist to the more evenly developed conscience of the community at large. It is for us as a people to declare that there are moral limits to every pursuit, that there are means which no end can justify. In the axiom that the infliction of torture upon any innocent creature whatever for the benefit of others is absolutely unjustifiable, we have an indefeasible rule by which to decide the case in point. The plea that it is for our own good rather aggravates the offence; for it is then no other than the apotheosis of that worst of devils, the devil of selfishness in his most detestable form, that of cruelty."

It is the old choice between the way of Righteousness and that of Mammon here presented to us; whether we shall strive to be worthy children of our Divine Father, whose love and compassion ever flows unto and sustains all His creatures; or whether in the spirit of cowardly and base self-seeking we banish light and pity from our hearts and condemn multitudes of our sub-human fellows to infinite suffering in the hope of acquiring some personal profit thereby.

I have written in the hope that some of my readers may be led to see this practice of vivisection in its true light, and be impelled to use their most earnest endeavour in promoting right knowledge, right feeling, and right action concerning it so that its abolition be not long delayed, its dreadful shadow be lifted from the lives of our lowly kindred, its stain cleansed from our nation's honour, its blighting influence upon all moral and spiritual growth cease from our midst, and the due and inevitable nemesis which follows such deeds may no longer affect us and our descendants.

For be assured that in respect to this meanest crime of our civilization, " God is not mocked, for *whatsoever* a man soweth *that* shall he also reap."

ROBERT H. PERKS, M.D., F.R.C,S.

(To be continued.)

THE OTHER WORLD.

It was given unto me to witness the state of the spheres occupied by the Creatures in the Spirit-world.

I beheld the awful anguish arising out of the sufferings imposed upon the Creatures in the Abattoirs and Physiological Laboratories.

I saw the features of many of them in the Astral World, and they were beyond all description, so intense was the anguish expressed upon them.

And I anguished with them in their distress, and cried unto Heaven that I might be permitted to help them.

Then it was shown unto me that the true way to deliver them was through the Redemption of all Souls unto the life of true Pity, Compassion and Love ;

For only by the Redemption of the Human Race could the full Deliverance of all the Creatures be accomplished from oppression and bondage through the true recognition of who and what they are, viz.— the little children in the Great Spiritual Household.

THE SEVEN-FOLD AMEN.

When the Visions upon the Celestial Kingdom were given unto the Soul, I also heard the voices of many joining in the Praise of the Eternal and ever Blessed One.

They sang of the Majesty of the Divine Nature, the Tenderness of the Divine Love, and the Glory of the Divine Wisdom made manifest in all the Heavens and shown forth in all Life.

And in their Song of Praise I heard the sound of the Seven-fold Amen, and felt the majesty of it—for it went through my life like a current of heaven-born magnetism—,and also the overawing grandeur of it as the sound filled the Heavens with the most wonderful harmony.

When my Soul was caught up by the Spirit so that I heard that grand Seven-fold Amen, my whole being would fain have taken a part with those who sang so sweetly of the Divine Love and Wisdom, and have for ever joined them in the Service of Praise before the Divine; for my whole being longed for the life which I saw.

But the burden of sorrow which lay upon me through the consciousness of my infirmities was so great that the wonderful sound and vision overwhelmed me, and I was only able to join in the language of the Seven-fold Amen.

Yet the Song of Praise unto the Divine and the wonderful music of the Spheres expressed in the Seven-fold Amen, I felt to be like long-lost treasures found again, the Song and its many chords issuing in that Finale which no human ear has ever heard on this world being even as the finding by the Soul of the Sphere of the Gods, the Kingdom of the Father.

PENTECOST A DELUSION.

THE effects of the story of the Day of Pentecost have
been disastrous. The story was taken to represent
the outpouring upon all flesh of the Life-stream of the
Divine foretold in the Ancient Prophecies, and the estab-
lishing from the Heavens of the outward Kingdom which
began to be erected in the name of the Master. It was
taken as an illustration of how the Divine outpouring
took place, and the nature of the results which followed
it. The extraordinary phenomena which were said to
accompany the outpouring, were accepted as testimonials
to the Divine nature of the blessing supposed to have
then been given, and the like testimonies have always
been sought for more or less. The influencing of some
thousands by the remarkable display, to believe on the
Master as the Son of the Highest sent to redeem Israel
first and the Gentiles afterwards, was taken to be the sure
proof of the Divine nature of the power which was at
work ; and the sign was so impressed upon the early
communities that they all looked for its repetition in their
own history as the sure and certain seal that the Divine
power was upon them—a sign which impressed itself so
deeply upon the early Church that its influence has been
not only present but always paramount in the whole
history of the Church, even until this day. For any
community in which the outward signs of success are
lacking is not regarded (however beautifully spiritual its
few members may be) as one having the true seal of the
Divine favour ; whereas in the community where such
signs are great, the phenomenal success is taken to be
the token of the Divine blessing and of real spiritual
prosperity.

That the story of the Day of Pentecost with its
wonderful signs, was a delusion, the whole history of the
Western World testifies when it is closely examined in
the light of the truths which it professes to accept and
practise. That the story had no real foundation will be

known unto all who know the nature of the Divine outpouring and who have realised within themselves the
meaning of the Baptism of the Spirit. But it is hard
indeed to convince any who have not yet passed through
these blessed experiences by which the Divine outpouring is understood and seen, and the Baptism of the
Spirit is realised, that the spectacular of the Day of
Pentecost was not only not in harmony with the Divine
ways, but was the repudiation of the methods pursued by
the Ever Blessed One who, when He pours out from the
fulness of His own Life upon all Souls, does so in the
manner described in one of the Gospel stories: "The
Spirit bloweth where it listeth, and thou canst not tell
whence it cometh or whither it goeth; and so is it with
every one who is born of the Spirit." So effectual was the
delusion presented in the story that it has continued to
deceive the members of the outward kingdom known as
the Church. Nay, its influences were of such a character
that even amongst themselves these members came to
view the phenomena differently, and even the manner in
which the gift of the Spirit was given, and the means and
channels through which it was conveyed.

What a sad history that is which the ages of polemic
warfare within the Church has written over the beautiful
gift of the Spirit! How spiritually tragic have many of
the results been unto Souls who were indeed seeking for
the light to break upon them; of the terrible polemics
during the past ages arising out of the darkness in which
the Church was as the result of following the delusion?
How utterly opposed to the experience within the Soul
of the blessed Baptism of the Spirit were the conflicts
waged between the various Communities, each of which
professed to understand the nature and operation and
experience of that Baptism? What a commentary that
awful history is upon the spiritual darkness within the
Church; the lack of spiritual understanding on the part
of all who professed to teach and guide Souls; the
absence of true spiritual perception by which alone
Divine things can be apprehended; and the utter mis-

conception of the meaning of possessing the Divine
Spirit? If the story of the Day of Pentecost were not a
delusion but a grand spiritual reality in which the Divine
Spirit was bestowed without measure, a reality to be
repeated in manifold ways unto all the Communities
which grew up in the name of the Master, then what
meaning is to be ascribed to all the fearful conflicts waged
between these several Communities over the questions
concerning the nature and operations and methods of
bestowal of the Gift of the Spirit? How shall we explain
these conflicts when we know that all such things are as
opposed to the presence and inheritance of the Holy
Spirit, as darkness is opposed to the light! When we
know what the true fruits of the Spirit are, and how these
fruits show themselves when the Soul has the Holy Spirit
for an inheritance, how can we reconcile such a spirit of
conflict, loveless and discordant, hostile where Souls
differed from it, and even showing a spirit of hate where
it could not triumph, with that beautiful spirit which is
ever meek and lowly, ever full of loving thoughtfulness,
ever seeking to be even as the Divine in its love and
service?

If the Day of Pentecost, as given in the Acts of the
Apostles, had been a grand and glorious spiritual reality
and not a delusion imposed upon the Soul from the
Astral Kingdom ; and if the Church ever since had
inherited as its very special gift the presence and power
of the Holy Spirit, so that it made manifest the fruits of
the Spirit in all its history, what spiritual potency would
have been its heritage! What majesty and power for
goodness and righteousness it would have possessed!
What beautiful peace and harmony would have been
shed wherever the Church rose! What a different Western
World we should have had to-day had it been a world
wherein the triumph of the Spirit of God was beheld!
For instead of the spirit of dominant force which makes
armaments for destruction and means by which communities are fearfully oppressed and burdened, we should
have had the spirit of love which builds up and imposes

no grievous burdens.   For the spirit of contention which makes discord wherever it is to be found, we should have had a spirit of harmony melting into a beautiful Brotherhood of all Souls.   For the thoughtless, unsympathetic spirit found in every sphere of experience, from the most commercial where men strive against one another, to the most sacred where Souls are supposed to seek and find the healing from the Divine Love which makes the entire life whole, but into which men and women carry the spirit which dominates them in the more outward spheres, we should have had made manifest the most beautiful sympathy born within the life from the presence of the Divine within the Soul.

J. TODD FERRIER.

THE SIGN OF THE SPIRIT.

The possession of the Holy Spirit may be known by the Soul in whom the consciousness of the Divine Love has been called forth.

For the Fruits of the Holy Spirit are ever the same in all ages; and they are these—Pity unto all Creatures, Compassion for all Souls, the Divine Love showing itself in all the ways of life so that they become pure, the Divine Peace making itself manifest in such a way that peace is shed abroad everywhere and the spirit that makes for strife and warfare subdued, the Divine Joy revealing itself in glad service for the Divine through ministering to the children of the Father.

THE WESTERN DELUSION.

AFTER more than eighteen centuries of the supposed manifestation and power of the Holy Spirit's operative presence in the Western World, behold what a spectacular is presented to us! It is a veritable Aceldama. Though there are fewer international wars, yet are the children of the Heavenly Father slain upon the altars of vaulting ambitions, national jealousies, racial rivalries, and false habits and customs. The very life-energy is wasted in evil, wicked and disastrous pursuits. The world groans beneath the burden of their strife, so great is it in almost every sphere. The burden of great fear lies upon the minds of men and women fashioned from their pursuit of evil, and those wicked ways which make nations distrust one another; for though there is the cry of *peace, peace*, the sounds which speak of great preparation for coming strife, are everywhere heard. Many groan beneath the awful burden, and feel how utterly opposed it is to Him whose name these nations all profess to love, reverence and serve : but at present the counsel of these Souls is rejected, so triumphant is the terrible delusion which has smitten and blinded the nations and led them to seek peace and strength in ways whose ending is warfare, the weakening and impoverishment of the people, the degradation of every noble and brotherly principle and feeling, and the unspeakable enervation of the Soul.

Why do the nations rage within themselves, and their peoples imagine vain things? Because of the sad and terrible delusion which overtook them when the true meaning of Human Life, of Brotherhood, of Nationality, of Race, of Life as an Organic whole, was inverted for them, and the beautiful spiritual meaning and vision of life as it was meant to be became lost to the Soul.

THE TRUE MEANING OF LIFE.

May we not with some show of reason ask the very pertinent question, What is the meaning of life in the

Western Mind ?   What view does the Western take of
life?   That it is not the view generally taken by the
Eastern is very true ; that it is not the ideal presented in
any of the Ancient Religions may soon be discovered by
examining the view of life which these spiritual sign-posts
presented ; that it is the very antithesis of that wonderfully beautiful ideal which the Christ gave in His own
Life and Teachings, any one who knows what that life
was, and what the meaning of the profound Sayings of
the Master implied for all who sought to follow Him,
may easily recognise.   The meaning of life for the
Western is the triumph of every elemental power, the
victory of the man in all the outer spheres of experience,
the conquest by the mind of everything material.
Success is counted according to such conquests ; and
failure is stamped upon all who cannot succeed in that
way.   Life means material increase, social uprising, the
gaining of power within the elemental kingdoms ; and all
who do not rise to these things are accounted the
world's failures—mere hewers and drawers for others.
The inner spheres of experience are almost forgotten.
The elemental powers shut out those powers of Heaven
whose influence is the reverse of everything elemental.
The culture of the Soul is a culture not included in the
Western curriculum.   It is a culture quite foreign to the
elemental life which is sought after.   For the Soul-life is
not a reality in the Western World ; at any rate, it is not
so to the majority.   True spiritual realisation is accounted
a strange phenomenon.   Indeed few believe in the reality
of the world of the Soul, in the realisations which proceed
to the life from the Spiritual World when the Soul seeks
unto the life which that World has to give.   They
relegate all such experiences to that time when life upon
the outer planes is closing, and even unto the time when
the Soul is supposed to pass away from all its old
conditions and associations and enter upon the life of the
Heavens.   They regard all effort towards knowing what
that life means, and what possible attainments the Soul
may acquire even here, as not only superfluous but

wrong. They think, when they think at all of such things, that any such endeavours are evil and not of God.

In the Western World the true meaning of life is largely unknown. Its original beautiful purpose is something undreamt of. The real nature of the being known as man yet remains unto nearly the whole of that World, an unknown quantity. The life born in the world when physical birth takes place, is as yet unrecognised in the West, since the life born is viewed as a new creation, a physical organism that contains elements which may unfold into what is thought of as a Soul, a life without any previous experience, without any spiritual history in the past, without any latent memories of earlier days, without any strongly marked individuality and character-istics peculiar to itself and which cannot be related to any parental influence. The Soul that once more rises upon the outer spheres when birth takes place, has had no place given unto it in Western Philosophy, Religion, or practice, as a spiritual being once more appearing in the world for experience in order that it might grow up towards the light of the Spiritual World, and find itself the stronger for having had the experience amid a true spiritual environment. For the Western World has never thought seriously of the nature of the Soul, the life unto which it is ever being called by the Divine Love and Wisdom, and the marvellous spiritual and Divine possi-bilities inherently latent in it; they have devoted their attention to the outer physical form, its organic history, its physiological construction, its culture as an instrument of physical and mental power. And so the real man has not been understood. The beautiful purpose for which the Soul was fashioned, has remained undiscovered. The transcendent life of which it was possible, has not been known. That it was meant to be a microcosm of the Divine Nature, has never been imagined. That it contains the potentialities of the Divine Nature, may be vaguely believed by some, but rarely realised in the sublimity of its meaning.

Who amongst the various Schools of religious thought think of the Soul as a spiritual organism quite distinct from the mere physical vehicle through which it makes manifest its longings on the outer spheres; a being who has had a long history upon this world; who once knew something of the glory of perfect life; who once walked in the Garden of Eden or that state of experience when no evil was known; who even communed with Angels and heard the voice of the Divine within His Sanctuary; who beheld within that Sanctuary the Vision of the Divine Love and Wisdom; but who lost the power to see Divine Visions, to hear the Divine Voice, and to commune with the Angels, through leaving the beautiful state known as the Garden of Eden, and passing outwards in desire and purpose of life into a veritable wilderness where the Soul has had to till the land in much labour and sorrow in order to be able to spiritually subsist, and from which mistake with all its grievous consequences it has to be redeemed? What great and noble heritage have these Schools given the Soul? None. They know of none. The past is unknown to them. The life the Soul once lived full of beautiful purity, joy and gladness when it knew the Divine Love and rejoiced in the life unto which He called it, is a thing of which they have never even dreamt concerning the individual born into the world. And knowing not the nature of that beautiful life which the Soul lived in the Golden Age when it is said that "All the world was young," they understand not the kind of life unto which the Divine is ever calling the Soul, the kind of life which the Master made manifest when He lived His beautiful Christhood.

BROTHERHOOD.

The life lived by the Soul prior to its descent into conditions which brought about the disastrous spiritual impoverishment whose results are still with us and most manifest everywhere, and nowhere more strikingly manifest than in the Western World, was one of beautiful Brotherhood. There were various orders of Souls, and various degrees of experience through unfoldment in each order, but one spirit ruled them. There were the Elder Brethren and the Younger; but there was no dominancy by the one over the other. The Younger Ones learnt from the Elder Ones, but they learnt through the loving service of the Elder. Many were great amongst them, but they knew it not; for when a Soul is great towards the Divine, it is unconscious of it. It feels no personal nor individual greatness, because it has the blessed consciousness that apart from the Divine it is even nothing.

It was not only a very real and true Brotherhood, but it was a Brotherhood of the whole Human Race. Even the Creatures shared in the blessings. It was a Brotherhood of Nations, Races and Peoples; for the true meaning of these terms is not what is now understood by them. The Nations represented the evolution of the Soul towards the Divine, the various stages of the Soul's growth Godward, so that the more advanced Souls formed the Older Nations. The various Races represented the different orders of Souls, and the Peoples the various degrees within each order. There was only one life manifested, though it was diversified according to the Nationality, Race and People. There was no difference between the Nations as to the great and sublime purpose in life, for all had but one great and beautiful end in view, namely, the attainment of the Divine Life unto which all were called. There was no subjection of one Race by another, no feeling of superiority by the Older towards the Younger, no line of conduct pursued that made the younger and less unfolded Races conscious of any inferiority; for the law of love prevailed: the greater thought much of the less; the stronger ministered unto the weaker; the Elder served, with beautiful devotion, the Younger in the Father's Household.

In those days no lack was known. No child of the Heavenly Father hungered in any sphere of experience without having his needs met. No one longed to rise higher in spiritual experience without the necessary assistance being forthcoming to enable the Soul to realise its beautiful purpose. No obstacles were placed in the way of any one who sought to attain to higher conditions of spiritual experience. No false ambitions were taught by which the Soul found itself hampered and even held in captivity, as so many Souls now are through the awful delusions born from their false view of life. The Path of the Soul was unobstructed by such hindrances as array themselves upon that Path now. The habits and customs of the people from the oldest Nation to the youngest, were all pure, and such as aided the soul in its Heaven-ward journey. The outer spheres were clean and pure, so that the Soul was not in any bondage to the sense-life, as it now is in all the Nations, and in a very special way in the West. The powers of the body were kept pure because the body was purely built up and nourished on the beautiful fruits of the Earth. All the senses and feelings and affections were obedient unto the Soul, so that no part of the system was at variance or out of equilibrium. All the powers upon every sphere within the system were obedient unto the central will, so that the individual was in a state of harmony. In those ages to rise up on to the Spiritual Heavens so as to behold the Angelic World, and receive from the Angelic ministrants those Teachings concerning the Divine Love which were and ever are essential to the Soul's true progress toward the Divine Life, was possible. And one Nation ministered unto the other, and one Race helped the other, and the various Peoples all aided towards this beautiful and sublime realisation.

In the light of these past experiences, where do the Western Nations to-day stand?

J. Todd Ferrier.

THE PYRAMID OF LIGHT.

When I was carried up out of the conditions of the Earth into the Heavens where I heard the Praise rendered unto the Eternal and Ever Blessed One by an innumerable host, and the wonderful Seven-fold Amen whose sound filled the whole Heavens with feelings of the Majesty of the Divine Awe, I likewise saw a Pyramid of most wonderful Light.

The base of it rested upon the upper Heavens, and, with the two sides, it glowed with a Light whose whiteness bespoke its Divine Nature.

Between the sides, and reaching from the base to the apex, I saw a multitude of points of beautiful light like Stars so grouped that they appeared to form a Constellation in the Celestial Heavens like a perfect triangle.

But the Pyramid of Light was quite distinct from them, though they were contained within its form.

As I looked upon the wonderful vision I became conscious that it was the expression upon the Divine Kingdom of the Divine Love and Wisdom, the sign of the Presence of the Eternal and ever Blessed One in whom all Souls and all true systems are contained, the symbol of the Fulness of the Divine Life, Light and Love, the testimony to the all-embracing and all-comprehending nature of the Eternal Father.

In this wonderful Pyramid of Light whose sides and base glowed with such pure white radiance, I feel that the true meaning is to be found of that most wonderful structure in the midst of Ancient Egypt, the Great Pyramid of Ghizeh. For that Pyramid originally was so built that its sides glowed with the powerfully reflected effulgence of the glory of the Sun, so that it was the symbol of the Divine Presence; whilst interiorly it represented the return of the Soul to the Divine Kingdom.

ACELDAMA.

THE delusion which overtook the Western World and led the Nations and peoples of it to the disastrous view of spiritual life which has influenced all the ways and actions of the various communities, turned that World into an Aceldama. In every sphere of experience it became a "field of blood." The fearful strife in the early centuries between the various schools of thought which had arisen within the Church over the meaning of the various doctrines enunciated in the name of the Master, not only led to the taking of the lives of many who entered into the arena of conflict, but, what was even much worse for the progress of spiritual life, made the very Soul shed its life upon the altars of warfare. For many centuries did the battle continue, only changing the scene as the occasion arose. The Saints were slain on the altars; whilst in a spiritual sense, the people covered the battle-field. The Western World which was supposed to have been conquered for Christ, became like that "field of blood" which was purchased by the betrayer; it became the home of the spiritually dead. Instead of conquest for Christ when the conquered would have become subject to the gentle rule and ways of the Christ-life, it was made a theatre full of actors whose whole action in the drama of the Soul was to turn what should have been a life of beautiful purity and goodness, into tragedy. For the Christ-life was constantly betrayed, and the Christ-spirit strangled. The Christhood yearnings of the Soul were continually crucified by those who should have been most anxious to aid their fulfilment.

Even unto this day the term Aceldama may be written across the threshold of the West. Though many of the conditions have changed, yet is it the scene of warfare upon every sphere. It is yet a battlefield where the slain lie in their millions, both Human and Sub-human. The lives of the multitudes are laid low in the conflicts, and the Saints are sacrificed still upon the altars of the leaders and lovers of strife. The blood of the Saints is shed as they endeavour to change the conditions and bring in the pure and beautiful reign of Christhood which would give new life unto all and shed peace and harmony everywhere. The blood of the Creatures cries unto Heaven against the cruelties of men and women who slay them for food, destroy them for clothing, and torture them with sufferings unspeakable in order to try to cure their self-created diseases. In a very real sense, the Western World "runs blood" through all the avenues of life, from the most sacred threshold of the Soul to the threshold of the outermost spheres of experience. Where are the blessings supposed to have become its heritage as the result of the outpouring of the Holy Spirit? Where is the Christ-life it was supposed to believe in and seek unto the finding? Where is the Christ-spirit whose very nature is opposed to strife, without the possession of which no one can know the Lord? Where is the Christ-ideal for the Soul, to realise which a man must give up *the whole world?* Where is the love which is the foundation of true Brotherhood, which loveth man like the Divine and accounteth no true service to him too lowly nor any service for his spiritual welfare too great; which reckoneth not of Nationalities and Bloods and Distinctions, but regardeth all as members of the one great Household to be ministered unto for the Divine? Where is the compassion of the Christ-love which breaketh forth in real pity towards all Creatures, sheltering them from every form of evil, defending them against all who would do them hurt, beholding them as the little children in the universal life of this world-system who are to be cared for and helped in their evolution towards that fuller life for which they have been generated?

Let the Western World which was supposed to have been won for Christ so many ages ago, answer these pertinent questions. Yea, let the Church reared in the name of the blessed Master, consider them well, and see whether they do not contain a message for her communities.

J. TODD FERRIER.

THE HERALD OF THE CROSS.

Vol v. New Series.   June, 1909.   No. 6.

REJOICE, O EARTH!

O sing unto the Lord a new song; let your hearts make melody unto Him: for He hath visited the Earth and redeemed her, that she should again show forth His glory and speak abroad His praise.

O sing unto the Lord all the Earth; let a song of gladness be heard within all thy palaces and upon all thy spheres: for the Lord hath visited thee in thy affliction, even unto the healing of thy wounding.

O sing unto the Lord ye dwellers upon the Hills; and from the Mountains let the joyful tidings be heard: then will all the dwellers within the valleys hear of the wondrous things which the Lord hath brought to pass, how He hath made Himself known unto His children and broken with them again the Bread of Life, and given unto them to drink from the Wells of Salvation.

O sing unto the Lord a new song; let the whole Earth resound with praise unto Him; and let the dwellers within the shadows hear of the wonderful Light which streameth from the Heavens, and the glory which breaketh on the Hills, that all may know that the Lord is near.

THE CONTRADICTIONS IN NATURE.

THE meaning of all the apparent contradictions in what is spoken of as Nature, is only to be found in a right understanding of the true history of the Soul and the Planet. They are only to be understood when seen in the light of the past history of the Planet and all her children. The extraordinary phenomena witnessed in all the physical planes and kingdoms find their true interpretation only from *within the Vail*, and not from the mere study of the phenomena themselves. For whilst observing the phenomena which are only results of hidden forces, the primary cause and secondary causes of the phenomena remain unseen and unknown. The forces lying behind the strange and ofttimes contradictory phenomena, forces which themselves are often only the secondary manifestations of other more deeply hidden elements and powers, are to be known and understood alone by those who have been permitted to see and behold " within the Vail " both their nature and their operation. They are of such a nature that only from the Kingdom of the Divine may they be understood. Their operations are so extraordinay at times as to appear unto the observer upon the outermost planes as if no true law directed them, but that they were a law unto themselves; whereas the contradictions which are beheld, and which are not only very real but also frequently disastrous in their results, are only in the phenomena produced upon the outer planes as the result of wrong conditions set up within these planes. They are the outcome of certain forces born from certain elements operating within conditions whose nature is such that they generate phenomena which are themselves in opposition both to the nature of the operating forces and the purpose for which they are in the world.

THE VEGETABLE KINGDOM.

The apparent contradictions in the observed phenomena within the Vegetable Kingdom are due only to wrong conditions resulting from the displacement of that Kingdom through the displacement of all the outer planes of the Planet. For the Vegetable Kingdom was originally perfect in every order of its life. It was beautiful in every sphere. All its forms were perfect of their kind, and the colours were true representations of the Seven Spheres wherein the Seven Sacred Colours were made manifest unto the Soul. All the trees and plants were full of the grace and beauty of the Divine Wisdom as that Wisdom was manifested upon the objective world. Their bloom was always beautiful and unfailing, and their fruits were always good and sure. The seasons had no uncertainty in their return; for even the objective world, in a very real sense, rejoiced before the Lord and praised Him. The conditions witnessed now within the Vegetable Kingdom were unknown in those ages. No grave contradictions existed to make it manifest that there was an unseen and unknown conflict between the various orders of life in the kingdom and the conditions amid which they had to grow and unfold and bear their fruit. The Seasons were always sure. The Earth gave her increase without the terrible travail which often now accompanies the giving of her fulness for the needs of all her children. Famine and drought resulting from blighted fruits and dried-up springs found no place amid the perfect and beautiful conditions which then prevailed. The tempest and whirlwind came not nigh the dwelling of the children. The elements were never out of Season nor in any way at variance with the life within the Vegetable World. The laws which governed the Earth were those established from the Divine, perfect always in their operations and beautiful in the results. The Earth moved in harmony with the Spiritual magnetic laws of the great Solar Household, and all her elements responded to the Divine attraction. Through moving in harmony with the Spiritual magnetic laws, no wrong conditions found any place amidst her elements, so that they performed their functions for which they were generated perfectly, and were never in conflict with one another in the performance of those functions, nor at any time wrought evil upon any of the orders of life within the Vegetable Kingdom.

It was a Golden Age for the Earth as well as for all her children.

J. TODD FERRIER.

A VISION OF THE EARTH.

When there was vouchsafed to me the Vision of the Earth as she was in her unfallen and pristine glory, I beheld her upon the Heavens within the Celestial Spheres performing her service before the Lord; and she was glorious to look upon.

She was clothed in garments of light, and her appearance was like an Emerald fashioned to reflect the glory of the Sun.

Her path was upon the Kingdom of the Divine: all her movements wrought only harmony, and filled her spheres with a music whose tones were grand in their sounding and glorious in the rhythmic colours which they revealed as the Spectrum of Elohim was broken upon her planes.

Her movements were as parts of some unspeakable Divine Symphony performed upon the Celestial Heavens, full at once of the infinite majesty and ineffable sweetness of the Divine Love and Wisdom, the Omnipotence and Gentleness of God, the Awe and Tenderness of the Eternal and Ever Blessed One.

Ten thousand times ten thousand voices filled her with songs of Gladness and Praise as her children rejoiced in her light and beheld her glory.

THE CONTRADICTIONS IN NATURE.

(THE ANIMAL KINGDOM.)

THE strange contradictions which are so apparent within the Vegetable Kingdom may likewise be found within the Creature Kingdom. The phenomena observed in the various zones of that Kingdom indicate that there are elements operating within it which are not conducive to harmony, and which often find their manifestation in very serious strife between the various orders, and even between members of the same order. Such will be obvious to every careful student of the remarkable phenomena witnessed within the various zones of the Creature Kingdom. For in almost every zone there may be found unseen disturbing influences; and in some zones the disturbance is so great that there is not only lack of harmony, but serious conflict. Warfare by one order is pursued against another to such an extent that it has been said that " Nature is red in tooth, and claw," because of the fearful strife and shedding of life. And the sad part of it all is that the observer whilst witnessing the awful phenomena can speak of the wonderful harmony of all Nature, so blinded is he by the illusionary theories of the phenomena propounded by Physical Science. For the conditions of the Creature Kingdom are accepted by Physical Science as the natural result of the operation of the evolutionary laws in which its adherents believe; and all who cannot accept the conclusions of Physical Science believe that the Creatures were originally fashioned by the Allwise and Beneficient Creator with the conditions which prevail in the various zones. They look upon the state of the Creature Kingdom as that intended by the Divine and Ever Blessed One; whilst the Scientist accepts the phenomena as the testimony of the evolutionary process.

But both positions are untenable in the light of any accepted belief in the Presence within the world of a Wise and Beneficient Creator and Ruler, or the idea of Harmony; for there can be no harmony where there is such fearful strife, and harmony must be found wherever the Divine operates. It were impossible to conceive of a Creature Kingdom at variance with itself in almost all its zones, and full of unspeakable strife, being the outcome of the operation of the Divine Presence. The Eternal One who fashioned this Earth with her Kingdoms, must surely ever stand for Harmony and not discord, for peace and not strife. In the world in which His Presence abides and His laws rule will be found beautiful order in every Kingdom, harmony within every sphere, gentleness and peace everywhere. His works could never be in conflict amongst themselves whilst His laws alone directed and fashioned them. The world when full of the Divine Presence must be the exposition and manifestation of the true Attributes of the Divine, and not otherwise; and the Attributes of the Eternal One must be perfect in Love, in Justice, in Compassion, and in Pity. We cannot conceive of any world fully ruled by Him, to be other than the interpretation of these beautiful and perfect Attributes. If He is Love, then where He is there must be love. If He is the All-Wise and ever Just One, then where justice is absent He cannot be present as the guide and ruler. If He is full of Compassion unto all Souls so that His Mercy floweth unto them at all times to help and heal them, then where He maketh His dwelling there must be the outflowing of true beautiful Compassion towards all. And if He pities all the Creatures and would fain help them out of their limitations, and the sufferings caused by the oppression resulting from the wrong conditions in the planes of their experience, then where pity dwells not but only such things as contribute to the hurt and oppression of the Creatures are found, His Presence must be absent. Whether it be in the Microcosm or the Macrocosm—that is, whether in the Individual or the Planet; if Love, Justice, Compassion and Pity are absent, or if they find no expression of themselves towards all Souls and the Creatures, then we may be sure that the Presence of the Divine is not realised there.

J. TODD FERRIER

THE CONTRADICTIONS IN NATURE.
(THE EFFECTS OF THE CHANGED ELEMENTS.)

THE history written upon the mind of the Soul was one full of the most terrible experiences. The effect upon the mind of all the new conditions which had arisen within the elemental kingdoms, was such as to bring down the mind to function within those kingdoms, to seek the life of the Soul in them, to reflect the things belonging to the changed conditions rather than the spiritual things thrown upon it from the Angelic Kingdom. The new conditions so affected the mind that it became of their nature, just as the magnetic plane of the Planet was changed from being purely spiritual to partake of the magnetic nature of the elemental kingdoms. It was quite true the process was a long one, and that the change within the mind was effected very gradually ; but it was so effectively done that the mind lost its power to truly reflect spiritual things, and was so influenced by the elemental kingdoms that it changed the beautiful thought-forms sent unto it from the Angelic Sphere, and made of them things pertaining to those kingdoms.

The changed elements changed the whole history of the Soul from the age in which the Earth's polarity was so altered as to make her leave the Ecliptic, until these days of the Redemption and the Regeneration. They took the Soul away from its true path upon the Spiritual Heavens to make it follow a path within the elemental kingdom. They gradually changed the desires of the mind so that it no longer only sought the life born from the Divine, but also the life born of the changed elements, until at last many only sought the latter life and went away from being spiritual Souls to dwell amid the lower forms which were generated as the result of the Earth's mistake. They took down into themselves many of the later generated Souls who had not the strength to resist the new influences, and these became lost as spiritual organisms : these may yet be found within the Animal Kingdom, and the wonderful forms which they knew how to fashion may be witnessed in the marvels of the whole of the true Crustacea; for the forms repeat those found within the Vegetable Kingdom. They prevented the older and stronger Souls of the second Generation from passing upwards to the higher Creature forms: these may be found in the pure Rodents and timid Creatures of the fields. They hindered the progress of the younger members of the first Generation through intercepting the spiritual influences without which they were unable to grow towards the higher forms; for the Soul could only pass from form to form and order to order as it grew in strength: these may be found within the beautiful Orders of the Birds. They prevented the stronger Souls of that Generation who had not reached the Human Kingdom, from doing so, because these Souls could not find the spiritual magnetism necessary to their unfoldment: these may be found within the various orders of the true Herbiverous Creatures. They not only thus prevented the true evolution of all the Souls who had not then reached the Human Kingdom, but they so influenced those who had reached that kingdom that these Souls lost all their power to resist the elemental attraction, and were gradually drawn down from the Human Kingdom into the terrible forms which had in the meanwhile been generated as the outcome of the grievous mistake of the Earth: many of these Souls, though they were lifted out of the then Animal Kingdom more than once, may be found to-day in the Creatures who serve and companion man so faithfully and constantly—the Horse and the Dog. The remaining Souls of that Generation are to be found on the Human Kingdom. But the true evolution of all the children of the Earth was effectually suspended; for when they were able to rise on to the Human Kingdom, the influences of the long ages within the elemental kingdom had to be overcome, and that has been a long and painful process. And it is only in these latter days that the process has brought the Soul to a state in which it may once more take up its true evolution, and grow towards the Divine through unfolding all its potential beautiful elements and crown itself with true childhood before the Eternal One, that childhood which bears His image and makes manifest His love.

But the results of the Earth's mistake in changing her polarity, and moving away from the Ecliptic, were further reaching. They not only affected all the kingdoms of the Earth and took away from the Soul's true path all the Earth's children ; but they included in the terrible disaster all the Christ Souls who were ministering unto the children. For though these Souls were not at first overcome by the powers introduced into the elemental kingdom through the mistake of the Earth, yet they were at last also drawn down into those kingdoms through dwelling near the children in order to minister unto them. For when the children of the Earth were drawn down into the forms which had been generated out of the changed conditions, the Christ-Souls followed them in order to bring them back. And when they were thus drawn away from the Spiritual Heavens out of their great love for the children to follow them down even into the monstrous forms of the Saurians, the disaster was intensified manifold ; for it was the loss unto the Earth of all those who were sent out from the Divine Kingdom to aid her in the generation of her children. What that loss has meant may never be expressed adequately. It is almost beyond the power of any one to conceive of it. But the long ages of awful spiritual darkness and strife, first in the Creature Kingdom in every zone and amongst almost every order, and then in the Human Kingdom, bear testimoy to that loss and the awful experiences through which all the Souls who went down from the Human Kingdom had to pass through, especially the Christ Souls. For their afflictions were unspeakably great : None could even dream of all that they passed through, so great were their tribulations. What they once were in their Divine Estate none but Christs could know. The terrible experiences imposed upon them by the conditions of the Animal Kingdom, only Christs could understand. What they suffered of spiritual loss, and the fearful anguish which for untold ages was their heritage, none but those who witnessed it from the Divine Kingdom could realise.

The strange contradictions witnessed in Nature have a history and meaning more profound than students of the phenomena wot of. But their explanation may now be known and their cause understood, for the Soul has beheld it all afresh.

J. TODD FERRIER.

THE NEW MANIFESTATION.

Behold what manner of Love the Father hath bestowed upon us that we should be again raised out of our low estate wherein no vision of Him came unto us, but only the darkness and sorrow !

For He hath healed us with His Presence, and restored unto us the Vision of Himself as in the Ancient Days before the darkness overtook us and shut out from us the light of the Glory of His Love.

Behold how He loveth all His children even unto restoring them through working for them a most glorious Redemption from the darkness and sorrow which overwhelmed them when they went down from His Presence into the land where the Light of His Countenance could not shine !

For He maketh their Path full of the Light of His Presence that they may return unto the land of their heritage to dwell there as His Children, bearing upon them His Image and beholding His Glory.

THE CONTRADICTIONS IN NATURE.
(SOME PLANETARY EFFECTS.)

THE full effects of the disaster to the Earth and her children and the Christ-Souls, did not end with the loss of the Christhood Community, for they went out beyond the Earth as a Spiritual System and wrought great and grievous changes in the elements of more than one of the other spiritual systems within the Household of Sol. They affected so greatly the magnetic conditions of the Moon that she lost her power to function on the Ecliptic, lost her children and her beautiful magnetic plane. They exercised so powerful an influence over Mars that he lost his power to function on the Ecliptic, and caused all his once beautiful planes to consolidate and girdle him in chains of adamant, and they thus drove all his children into another system. They caused the little systems which accompanied him to lose their equilibrium and their Celestial Estate, and become as dead worlds. They wrought grievous harm to the planes of Jupiter and compelled the Planet to so act as to throw his entire system out of harmony. They even affected the wonderful system of Saturn so that the Planet's planes were prevented from performing their office. And they caused the system of Venus to be changed, drew down some of her children into the conditions, and even affected the motion of Mercury. They thus practically affected the whole of the Solar System, and brought about the strange conditions which prevail to-day.

Yet that was not the end of the results of the disaster to the Earth ; for the influence reached unto the Divine Kingdom of the whole system and brought about the change in the Sun Himself which necessitated the generation of the photosphere for the purpose, first, of protecting the Divine Kingdom from the influences of the changed conditions, and secondly, of providing a way whereby to aid the Earth to recover herself, and restore the other members of the System.

We have only been able to indicate the Celestial

disasters which were the result of the change in the Earth's polarity that caused her to move away from the plane of the Ecliptic (the Divine Kingdom); yet sufficient to show that there is not only a reason why the whole of the systems appear to be out of true harmony (though perhaps some scientists would not acknowledge that they were), but that the reason for it is to be found in the conditions of the Earth in past ages. The day when Science will behold with the understanding opened the profound meaning of all these marvellous and mysterious conditions of the various Planetary systems of Sol, is hastening. The age of the unification of all things is with us in the which the strange and contradictory conditions so apparent in the entire Solar System, will find their true interpretation. And then will it be known how wonderful are the works of the Divine Love, how unsearchable are His ways, how they are past finding out by the methods of material science and can only be known and understood and interpreted from the Divine Kingdom itself. Only from that Kingdom may all the meanings of the various conditions be received by the Soul ; for no one knoweth these things of himself, only from the Divine can he know,   J. TODD FERRIER.

O Love, Divine and Glorious !   Unto whom may Thy children go, if not unto Thee, for all succour, strength and light ?   In Thee alone is their true life found, and apart from Thee spiritual darkness and desolation overtaketh them.   With Thee is the mystery of their being, and alone from Thee may that mystery become knowledge unto the Soul.   How full of grandeur are all Thy Works !   How perfect is every one of them !   They all praise Thee in showing forth the wisdom and glory of Thy Love.

We are Thy work also though the darkness afflicted us in the days when we lost the vision of Thee : help us that we may again know Thee and shew forth Thy glory.   Amen and Amen.

A VISION OF THE EARTH.

When I was lifted up out of the conditions of the Earth and shewn the glories of the Spiritual Heavens, I also beheld the Earth as she once was in the days of her former and pristine glory.

Her Kingdoms were full of harmony, and all her planes performed their evolution in response to the attraction of the Divine Kingdom whose energy is poured forth through the Sun for the upholding and sustaining and guiding of all life within the Solar System.

The Earth was glorious to look upon, so full of light was she when all her planes moved in response to the Divine Magnetic attraction, like the Wheels in Ezekiel's vision : for they followed the Spirit whithersoever it went, upwards and forwards—i.e., the spirit of the Divine attraction.

And I saw upon her planes the beautiful forms which she had generated for the use of all her children in their evolution towards the Divine Consummation of their Life when they should have attained unto the beauty of the Angels, and the glory of the Sons of God : and the forms were wonderful in fashion on all her planes, and expressed by their fashion and colour the life unto which the Soul had attained.

And I also saw all her Kingdoms with the various Orders of Souls upon them, and the manifold spheres within each Kingdom upon which the different Orders of Souls dwelt and grew up before the Divine : they were resonant with a gladness the Earth now knoweth not, and all the activities within the Spheres made music before the Divine.

THE CONTRADICTIONS IN NATURE.
(THE MEANING OF THEM.)

THE great mystery observed in the contradictory phenomena of Nature is understandable when the mind is able to pass from the objective world wherein the phenomena are observed, to the subjective world where all the causes of the contradictions are to be discovered and known. For it is in the subjective spheres, which have been spoken of as the Unseen World, where the causes are to be found. And they are only to be discovered by the Soul who is able to rise above the objective and semi-objective spheres to function on the Spiritual Heavens. For all the Mysteries concerning this Earth, the Solar System, and all the Children of the Divine Love upon the System, find their interpretation alone from the Heavens, and are not to be otherwise understood. They cannot be discovered from the objective world, however carefully the phenomena may be observed. Nor can they be understood from observation upon the semi-objective spheres where the phenomena are reflected upon the magnetic plane. Only from the Kingdom of Causes can the effects be truly understood, and that is the Kingdom in the Heavens. For *all things have a spiritual origin,* though they may not seem to have such an origin to the observer upon the objective and semi-objective spheres. So accustomed are we to hear the objective world spoken of as Material, men and women forget its Spiritual and Divine origin. So accustomed are they to view every objective thing as mere matter, they have lost even the thought that once all things were spiritual. The difference between things as they are and all things as they were, remains unknown to them. What Spiritual Substance is and what mere Matter is, they do not understand. So much have they been impressed with the idea that matter as now known was a primary substance, that they have come to regard it in its present conditions as in that state in which it was generated by the Eternal One when He is said to have fashioned the Earth. And accepting it as such, they have likewise to accept all the remarkable contradictions and even incongruities in Nature as the outcome of the Divine Handiwork. They behold the contradictions and wonder at them ; but they find no explanation for the strange incongruous phenomena.

THE DREAM OF THE PROPHETS.

That the phenomena cannot be the work of the Eternal and Ever Blessed One, we have already shown. That they are not in harmony with the idea of a perfect world must be obvious to every one who thinks deeply and seriously. That they are at variance with the Vision of the Earth Redeemed given by the prophets and teachers in all ages—Hebrew, Egyptian, Brahminical, Persian, Buddhistic, Grecian and Christian — may be gathered from a study of their writings. That they were not always as they are will be seen from the perusal of all the Sacred Books. That they are not to remain as they are, but to be changed by a process spoken of as Redemption, will be learned from these Books. That the day is to dawn when the Earth will yield her increase in the Vegetable Kingdom without fail, and when the full glory of her life within that Kingdom shall be again manifest, has been anticipated and sung of by all true poets. And that all the terrible incongruities and war-fare within the Creature Kingdom are no more to find a place in the spiritual economy of the Redeemed Earth, has been the theme of all spiritual Prophets.

These things are self-evident unto all who have read the teachings of all the great Religions, and they testify to the great longing of the Soul for a perfect restoration to a true state of equilibrium of all the spheres of the Earth, and the realisation of the Golden Age. But that very longing for the restoration, and the fact that such a restoration must needs take place, show that the present state of the spheres referred to is not a true state, not that which was intended. And the cause of the wrong state is thus seen to be at variance with the Divine

Purpose and the true harmony of the Earth. And so we have to seek for the meaning of the strange and often incongruous phenomena, to inquire as to its nature, and how it came to play so great a part in the history of the Earth.

THE PURPOSE OF THE VEGETABLE KINGDOM.

In earlier ages before any evil overtook the planes of the Earth or any of her children, the two Kingdoms of which we have been speaking—the Vegetable and the Creature—were in a perfect state. Harmony reigned in all their spheres. Every order was perfect, from the lowest to the highest; and in each Kingdom they were all the various stepping stones, so to speak, along which the Soul travelled in its evolution from an elementary spiritual organism to a true Human Soul. In the Vegetable Kingdom the Soul passed through the various spheres, from the simplest forms to the more complex, receiving from those forms impressions which in after days were helpful unto it. And the wonderful colours of the flowers, the most objective expression of the glorious tinctures of the Elohim, gave to the Soul such influences as it required to enable it to rise from sphere to sphere until it reached the Creature Kingdom. For the beautiful forms and colours in the Vegetable Kingdom were all the expressions of the Divine Love and the manifestations of the Divine Wisdom, and were fashioned for the purpose of educating the Soul during the ages of its infancy. The inherent love of beautiful form and colour has had its origin in the Vegetable Kingdom long ages ago. The wonderful forms and colours after which the true artist ever seems to strive, as for the recovery of some ancient knowledge and power within himself or herself may be traced back to the dwelling of the Soul within the Vegetable Kingdom in the ages when that Kingdom was in its pristine glory.

The Vegetable Kingdom had a very much more wonderful office than simply that of supplying the necessary elements for the sustenance of the Creature Kingdom, and the Human Kingdom when that higher development was reached by the Soul. All its wonderful forms and even more wonderful colours were engaged in a service of far greater moment than merely growing and blooming and fructifying. For the entire Kingdom was engaged in educating human Souls during the years of their infancy. All its forms, from the elementary heath now so wild, to the most complex and beautiful plants and flowers, were the instruments by which the Soul was taught as it passed from zone to zone. It was not only a Kingdom full of the most beautiful expressions of the Divine thought, but a Kingdom performing a most wonderful and beautiful ministry. It did not exist simply for itself, but was fashioned for the education of all the Souls to be generated upon the Earth. Its purpose was not merely to adorn the Earth in her outermost spheres, but rather to adorn all the Souls who would pass through the manifold forms. Though an objective Kingdom, its elements were essentially spiritual. Within its various zones the Soul found nothing to militate against its progress toward the Human Kingdom. All the conditions were such as to contribute to its true education and growth. The Vegetable Kingdom was thus the nursery of the Soul in the Household of this Earth as a Spiritual System. And it was a nursery in which the ministry of the Angelic World was performed unto the little children in the Heavenly Father's Household. For the original Vegetable Kingdom was the outcome of the Angelic ministry for the Divine on the outermost spheres of the Earth, the kingdom wherein the thoughts of the Divine Love and Wisdom were objectivised for the help of the child-Soul to impress it with the beautiful forms and colours which took form and expression as the outcome of the Angelic Ministry.

THE PURPOSE OF THE CREATURE KINGDOM.

What we have said concerning the original Vegetable Kingdom may likewise be written of the original Creature Kingdom. It was not such a Kingdom as we have on the Earth to-day. Its manifold forms were the ex-

pressions of the loving care of the Divine for all His
little ones, helpful and beautiful vehicles for the Soul to
pass through in its evolution toward the Human Kingdom. The Creature World was not an animal world in
the sense in which that term is now used. Within it
were none of those elements which are now accounted
animal, those destructive conditions which make the
Creature World a Kingdom at war with itself. All its
orders were in perfect harmony, and nothing militated
against the progress of the Soul as it passed from order
to order as it grew in experience. The various zones
were all in perfect equilibrium so that the higher did not
in any way oppress the lower. The passage of the Soul
from the lower to the higher was facilitated by the way
in which the various zones overlapped each other like
circles intersecting one another. And in this way the
whole of the Creature Kingdom, from the simple forms
up to those most nearly allied to the Human, was like a
chain stretching from the Vegetable Kingdom up to the
Human. And the Soul moved upward along the links
of the chain from its passing out of the Vegetable Kingdom until it attained the experience necessary to enable
it to function through the complex human form.

In those ages there were no wrong links, nor any links
missing. There were no perverted orders nor any zones
out of harmony. The Soul was able to rise from order to
order without unnecessary hardship and inherent dread.
Indeed, the passage of the Soul from one order to
another and from the lower to the higher zones in each
order, was perfectly natural. For all the forms were
perfect of their kind. They also were the outcome of a
ministry concerning which we have often written, the
ministry of the Christ-Souls who came to this Earth to
aid her in the evolution of her children, and who
fashioned forms through which the Soul might pass in
the performance of its evolution. They were thus forms
which expressed the most beautiful meanings, being the
expressions of great spiritual truths whose interpretations
could be found upon the various spheres of the Heavens.

And they were of such a nature that as the Soul functioned through them it was impressed by the form, and its attributes were influenced and moulded by it. By this means were the powers of the Soul increased as it rose from order to order, until it reached the Human Kingdom when it became capable of receiving a direct conscious ministry from the Angelic Kingdom, and so upward, ever upward, until it could *within itself* receive direct from the Divine Kingdom the realisation of the Divine Love and the knowledge of the Divine Wisdom.

The original Creature Kingdom will thus be seen to have been a most wonderful and a most beautiful part of the constitution of the Earth as a Spiritual System; a Kingdom whose zones had all a beautiful purpose to serve as the Soul entered and passed through them on its way to those great and blessed realisations which are the heritage of the illumined Human Soul; a Kingdom whose orders ennobled the attributes of the Soul so that all the influences gathered within it were of true helpfulness and value as the Soul rose ever higher in the chain of its evolution ; a Kingdom full of the most useful experiences for the Soul prior to its attainment of the Human Estates.

The Cause of the Contradictions.

What was it then which changed both the Vegetable and Creature Kingdoms, threw out of equilibrium their various zones, introduced the strange contradictions which are so apparent, and, in the case of the Creature Kingdom, generated such opposition between the various orders as may be witnessed ? How did it happen that the perfect Earth fell from her first Estate and found her planes all disturbed, thrown out of equilibrium, so much so that her Kingdoms became changed ?

It would appear almost incredible that such a thing could have it overtaken a world fashioned and ruled from the Divine Kingdom, for unto many such an experience would imply that the Divine Love and Wisdom had been frustrated in His beautiful purposes concerning the

Earth and all her children.   And such usually accept the
astounding conditions which exist in all the Kingdoms as
the way the Divine Love purposed the Earth and all her
children should travel ; and they do this notwithstanding
the fact which must be obvious to them, that a world
full of discord and strife, not to name some of the results
of these things, is a negation of all that we conceive concerning the Nature and Ways of the Divine Love.

The Earth was in the act of generating her second
Race when the change overtook her planes.   That act
had many stages and was a long process which took her
untold ages.   Her first Race had all passed through the
Vegetable Kingdom, and many of the orders of that
Race had passed through the Creature Kingdom and
reached the Human Kingdom.   And a few orders or
Houses had almost attained the full Human Estate when
the sad change overtook the Earth.   The Second Race
had also passed through the Vegetable Kingdom and
entered that of the Creature ; but it had not progressed
far in that Kingdom when the Earth changed her polarity
and went into a state in which she failed to fully respond
to the Divine Magnetic attraction to move on the Divine
Kingdom expressed in the scientific term " The Ecliptic."
Her purpose in moving so as to change her polarity was
beautiful ; though it was her great mistake, as the subse-
quent history has testified.   Why she should have made
the mistake is one of those mysteries which are unknown.
But it was her intention to hasten the generation of the
Souls comprising the second Race.   Yet her well-meant
action only wrought upon her grievous harm ; for when
she changed her polarity and, as a result, was no longer
able to move on the Ecliptic, all her beautiful planes
were thrown out of equilibrium and failed to respond to
the magnetic attraction of the Divine Kingdom.   And
the ultimate effect of that failure was to throw all her
Kingdoms out of equilibrium, and cause such conditions
to arise within them that not only was the whole process
of the evolution of the Soul suspended, but the conditions took the Souls even of the First Race away from

the path.   And when they lost their true spiritual equilibrium, they became the subjects of the new opposing
conditions.   The changed elements were in opposition
magnetically to the spiritual state necessary for the true
growth of the Soul, so that the Soul had to contend
against them.   And as these changed elements set up
false conditions within the various zones and orders of
conscious life, contention, strife and warfare gradually
crept in amongst them.   And in this may be found the
explanation of the contradictions in every Kingdom.

J. TODD FERRIER.

BEFORE THE DARKNESS.

*When the Earth was young in her spirit, then
were her Kingdoms full of the laughter of children
who knew no pain nor sorrow, and all her planes
were resonant with the gladness of life crowned with
goodness.*

*For the Earth was young in her spirit because
she was pure in her Kingdoms, knowing not the pain
and anguish which are her heritage now, nor the
darkness which like a pall has enmantled her and shut
out from all the Souls within her Kingdoms, the
glory of the Lord in His Love and Wisdom.*

*Then was she yet unfallen.   Her Kingdoms were
glorious with the Light streaming from the Divine.
Her planes were all beautiful like perfect moving
terraces whereon her children walked before the Lord.
And her palaces were radiant homes for the unfoldment of the Soul.*

*For the Earth was a Spiritual System before the
darkness overtook her, a world full of Heavenly
Light and Life, a true Paradise wherein the children
grew up into the knowledge and life of the Divine
Love and Wisdom, a Land which was fairer than
our day.*

THE CONTRADICTIONS IN NATURE.
(THE PAST HISTORY RECOVERED.)

THE contradictions so apparent in the Vegetable and
Creature Kingdoms whose presence in the Earth are
themselves the negation of the Presence of the Divine in
the sense that the elements and magnetic forces are all
the expression of that Presence operating in the world,
may be traced to the elemental changes which overtook
the Earth when she changed her polarity. They may be
traced to that event through tracing the Soul in its history
since those ages, as that history has been written upon the
mind of the Soul itself. For the whole of that history is
yet to be discovered by humanity ; and it can only be
known through the recovery by the Soul of all the way
travelled by it since it was a dweller upon the Spiritual
Heavens. The history of the great change which came
over the two Kingdoms was written upon the Magnetic
plane of the Earth, that plane where all things are imaged
and reflected. But the original magnetic plane was
destroyed afterwards in what is now known as The Deluge,
and so the history of all that took place prior to that awful
disaster was lost. But all the changes which took place
in the two Kingdoms were deeply impressed upon the
magnetic plane or mind of the Soul. They were all
witnessed by the Christ-Souls who were present ministering unto the Earth's Children. And the results of the
Changes were all impressed upon the children of the Earth ;
because, until they had reached the perfect Human Estate,
they were subject to the elemental kingdoms. Even the
Christ-Souls came under the dominion of the new
elemental conditions through their great love towards the
children of the Earth ; for they descended into the changed
Creature-Kingdom after them that they might be able to
rise up out of the conditions and find the true Human
Kingdom. And through their descent in their ministry
of love, the whole history of that terrible period was
written upon the Soul. And it is through the unfoldment
unto the Soul itself *through the process of recovery*, that the

events which followed the mistake of the Earth may be known. For the mind of the Soul is a magnetic plane upon which all the Soul's history is written, and from which is reflected into the Soul the thought forms thrown upon it from the Spiritual Heavens. As is the Macrocosm so is the Microcosm. The mind of the Soul corresponds to the magnetic plane of the Planet which was originally purely Spiritual. It corresponds to the magnetic plane of the Spiritual Heavens whereon images are thrown from the Angelic Kingdom by means of which those Souls who have risen into those Heavens are taught Divine things.

Hence the whole history of the Soul is engraven upon the mind. And when it is able to recover the knowledge of the past, which it does when it lives the Redeemed Life and enters upon the Higher Path of Christhood, the entire path along which it has travelled unfolds to its view. And in that view the vision of the disaster which overtook the Earth, with all the tragedy that followed for all the Souls upon the system, is only too vivid even now.

J. TODD FERRIER.

A PRAYER.

O ever Blessed One from whom we all came forth, the Source and Fulness of our life in whom we live and move and have our being, we flee unto Thee for refuge and comfort in the hour of our affliction and sorrow. None shieldeth like Thee in the greatness of Thy Love; none healeth our wounding as Thou doest. For Thou hidest us in the Pavilion of Thy Strength and dost anoint us with the balm of Thy Love Nearer unto Thee would we come in all our thoughts, desires and ways; upward still more and more towards the glory of that Life unto which Thou hast called and fashioned us, would we rise; nearer and yet nearer to Thee in our nature would we come, until crowned with the Crown of Life Immortal and Eternal, the gift of Thy great Love.

Amen and Amen.

A VISION OF THE EARTH.
(AFTER THE DARKNESS.)

Behold the kingdoms that once were the kingdoms of light and goodness were all changed and turned into kingdoms of darkness and suffering !

I saw the once glorious Vegetable Kingdom bereft of spiritual succour through the loss unto it of the magnetic rays by means of which all its manifold forms were quickened, sustained and adorned ; and I felt the impoverished conditions that came over the Kingdom through the loss of the magnetic rays. The vision was overwhelming in its sadness, and painful in its tragic conditions.

I saw the Creature Kingdom which once was full of music, become discordant through the strange conditions which came upon all the Souls within it, as the elements more and more refused to vibrate to the magnetic rays streaming from the Divine Kingdom. For all the Creatures also suffered the loss of the magnetic rays, became impoverished in their life and subject to the changed elements, and then gradually grew less and less spiritual from lack of the magnetic currents whose flow was intercepted by the changed elements, until, at last, they became what they so largely are to-day, full of the spirit of contention and strife : and the Vision filled me with dismay, and great fear came upon me as I was witnessing the changes wrought upon the Kingdom ; for I felt like one of the Creatures passing through the ordeal which befell them when they were all drawn down into the strange ways born from the changed elements, and suffered in my feelings the awful change which came to them.

SOME MEDICAL TESTIMONIES AGAINST VIVISECTION.

Appendix I.

LAWSON TAIT, F.R.C.S., M.D., LL.D., *Ex-Professor of Gynæcology, Mason's College, Birmingham.*

"SOME day I shall have a tombstone put over me and an inscription upon it. I want only one thing recorded upon it, and that to the effect that 'he laboured to divert his profession from the blundering which has resulted from the performance of experiments on the sub-human groups of animal life, in the hope that they would shed light on the aberrant physiology of the human groups.' Such experiments never have succeeded, and never can ; and they have, as in the cases of Koch, Pasteur and Lister, not only hindered true progress, but have covered our profession with ridicule."—From a letter in the *Medical Press and Circular*, May, 1899.

" Syme and Fergusson were the greatest surgeons I have ever known, and they were right in stoutly asserting that Surgery has in no wise been advanced by vivisection."

SIR WILLIAM FERGUSSON, F.R.S. (*formerly Sergeant-Surgeon to the Queen*).

" I am not aware of any of these experiments upon the lower animals having led to the mitigation of pain or to improvement as regards surgical details." (Evidence before Royal Commission, 1876).

SURGEON-GENERAL SIR CHARLES ALEXANDER GORDON, K.C.B. (*formerly Honorary Physician to the Queen*).

" I hold that the practice of performing experiments upon the lower animals with a view to benefitting humanity, is fallacious."—(Speech at Westminster Palace Hotel, London, June 22nd, 1892).

SIR CHARLES BELL (*Physiologist and Anatomist, formerly Professor of Surgery, University of Edinburgh*).

" Experiments have never been the means of discovery,

---

* " Why I condemn Vivisection," by Robert H. Perks, M.D., F.R.C.S. *Vide* advertisement pages.

and a survey of what has been attempted of late years in physiology will prove that the opening of living animals has done more to perpetuate error than to confirm the just views taken from the study of anatomy and natural motions."—(*Nervous System of the Human Body*, p. 217).

HENRY J. BIGELOW, M.D. (*Member of the Massachusetts Medical Society, Emeritus Professor of Surgery, in Harvard University.*)

"There is little in the literature of what is called the horrors of vivisection which is not well grounded on truth. . . . A torture of helpless animals—more terrible, by reason of its refinement and the effort to prolong it, than burning at the stake, which is brief—is now being carried on in all civilized nations, not in the name of religion but of science. . . . By far the larger part of vivisection is as useless as was an *auto-da-fe.* . . . The law should interfere. There can be no doubt that in this relation there exists a case of cruelty to animals far transcending in its refinement and in its horrors anything that has been known in the history of nations. There will come a time when the world will look back to modern vivisection in the name of science as they now do to burning at the stake in the name of religion."—Extracts from *Anæsthesia, Addresses and other Papers*, 1900, p. 363.

FORBES WINSLOW, D.C.L., OXON, M.R.C.P., LONDON (*Physician to the British Hospital for Mental Diseases ; Physician to North London Hospital for Consumption, etc.*)

"In my opinion Vivisection has opened up no new views for the treatment and cure of diseases. It is most unjustifiable and cruel, and in no way advances medical science."—(American Humane Association's *Report on Vivisection*, p. 13).

CHAS. BELL-TAYLOR, M.D., F.R.C.S.

"If anything could exceed the hideous cruelty of the whole business, it would be the childish absurdity of the claims to benefit which are being constantly put forth by the advocates and promotors of the system."—(Address before Medico-Chirurgical Society of Nottingham, November 16, 1892).

JAMES E. GARRETSON, M.D. (*Senior Professor of Surgery, Medico-Chirurgical College, Philadelphia*).

"I am without without words to express my horror of vivisection, though I have been a teacher of anatomy and surgery for thirty yeass. It serves no purpose that is not better served after other manners."—(Letter to American Humane Association's *Report on Vivisection*, 1895, p. 13).

WILLIAM J. MORTON, M.D. (*Professor of Nervous and Mental Diseases at the N. York Post Graduate Med. School and Hospital.*

"If mankind suffers from disease it is its own fault, to be cured by the rectification of the causes which lead to it ; and it is subversive of the high and moral order of the progress of humanity to inflict pain or death upon other living animals to abolish or minimize disease or suffering due to mankind's own faults. In the end, the retribution to the race which does this will equal and offset the advantages temporarily gained. One crime or fault does not excuse or justify another."—Letter to American Humane Association's *Report on Vivisection*, 1895, p 13).

GEORGE WILSON, M.D., LL.D., EDIN., F.R.S., D.P.H., CAMBRIDGE.

"There are not a few who doubt whether all the agonies, inflicted on animals sacrificed in the laboratories of Continental workers in bacteriological research, or even those at home. . . . *have saved one single human life, or lessened in any appreciable degree the load of human suffering.*" Page 443 of the 8th Edition, 1898, of the *Handbook of Hygiene and Sanitary Science.*

"I accuse my profession of misleading the public as to the cruelties and horrors which are perpetrated on animal life. When it is stated that the actual pain involved in these experiments is commonly of the most trifling description, there is a *suppressio veri* of the most palpable kind, which could only be accounted for at the time by ignorance of the actual facts."—From a paper read before the Section of State Medicine, British Medical Association Annual Meeting, Portsmouth, August, 1891).

FRANCOIS ACHILLE LONGET, VIVISECTOR (*Late Professor of Physiology at the Medical Faculty of Paris*).

"Experiments on animals of different species, so far from leading to useful results as regarded human beings, had a tendency to mislead us. In seeking to benefit mankind by vivisection, it would be necessary to have recourse to pathological facts founded on experiments on human beings."—(Quoted in Prize Essay on Vivisection, p. 23, by George Fleming, F.R.G.S., F.H.S.L., of London, published in Philadelphia, 1874).

CHARLES CLAY, M.D. (THE LATE).

"As a surgeon, I have performed a very large number of operations, but I do not owe a particle of my knowledge or skill to vivisection. I challenge any member of my profession to prove that vivisection has in any way advanced the science of medicine, or tended to improve the treatment of disease."—(Letter in London *Times*, July 31st, 1880).

GORDON STABLES, M.D.. C.M.

". . . I have never yet met a truly brave man who was not kind to God's lower creatures, nor do I believe that a man can be both cruel and brave; but the amount of cruelty that takes place in this country under the title of legalized experimentalism is horrible to contemplate. It is ten times worse on the Continent, especially in such institutes as those in Paris."—(Letter in London *Daily Telegraph*, August 31, 1892).

JOHN H. CLARKE, M.D., LONDON.

"Our country, I trust . . . will purge itself from this, the meanest of all its crimes."—(In a paper read before the Church Congress, at Folkestone, October 6, 1892).

STEPHEN TOWNSEND, F.R.C.S.

" I contend that these experiments, from a moral point of view, are criminal, inasmuch as they often involve the unnecessary torture of sensitive animals, and that from a scientific and didactic point of view, they are worse than useless."—(Article in *The Animals' Friend*, April, 1896).

F. S. ARNOLD, M.A., M.B. (OXON).

" I believe that vivisection is a barren and misleading method of research trom whose practice no benefit has accrued to humanity which would for a moment be considered by any unbaissed person, cognizant of all the facts, to out-weigh the animal suffering and human degradation it has caused, and still causes."—(From article in *The Animals' Friend*, January, 1895).

"I believe that medicine and surgery have gained nothing by vivisection, that it is, considered as a method of research, utterly barren and misleading, and bound in the nature of things always to be so. I am, however, not putting forward an opinion but stating a fact when I say that there is not one of the ' triumphs of vivisection,' such as the antitoxin treatment of diptheria, Pasteurian inoculation for anthrax, hydrophobia, etc., whose utility is not strenuously denied by eminent physicians and surgeons who are themselves supporters of vivisection. Vivisection, that is to say, has produced absolutely nothing whose utility to ' suffering humanity' is unanimously affirmed, even by the vivisecting fraternity itself."—(Letter to *Abolitionist*, September 15th, 1903).

JOHN ELLIOTSON, M.D., F.R.S. (*Physiologist*).

" A course of experimental physiology, in which brutes are agonized to exhibit facts already established is a disgrace to the country that permits it."—(Elliotson's *Human Physiology*, p. 428).

EDWARD BERDOE, M.R.C.S., L.R.C.P.

" I have seen the rise and fall of Pasteurian quackery, the fiasco of Koch's tuberculin and the diptheria antoxin nostrum, and every day confirms my belief that vivisection founded on cruelty, supported by falsehood, and practiced for selfish ends is not the method by which the merciful art of healing can be improved ; nor can it be shown that any disease can be cured by any method derived from it."

S. MILLS FOWLER, M.D. *Professor of the Practice of Medicine in Dunham Medical College, Chicago).*

" I am utterly opposed to the practice of vivisection. The brutality manifest in its employment is a disgrace to our civilization.   It disgraces not only those who employ it, but also those who witness it.   It should receive the unqualified condemnation of every civilized person."

ARTHUR GUINNESS, M.D., F.R.C.S.

"When I reflect on the abominable cruelties inflicted on them (animals) by such callous beings as M. de Cyon and many others, I regret to say, of my own countrymen, I can truly say a thrill of horror comes over me, and also disgust when I think that mankind can be so degraded as to commit such horrors."—(From letter in *Oxford Times*, October, 1902).

DEP. SURGEON-GENERAL THORNTON, C.B.

" There is no doubt that vivisection is an immoral practice, and can only be defended on the principle that the end justifies the means—a principle which has been used in past times for the defence and justification of all kinds of cruelty. . . . *This principle undermines morality itself*, and opens the door to crimes of every description, all of which can be defended if we once admit that it is right to do evil that good may come."—(From the *Principal Claims on behalf of Vivisection*, 1901, p. 10).

PROFESSOR SPOONER (*of the Royal Veterinary College*).

" Gentlemen, allow me to protest in your name and mine against all attempts to raise up Schools of Vivisection.   The act is an abomination to all our most enlightened feelings—a torpor and darkness extinguishing our best sources of knowledge ; in short, it is arrant and horrible sepoyism wearing the mask of Art and Science."
—(*Veterinarian* for 1858, p. 614).

ROBERT H. PERKS, M.D., F.R.C.S.

(*To be continued.*)

WHAT ARE THE CREATURES?

THE Coming Congress on the question of Vivisection from which we hope so much, raises the larger and even further-reaching question regarding the nature of the Creatures and the uses to which they were meant to be put. That the doctrine of Vivisection has DIABOLUS engraven upon it, and that all its works are satanic, may be known by a true understanding of who and what the Creatures are. Indeed a consideration of that question which leads the student to a true understanding of the nature of the Creatures and their place in the Earth's economy, will compel the student to marvel that the Creatures could ever have been taken advantage of by man to minister to his appetites and fears in the way of making use of them for diet and the healing of disease. It is one of the strange contradictions so observable in many of life's experiences, that the greater number of those who lift up their voices against the tragedies wrought by Vivisection, and who devote their gifts and energies towards securing its abolition, should continue to make use of many of the Creatures for the sustenance of their own bodies and for articles of adornment. They do see the terrible evils of the Physiological Laboratories, but not the evils of the Abattoirs and Shambles. They behold the sufferings of the Creatures at the hands of the Vivisector, but not those through which the Creatures pass in the awful traffic in their lives. They call aloud to the Vivisector to withhold his hand whilst they encourage the labours of the Abattoirs and the service of the Shambles. They hear the terrible cries, the heart-anguishing, of the Creatures in the Laboratories, and would fain accomplish their healing ; yet they contribute day by day to sufferings of a like nature through having the lives of the Creatures taken to minister to their physical requirements. Thus on the one hand, and that the least part of the awful evil, they would heal; whilst on the other hand, one unspeakably larger, they would have the afflictions continued. What a strange contradiction in experience! It makes us often wonder that those who see so much of the evil should not be able to see all; and that they can eat the flesh of the Creatures and have their coverings as garments and adornments, even whilst they labour to deliver them from the hands of the Vivisectors. Was there ever in the name of Compassion a more illogical position, a more enigmatical service wrought? Until those who would deliver the Creatures who suffer at the hands of Science (falsely so called), learn that true Compassion sees all the evils and puts them away from its own door, and makes the service on behalf of the Creatures full-rounded because it recognises that they are sentient beings who not only feel the burdens imposed in the Physiological Laboratories, but who feel any wrong that is inflicted upon them, their labours will not accomplish the true deliverance of the Creatures.

For what has been done for untold ages unto the Creatures will all have to be undone through redeeming them from the awful dread, the latent conscious feeling that they are the subjects of man's power, and that that power is used to afflict them and fill their lives with anguish. For the Creatures are more in their nature, much more in the original purpose of their lives, than even the champions and defenders and would-be saviours of them know. They are not mere goods and chattels having a commercial and social value, but elementary Human Souls : Souls who once were like the most joyful little children in the days when the world was yet unfallen and its beautiful spirit was young with the youthfulness of spiritual being. They are Souls whose progress was suspended ages ago, spiritual beings as truly and surely as man is a spiritual being, the little children in the great Spiritual Household of the Earth.

They should be viewed, yea, they *must* be viewed, as parts of the Organic Whole.

                                        J. TODD FERRIER.

The Herald of the Cross.

Vol. v.   New Series.   July, 1909.   No. 7.

PSALM XXIX.

(*A NEW READING.*)

Give unto the Lord, O ye sons of the Mighty One ; give unto Him the glory of life !

Give unto the Lord the glory which is His due, even worship within the Beauty of Holiness, His glorious Sanctuary.

The Lord sitteth upon the Great Waters whose out-flowing nourisheth the Earth. Upon them is His Voice heard, and the sound thereof is as when it thundereth.

The Voice of the Lord is full of Majesty. When He speaketh from the Heavens, it is in power and great glory.

He maketh the Cedars of Lebanon[1] to bow before Him ; even Lebanon and Sirion[2] to rejoice in His ways.

The Voice of the Lord divideth the Tongues of Flame[3] ; He causeth His Spirit to go forth Sevenfold[3].

The Voice of the Lord breaketh up the wilderness, even the wilderness of Kadesh[4], and maketh it blossom abundantly and rejoice before Him.

He giveth strength unto His people, and blesseth them with His Peace.

---

[1] *Those who are in the Divine Kingdom.*
[2] *The Divine and Celestial Spheres.*
[3] *The Holy Spirit and Elohim.*
[4] *The hard conditions around the Soul.*

TELEPATHY IN RELATION TO PRAYER, MIRACLE, AND THE REALIZATION OF GOD IN THE SOUL.

TELEPATHY is in the Air. Marconi's system of wireless Telegraphy seems almost miraculous; yet it is only the application of knowledge to the laws in Nature which already exist, the re-discovery of a long-lost knowledge of the powers in the Earth. Yet it is not more wonderful than the power which is understood by the term Telepathy. For that also is an ancient power, one which men and women once knew the right use of, one which also, alas! they have greatly abused in the history of this world. *For true Telepathy is Mind-force by which thought images and influences are transmitted to any given object upon the physical planes, the Astral Kingdom, the Occult plane and the Spiritual Heavens.*

THE VIEWS OF PSYCHICAL SCIENCE.

In the Journals of the various Societies founded for Psychical Research, the subject of Telepathic action is found freely discussed with unfailing interest; but whilst all of them give abundant evidence of the fact that there is such a thing as Telepathic action and influence upon the Physical, Occult and Astral planes, yet no approach to a definite basis of the nature of the Force is given, nor any sure or adequate explanation. There are scientists who think that its basis is material, that it is effected through changes in the brain-substance by which are produced certain extra and increased vibrations; and that these vibrations send through an unknown medium the Idea, or Thought, or Vision to be transferred.

With all this we may agree. But if we cannot be carried further into the true meaning of the nature both of the Power itself and the medium through which it is communicated, then we must look elsewhere than to these various Societies for the true explanation. If Telepathy, truly undertsood, were a force whose basis was material, then material Science ought to be able to explain both its nature and its medium ; and if it does not explain anything beyond the mere phenomena as to their character, and seems powerless to explain more, then we may take it for granted that by no material means shall we ever arrive at any sure knowledge of the true nature and operation of the power known as Telepathy, and that we shall have to seek in another direction.

A TRUE PSYCHIC FORCE.

We have every reason to think that the power known as Telepathy transcends the material plane as surely as the real being known as Man transcends the brain-substances which are the media of his thoughts. We have strong ground for thinking that *the basis of the power lies within the Spiritual Nature of Man,* and that the manifestation of the power upon the various planes of his experiences is the exposition of a potential force latent in all men, and revealing itself upon the plane on which the man or woman is functioning, *viz.* : the Material, the supersensuous or Astral, the Occult and the Spiritual. As we approach it from the Spiritual standpoint the significance of the power grows greater and the meaning of it clearer ; for we behold in it that latent energy within the Soul by which men and women rise to higher things when it is directed to the highest, but which brings upon them sadness and sorrow, and even deep suffering and tribulation, when directed outwards and towards things whose nature fails to ennoble the life and fill the Soul with pure and beautiful Visions.

" In Man's (true) self arise
    August anticipations, symbols, types
    Of a dim splendour ever on before,
    In that eternal circle run by life."

These are born within the man in the very centre of his being ; and his earnest endeavour to realize them is of the very nature of that force and power which is expressed by the term Telepathy. Human Philosophy seeks so much for the explanation of the hidden forces of the world and of the Soul upon the outward

material and the supersensuous or Astral and purely
Occult planes, instead of turning at once to that plane
from which alone all things of a spiritual order can be
understood and beheld in their true relationships.   But
the saying is true that there are more things in Heaven
and on Earth than are dreamt of in Human Philosophy ;
and the only way to understand them is to view them in
their operation upon the planes to which by Nature they
belong.

I.

IN RELATION TO PRAYER.

ONE of the most beautiful forms of Telepathic
action is what is spoken of as Prayer.   By means
of the intense yearning of the whole being of man towards
some given purpose, is the purpose itself realized.   It
has been said that by prayer " the whole round world
is everyway bound by gold chains about the feet of
God."   And, were that true, it would be beautiful
indeed, for it would bespeak a world redeemed, the
Golden Age returned when all the children of the Divine
Love were experiencing the rich and full life born from
the consciousness within them of the Divine Presence,
when the whole world was full of wonderful harmony,
discord and all that proceeds from it being unknown.
Then would the whole world be guided by the magnetic
conditions born of prayer, and be the scene of such
out-flowing of Telepathic force as the true man longs
for, hopes for and labours to accomplish.   For the
world would be full of thought-forces, streams of spiritual
power passing to and fro, flowing Eastward and West-
ward, Northward and Southward, encompassing the
four-fold nature of man, acting upon the Soul, upon other
Souls, upon the life lived, upon the environments of life,
upon the conditions in the world, and upon even the
substances of the Earth.

WHAT THEN IS PRAYER ?   AND WHAT IS THE
RELATION OF TELEPATHY TO PRAYER ?

Prayer is the language of the Soul expressed in the

aspirational attitude of the whole being of a man or woman. It is the innermost and deepest feeling of the Spirit within growing into desire, and seeking expression for itself ; and it must never be confounded with so much that passes for prayer where repetitions are vain and expressions are used without deep feeling and meaning. And the relation of Telepathy to Prayer is this, that the vibrations set up are such as to influence all the conditions around the Soul itself, the environment amid which the life is cast, the object of the Soul's solicitation, and the conditions of even the Astral Kingdom. So that Telepathy, rightly understood, is the power generated from that state of the spiritual man known under the expression Prayer, and is in itself an effect of a great spiritual cause, though it likewise is the cause of other far-reaching effects upon the various spheres of experience. And in its primary action it affects our own life and environment, and in its secondary action the environment and life of others. The Soul-desire, which passes from us into Telepathic action, finding its objective more speedily even than the magnetic rays reach the Earth from the sun, passes first through the spheres of the world within us, influencing them divinely or otherwise, according to the nature of the desire. If the purpose of the Soul-desire is to lay hold of the beneficent powers of Heaven and cause them to embrace in their blessings the objects and friends who are beloved, then the desire, as it passes through the various spheres of our own spiritual system, will gather unto itself the influences prevailing upon these spheres, and will seek to make of them instruments for blessing upon the objects ; but should the Soul-desire be of an impure or selfish order, then the whole influence will be against the true life of every sphere of experience. The vibrations set in motion within the Soul will affect the life of the operator first and most, though at the moment he or she may be unconscious of any change ; and then it may affect the objects or friends according to the spiritual state in which they are. And should the objects of the Telepathic influence be in spiritual states in which they are open to the incursions of adverse influences, great and very terrible afflictions may be thrust upon them ; but should they be able to resist the vibratory influences sent to them, then the rebound of these impure and evil influences will be upon those who sent them forth.

THE INFLUENCE OF THOUGHT.

This is a great truth which requires to be set forth so that men and women may understand what they are doing when they desire that which is evil to befall any object—that on the one hand ; and on the other, the great blessing which descends upon all who will any good unto other Souls, whose desires are all of a true spiritual order, full of the harmony generated from the spiritual conditions which are always present when the Soul desires God-ward, beautiful with the scintillating and healing colours generated through the spiritual realizations within the Soul. For the willing to bless or otherwise is *within us,* and is dependent upon our own spiritual state, the motive by which we are swayed, the purpose of the influence which we send forth, the nature of the end sought. An impure fountain cannot give forth pure water ; though the impure fountain may be purified, so that the waters be made clear and sweet. And so the Soul-desire may become pure and beautiful, and make its sally through the various spheres bearing within itself great power of blessing.

No one ever prayed with all their being fervently and purely without accomplishing good, though it may not seem to have accomplished all that was meant. For spiritual conditions are generated through such true and pure Telepathic action ; and, as a result, those conditions which make against the true upwardness of all life are influenced and at last changed in their nature. Even those beautiful things in this world which at present seem to possess no more vitality than did the wonderful form which Pygmalion fashioned, may at last also come to possess a life beating in harmony with all that is truly spiritual and Divine, through the intense Soul-yearning and noble purpose of a life passing forth to make pure and hallowed with its own beautiful blessing, all things and all Souls within the Heavenly Father's House. For, when the Holy Goddess of Prayer fires the Soul so that all its images take living form and breathe a life born from the Divine, then will the whole world be girt about with " golden chains " from God, girdled with a magnetic power full of a beautiful ministry of healing and uplifting : for the true prayer is the Divine in man rising unto the fulness of spiritual realization ; and Telepathy is its out-going energy seeking to find that realization within all its own spheres, and within all the spheres wherein Souls operate ; and together Prayer and its Telepathic Energy are the fulfilment of the Divine Purpose within the Soul itself, and the means whereby that Holy Purpose is to be accomplished in the world.

II.

IN RELATION TO MIRACLE.

WE now turn to the second part of our subject to consider the relationship between Telepathy and Miracles. Having observed that Telepathy is the power which goes forth from the Soul as the result of intense desire, we must, in order to understand its true relation to Miracle, understand first of all what a Miracle is. For the term has come to be associated with certain phenomena of an extraordinary nature, phenomena which are considered to be contradictions of what is understood as Natural Law, or to supersede it. All the incidents which are called miraculous and which may be found recorded in the Bible, as well as in many of the books wherein the Ancient Religions are taught, are not to be so understood, but rather as spiritual allegories and parables wherein profound things are set forth— things relating to life's experiences as the Soul evolves from one stage to another ; things relating to the history and progress of the Soul itself as it rises from sphere to sphere, and to the Divine Power made manifest both in the Soul as an individual unit, and in the whole of the House of Souls comprising the Spiritual System of this

Planet. And the wonderful works said to have been wrought by the Master during the manifestation of the Christhood through Him, and which were afterwards related to outward events and changed into material history, were works of an entirely spiritual order, though they had manifestations upon the different spheres of experience. For a true Miracle is not a mere physical phenomenon resulting from the laws of nature having been intercepted and superseded; but it is the sign of a presence which makes for the true fulfilment of Natural Law, by which the already intercepted or superseded law is brought once more into true and full operation, so that the cause of the natural order of things having been obstructed, is removed, and restoration again takes place of the true powers inherent in the object on behalf of which, or upon which, the miracle is supposed to have been wrought.

A miracle is, therefore, the sign of the presence of a power through which is effected the restoration to their true and perfect function of the Laws by which this world is governed; the laws by which man's life should be regulated; the laws of the true evolution of the Soul, obedience to which is a necessity for the World and the Soul in order that they may be able to fulfil their true destiny. So that the very idea of a miracle taking place in Nature herself or within one of the spheres of man's experience, testifies to the wrong condition within them, and the need for the approach of some power external to themselves to operate within and upon them in order that the true balance of all their forces may be restored and they themselves equilibriated.

The intimate relationship between such Miracles (so called) and Telepathy may be easily recognised. For if Miracles be the restoration to a true balance of the forces within the world of the Soul through the approach of some higher power, the changing of the condition of the elements of Nature, the life of man, and the Soul itself, so that true equilibrium is again experienced and health of life in body, mind and Soul gained; and if

Telepathy be that power generated from intense Soul-desire known as Prayer, which passes through the spiritual system, affecting every sphere from the innermost to the outermost, and then passing from the individual to some object to effect good upon it, to help some life in its ways to grow nobler, to aid the mind of some one towards a truer state of vision, to bring powers of true healing to act upon and within some afflicted one, to bring into the whole life the blessed experience of Redemption ; *then the relationship of Telepathy to Miracle is as real and as intimate as its relationship to Prayer.* For no true Miracle could otherwise take place. It would be no true Miracle to merely supersede the laws of Nature without accomplishing spiritual good, though it might seem a most wonderful performance in the eyes of the world which ever seeks after the phenomenal. It would be no true Miracle to work what came to be written of as "black magic," by which other lives have been grievously afflicted. Such works would be the very antithesis of true Miracle ; the perversion of the beautiful spiritual power born within the Soul through which the Miracle is wrought ; the turning of the Divine Life-stream within the Soul from its true and beautiful function ; the degradation of the Soul itself with all its wonderful powers; the changing of its very aspirations from being those of pure spiritual feeling and desire to be those of evil purpose. But where true Miracle does take place, *i.e.*, where there is real good effected in the conditions around any life and within its various spheres of experience as the outcome of the earnest longing of some Soul to effect upon or within another life a beautiful and healing ministry, there true Telepathic action has taken place, and the powers of the Soul directed to a pure and beautiful service. *The true Magic* has been wrought, "the white Magic" of pure and noble intention, through which healing will be accomplished upon all the spheres of experience, and even a noble love begotten within the heart. Such Telepathic action will, indeed, at last gain the power to heal the sick and the afflicted ; to take away the diseases by which the whole world is burdened to-day ;

to effect the restitution of all who have gone down into
the bondage imposed by the senses ; and even to raise
the dead who are unconscious of the glorious spiritual
forces around and within them, unto the consciousness
of a new life.

Viewed in this light the so-called Miracles of the
Master will have a new meaning for many. The merely
phenomenal will give place to the truly spiritual. The
visible manifestations of power will cease to cast a false
glamour over the mind, and the invisible spiritual and
Divine influences will command the attention. The
outward results will no longer have the mysterious
significance attached to them, whilst the inward cause
is unseen and unknown. Rather will the meaning of the
Miracles become clear both as to their nature and the
means by which they were accomplished. The mere
outward histories of the events will become only the
stories and signs of great spiritual events. And many
of the supposed events upon the outermost spheres will
be beheld as having relation only to interior spiritual
experiences, wrought within Souls as the result of their
contact with the Master. For His Soul-yearnings were
Divine, and they proceeded in their out-flowing from a
Soul in whom the Divine Presence was fully realized, and
who, therefore, knew and understood the burden of the
beautiful mission on which He had come. And His
Prayers being always in harmony with the Divine Purpose,
set up vibrations which had such an effect upon seeking
Souls that they became conscious of the healing which
flowed from Him to them, and which entered into the
various spheres of their life. And in this way were many
healed of divers afflictions through the restoration
within them of their own spiritual forces to a state of true
equilibrium. For when the Soul is in the state when all
its powers are equilibrated, there can enter into its
system no such diseases as those with which human history
has made us familiar. It was thus that the Master
wrought His wonderful works ; and it is in this same way
that the "greater works " are to be accomplished.

III.

THE DIVINE REALIZATION.

We have now to speak of the Divine Realization within the Soul, and what relationship Telepathy bears to its accomplishment. Having observed that true Prayer is intense Soul-desire towards the Divine, and that Telepathy is the power generated from that intense desire flowing through all the spheres of experience and reaching the spheres of other lives to aid them ; that Miracle is not merely a material phenomenon, but is rather a great spiritual experience accomplished within the spheres of a man or woman's life, or in the conditions of the elements of the Planet as the result of the spiritual influences generated by the Telepathic action of one who contains within himself, as the Christ did, the spiritual power born of the consciousness of the Divine Love, and the knowledge and meaning of all the conditions found within the Earth's elements and the various spheres of the life of the Soul ; WE HAVE NOW TO ASCERTAIN WHAT IS MEANT BY THE REALIZATION OF GOD IN THE SOUL, AND IN WHAT RELATIONSHIP TELEPATHY STANDS TO IT.

To realize the Divine the Soul must come to know the Divine, and to know the Divine the Soul must needs grow like the Divine, and to grow like the Divine the Soul has to perform its evolution upon the various planes and spheres which rise tier above tier in the path marked out for its progress, from a Creature Soul up through the elementary Human, till the full Humanity is reached in the Angelic, and the full Angelic manhood is crowned with what is known as Celestial Christhood—the Christhood of the Master—and which is true Sonship to God, and even then still pass upward to be even as the Divine. It is the Spiral Staircase whose lowest step rests upon the base where the Soul begins its life of ascent, and whose highest step is upon the Divine Kingdom. That bespeaks a long process for the Soul ere its life is crowned with Divine fulness ; but the process should have been always one full of real blessing and blessedness, and would have been had the true path always been followed by the

Soul. Nor would the process have been so long as it now has to be; for the untold ages during which the entirely Spiritual System of the Planet has been lost in materialism would not only not have been lost to the Soul, but the terrible conditions which grew out of the materialization of everything spiritual, and which have afflicted the Soul upon every sphere of its experience and militated against its true progress, would not have had to be endured and overcome. But now the Soul has to contend against all these adverse influences in order to rise even a little out of the conditions amid which it finds itself; and it is often conscious of the fact that unless there are generated new conditions whereby its endeavour will be aided, its spiritual progress must be slow indeed. Nay, there are many Souls who are unable to rise and who will never rise out of these terrible material conditions which make the Soul a mere vassal of the sense-life and keep it in perpetual bondage, unless the new and purer conditions be found for them by those and through those who have been able to rise even unto the Realization of the Purified Life, and especially those who have entered into the Realization of the Divine Love within the heart and the Divine Presence within the Sanctuary of the Soul itself. On their behalf such require real Miracles to be wrought in which the elements around them will be all changed in their nature, and the conditions purified so that they may gather the power to rise into a nobler way of life. And that these new and nobler conditions are being provided through the loving ministry of many Souls who have found the Redeemed Life themselves, and the beautiful spiritual teachings for the enlightenment of the mind and the upliftment of the heart through many who have come to know the Divine Love as a Realization, will be apparent unto all who are associated with the beautiful Reform Movements which are touching unto purification every sphere of experience.

I have thus spoken of the Realization of God in us so that we may first behold the phenomena of the Divine Presence within the Soul in its manifestations upon the outer spheres ; and also to show what is the effect of the consciousness of the Divine within the Soul upon the life of those in whom that blessed Realization has become known, and also upon the conditions and elements and lives around them. And now we may speak a few words concerning the meaning of that Realization and the relationship of Telepathy to it.

In every Soul are latent the forces by which man may rise up even until he reaches the Kingdom of the Divine. These forces are of a nature such as no one can fully understand, though they may be fully apprehended in their wonderful operation. But they are of such a nature that they must ever seek for the full realization of themselves in the perfect unfoldment of the Soul. And their perfect unfoldment is found only when the Soul finds the Divine Presence within it, *i.e.*, becomes conscious of that Presence ; feels its hallowing and uplifting and beautifying influence ; has found the Divine meaning of its own life in a life and service of pure and beautiful love on behalf of other Souls, and the testimony to that wonderful power within itself in the knowledge and understanding of the Divine Wisdom, and the perpetual light from the Divine burning and shining within its Sanctuary. So that to know the Divine Love as a possession and the Divine Wisdom as an inheritance is not only possible unto the Soul, but is the perfect fulfilment of its own true life, the crown of its complete evolution upon the manifold spheres upon which it lives its life from an elementary human Soul until it climbs to the Kingdom of the Divine. And the great motive power within it which moves it upwards, the fulcrum by which it is raised up from State to State, Sphere to Sphere, and Kingdom to Kingdom, is the intense natural yearning within it which, as we have observed, passes into spiritual force and vibrates through the whole being, lifting it upward, still upward, ever upward to the Divine.

J. TODD FERRIER.

PSALM XLV.

(A NEW READING)

The Heart is indicting what is good : it speaks of the things which concern the King : my spirit shall be as the pen of a ready writer in telling abroad the glories of His name.

Fairer art Thou[1] than the children of men : from Thy lips is Grace poured forth : upon Thee is the Blessing of God for evermore.

Thou lovest Righteousness and abhorest wickedness : God, even the Lord, hath anointed Thee with the oil of gladness and set Thee above the sons of Earth[2].

Thy raiment is fragrant with Myrrh, Aloes and Cassia[3] as Thou walkest within the Sanctuary wherein Thy gladness is found.

Kings' daughters[4] are amongst those who love Thee : upon Thy right hand once stood the Queen[5] clad in raiment made of the Gold of Ophir.

Hearken unto me, O Daughter of Zion[6] ; consider and incline thine heart.

Forget not thine own people and thy Father's House; for the King greatly desires that thou shouldst be beautiful : He is thy Lord, therefore worship thou Him.

Though the daughters of Tyre entice thee with a gift, and the rich amongst their people intreat thee to go with them, see thou do it not[8] ;

For the King's Daughter must be glorious within her Sanctuary, and her garments fashioned of pure Gold.

---

[1] *The Christ-Soul through whom the Adonai is made manifest.*

[2] *The Christhood attainment transcends the life upon this Planet, and so stands above the sons of Earth, though these may reach up to it.*

[3] *Graces of the Spirit belonging to the Christhood.*

[4] *The Souls of the Celestial Spheres who are spoken of as the children of the Kings or Rulers of those spheres. These are all of the Divine, and love the Adonai.*

[5] *The Intuition of the Soul when the Soul was in a state of Christhood, clad in the garments of Spiritual Love.*

[6] *An appeal to the Soul who once knew the Christhood.*

[7] *The Christhood Order and the Divine Kingdom.*

[8] *The influences of the outer spheres which now are non-spiritual and materialistic.*

WHAT WAS THE FALL?

THE hour has come when we must needs make plain much that has been only as yet presented in hieroglyph form. For what has hitherto been written concerning the fall of this system into conditions known as matter, was the necessary statement of the great mystery in order to impress upon the minds the nature of that fall, and the fact that it was, in very deed, a descent from higher conditions of spiritual experience into states of experience which militated against true spiritual being. For the fall was not only very real, having most real and far-reaching issues; but it was not such an experience as was necessary, however plausible the theory may seem, which includes it in the history of the evolution of the Soul. That it is too great a mystery for many to comprehend, we recognise. But it may be comprehended by the Soul who rises on to the Divine Kingdom. Nor is it much more difficult to understand how the Planet could move away from functioning on the Divine Kingdom than it is to understand how it is that the individual Soul goes away from functioning on the Spiritual Heavens. To be able to conceive of the latter implies the possibility of the former. In relation to the Planet, the Microcosm is the expression of the Macrocosm. "As is the Macrocosm, so is the Microcosm." And how could it be otherwise since within the Macrocosm the elements essential to the true evolution and unfoldment of the Microcosm are found? Without them the evolution of the Soul could not continue, for it is built up from them. But if the elements within the Macrocosm become changed in their nature and action, then it is only natural that the individual Soul or Microcosm must suffer as the result. And if the elements out of which all the future of the Soul as a spiritual organism has to be built up have become so changed in their nature and action as to affect the Soul, even to the extent of preventing it from growing into fulness of spiritual being, then what is known as " the fall " of the Human Race must be regarded as a calamity which was not only unnecessary, but which has hindered the Soul from accomplishing the purpose of its creation, and has clothed it with experiences so dark and sorrowful that its life upon the Planet has been one of suffering.

The mystery of the Soul's pain is to be alone found in that fall through the elements, though it may not be able to fully apprehend that mystery. For the mystery of pain and suffering, which is so constantly attributed to the Divine Purpose, is the mystery of the conflict between the Soul and the Elemental Kingdoms. The elemental conditions, out of which in their pure magnetic state the Soul should have been built up, have caused the Soul to suffer unspeakably. Not only was its true spiritual unfoldment intercepted by them, but the new and strange magnetic influences set up through the changed elements so acted upon the magnetism of the Soul as to weaken it in all its beautiful and natural desires towards the Divine Fulfilment of its life. And through weakening the inherent spiritual magnetic forces within the Soul by means of which it responded to the Divine, the Elemental Kingdoms gradually gained dominion over the Soul.

It was in this way that the Soul fell from its first estate, *i.e.*, from being pure in its magnetism and correct in its equilibrium before the Divine, to being a spiritual creature subject to the elements whose wrong (because perverted) magnetic conditions greatly afflicted it, causing it to pass through chambers (or lives) of terrible ordeal as it sought to rise out of the antagonistic conditions amid which it found itself.

J. TODD FERRIER.

WHAT WAS THE FALL?

(PHILOSOPHY AND ORTHODOXY.)

THE mystery of evil in the world is one which has arrested the thought of all earnest students. The evil is beheld in its manifold forms, being too evident to be passed over without recognition ; but the reason for its presence is not so obvious, and its meaning is largely guessed at, sometimes with disastrous results both to Philosophy and the Soul's Vision of the Divine. On the one hand, Philosophy has assumed that it is a part of the process through which the Soul was meant to pass in its evolution from a simple spiritual organism to the full estate when its life should be crowned with the Divine, and that it is very largely, if not altogether, born from the limitations naturally associated with such an evolutionary process ; and on the other hand, it is thought to be the result of some mistaken action on the part of the first pair who attained unto the true Human Estate, a curse which was made to overshadow the whole of their descendants, and which was pronounced upon the unborn generations by the Divine Love. Philosophy assumes it to be the outcome of the Divine Presence in the World, the result of the Soul moving along and upward through the Elemental Kingdoms towards the fulness of its life, and thus, by inference, attributes all the manifestations of wrong to the Eternal and ever Blessed One ; and Orthodoxy affirms evil to have been introduced into the world through the unknown mysterious action of the first human pair, and all its terrible issues to be the outcome of a curse spoken from the lips of Him whose very nature is Love immeasurable, unfathomable, and which is unspeakable in its infinite tenderness. Philosophy beholds the awful issues of the evil present in the world, and in their best moments its adherents mourn over them ; yet it calls the evil only another form of good : and Orthodoxy attributes them all to the anger of the Divine Love against the first human pair and all their issue. Thus Philosophy mars the Divine Government of the World by making the presence of evil part

of that Government, and the unspeakable issues of that
evil the necessary experiences through which the Soul
had to pass in its evolution, and consequently all the
unnameable conditions amid which so many lives are cast
as the necessary instruments by means of which the Soul
passes through its manifold ordeals ; and Orthodoxy in
its many forms inverts the beautiful Love of the Eternal
One, changing the image from being one of *Blessing* to
one of *Cursing*, where the very work of its hands are
henceforth smitten with such evils as have followed
the Human Race for untold ages.

An impure fountain giveth forth impure waters, but
a pure fountain pure waters. Of the Eternal One which
shall we postulate ? Who would care to lay at His feet,
as the direct outcome of His Government of the World, all
the experiences which have befallen the Human Race,
all the physical, moral and spiritual sores by which the
Race to-day is burdened and afflicted ?   And how can
anyone who thinks seriously concerning the Divine
Nature, and who understands from experience what a
beautiful thing even imperfect Human Love is, and how
such love can never do anything but bless in its thoughts,
purposes and service, attribute unto Him whose great
Love is only dimly expressed in our own, the blighting
of the life of the Race because of the failure of two of His
children ? If such an action on the part of any Human
Soul would be viewed as the very negation of love, can
we not see to what a state the awful doctrine perpetuated
by Orthodoxy reduces the Divine Love ? It changes
its very nature, takes away the beautiful Father-
Motherhood of the Divine and sets up in His place a
judicial Ruler, with such attributes as may be found taken
up by one who is appointed to judge between man and
man in the various civil and criminal courts. It inverts
the image which is implied in the thought of the Divine
Father-Motherhood, and brings down the whole Government of the World by the Eternal and ever Blessed One
to the kind of government with which the history of the
Nations has made us acquainted. It takes away from
the seeking Soul *the Vision of One whose Gentleness makes*

the Soul great, and puts in its place a vision which fills it with the fear of a great dread.

And thus have Philosophy on the one hand and Orthodoxy on the other, and both as representing the East and the West, failed to apprehend the profound significance of the interpretations which they give to the presence of evil in the World.

Whatever answer is given to the questions, Why is evil in the World ? and, Why is evil permitted by the Divine Love ? it must always be in harmony with the Nature of the Eternal One and His beautiful purpose in Creation. It must also be in harmony with the constitution of both the individual Soul and the Planet-Soul. It must be such an explanation as will not reflect upon the Divine Government of the Celestial Worlds, though it may reflect upon the Planet for the way which it went. It should rather show up the true manifestation of goodness and love on the part of the Divine towards both Planet-Soul and the Human Race. And such an explanation is not only possible, but it should have been known long ages ago. Indeed it once was known, and the knowledge would have been perpetuated had not the Vision of the Soul been darkened through the loss of the inner meaning of spiritual and Divine truths through their Materialization and the perpetuation of false views of the Divine Nature and Purpose.

J. TODD FERRIER.

A PRAYER OF BLESSING.

O Love, Ever Faithful and True ! How shall Thy children fully acknowledge all Thy Goodness, made manifest unto them throughout all the ages ? With Thee has been no failure. There has been no withholding of Thy hand. The outflowing of Thy Great Love has never ceased. Only through its finding us and imparting nourishment and strength have we found our way back to Thee. With all our being we would bless Thee. Amen and Amen.

PSALM XXXIV.

(A NEW READING.)

I will bless the Lord at all times. The Praise of Him shall be with me continually.

O magnify the Lord with me! Let us together exalt His Name:

For His Name is glorious: it is full of honour and majesty.

The humble in heart learn of Him: in Him only hath the Soul glory.

O come, ye children of men! Taste and see the goodness of the Lord, how He maketh the land goodly to live in, and supplieth all our needs.

Though the young lions hunger and roar for their prey, yet shall they who wait upon the Lord fear not lest they should lack any good thing.

For the Angel of the Lord encampeth around them whose fear is unto Him.

Who is he who would possess Life in Him? Whose desire is to have all his days crowned with Good?

Let him keep his lips from evil and his heart from thinking guile.

Let him make evil to depart that he may seek only good, and know the peace of the Lord.

The eyes of the Lord behold the righteous whose ears are open unto His call.

He heareth when they cry unto Him, and delivereth them from all trouble.

He is ever nigh the broken life to redeem the contrite spirit.

I sought the Lord, and He heard me; He delivered me out of all my fears.

WHAT WAS THE FALL?

(THE TRUTHS GUESSED AT).

GREAT truths underlie the statements of both Philosophy and Orthodoxy, though the interpretations of these truths are not only mistaken ones, but are grievously at fault in the meanings which they give to the past history of the world, and the reasons they assign for the presence of evil in our midst. The interpretations of the two schools of thought, though apparently so much at variance with each other, have nevertheless a point at which not only their reconciliation becomes effected, but also one where the truths which lie behind both of the positions they have taken up, are made quite clear, the erroneous meanings removed, and the real history of the World and Humanity is presented. They have taken two distinct standpoints from which they try to view the World and Humanity, the one being apparently supported by the theories of Physical Science, whilst the other appears to be confirmed by the inward experiences of mankind. For Physical Science, in so far as it is able to observe the phenomena of Nature and relate it, lends its weight to the doctrine of even a spiritual evolutionary theory of the history of the Planet and its inhabitants, though it confines its observations to the physical plane and tries to relate the phenomena it finds there. But true experimental Philosophy beholds something lying within the experience of the individual life which is not in harmony with any theory of the evolution of man, such as material Science has to propound, or the interpretation put upon the doctrine of evolution by Eastern Philosophy. It beholds in the experience of the individual Soul the dim echoes, not only of all the past, which the Soul has gathered up into itself on its way up through the Animal Kingdom, but it sees in that experience dim histories of a life far removed from all that could be associated with the Animal Kingdom, as Science and History know it ; it finds echoes of a past which must have been indeed beautiful, a past life when the sword of evil was not driven through the life of the

Race, nor wrong in any form was present to mar and embitter the Soul's experience, but when only good prevailed, when love reigned, and when the World within and around the Soul was full of sweet harmony. The very longing of Man in his best moments for a life of pure and beautiful experience, his dreams of a redeemed World in which evil will not find any more a resting-place in human life, his endeavours to purify the conditions around him, and his inherent faith in the vision that now seems so far off becoming a reality, all testify to the possession by him of some inner spiritual power which ever craves for its fulfilment and realization, and some dim memories from which his beautiful ideals are born and his hopes spring.

The reconciliation between these two distinct views of the World's history is to be found in the recognition of the fact that both are true in their special sphere ; that they both relate to different parts of the World's history ; that both are only segments of the circle which has been run by the Human Race, and are, therefore, not only incomplete by themselves, but even when joined together ; that the phenomena observed by Science are not material, though the manifestation is upon the material plane ; that the experimental history beheld by Philosophy has its origin in a long past when the Soul had reached the Human Kingdom, and prior to the time when it went down into the Animal Kingdom known to Science and History ; that together Science and Philosophy fail to account for the presence of evil in the history of Soul evolution, and for the remarkable inherent spiritual potencies of an advanced order possessed by the Human Race, and the strange out-reaching towards some long-lost vision, whose realization would change the entire conditions of the World and lift up all Souls into a life whose manifestations would be pure, true and good.

The true reconciliation between the divergent views of Science and Philosophy ; between the theories of the World's past history pre-supposed and affirmed by the evolutionary doctrine of Man's ascent from and through the Animal Kingdom, and that guessed at by experimental Philosophy as it tries to read the meaning of the strange sublime nature of Man when at his best, and the evil which it recognises running through the whole History of Humanity in so far as it is able to trace that History, will be accomplished only from the spiritual view which must be taken of the whole of the past of this World and its denizens. Only from the spiritual standpoint can the true history written and made manifest on the material planes in the phenomena observed by Science be understood, and the true meaning of the remarkable spiritual manifestations in Human experience even amid the most terrible evils, become known. For it is the true spiritual view of Human History which is most required to-day to carry the thought of the age away from the mere material and objective spheres, and take it to the sphere of the spiritual nature of Man ; to throw light upon the path where no material Science can illumine the darkness to explain the remarkable phenomena observed along the physical planes ; to unravel the even stranger phenomena observed by students of experimental Philosophy upon what may be called the planes of Man's religious experience, wherein evil and good are manifest, and often times as opposing forces ; to explain the meaning of the presence of the evil, and truly interpret the sublime aspirations and visions of the Soul. And when the light which breaks from that Kingdom is seen, then verily are all the strange contradictions in the History of Humanity made clear in their cause and meaning. The grievous burden of the Race is understood ; the travail of the World has new light thrown upon it ; and the travail of the Divine Love on behalf of the World and all its children stands forth in a new light, and becomes luminous and transfigured with unspeakable glory.

J. TODD FERRIER.

WHAT WAS THE FALL?

(HOW THE SOUL KNOWS).

THAT which Science cannot give us, and which Philosophy seems unable to discover, is made clear for us from the Spiritual Heavens. For only from that source can we come to know the true nature of the evil that is in the World, how that evil came first into the World, and the meaning of the sad History of Humanity all through the ages. And only from that source can the Soul recover the history of its own past as it functions upon the spiritual planes, endeavours to live the Angelic Life in all its ways and service, and seeks unto the full Realization of the Divine Vision within the Sanctuary of the Soul.

The history of the Soul's past is the history of its Travail through the spheres of the Elemental Kingdoms prior to the great change which came over these Kingdoms, and which resulted in the generating of evil conditions through the inversion of their polarity; the Travail, sad and terrible in its suffering and anguish, of the Soul amid these foreign conditions, whose whole tendency was to bring the Soul down into their own state; and the Travail of the Soul's return through what is known unto Science as the Animal Kingdom till it reached the Human Kingdom, its Travail through that Kingdom during all the long ages of conflict within it, then the return of the Soul within the Human Kingdom in what is known as its Redemption, until it reaches the Estate of Christhood when all the past breaks upon it, so that it recovers the history which it wrote in its Travail.

J. TODD FERRIER.

PSALM LXXXVII.

(*A NEW READING.*)

Within His Holy Mountain[1] hath the Lord laid deep the foundations whereon Zion[2] is built.

He loveth Zion more than the tabernacles of men, and her Gates[3] more than those which leadeth unto earthly temples.

Of her have glorious things been spoken : for she is the Holy City of God.

Behold in Philistia, Tyre and Ethiopia are born those who know the ways of Babylon and Rahab[4] !

But in Zion shall it be said of me, " This man was born within her Gates ; therefore the Lord will establish him."

" In the day when the Lord numbereth the Children of Zion[5], that man shall be remembered as one who was born there[6]."

All our springs are in Thee, O Lord. We are Thy instruments sounding forth the Praise and glory of the Life unto which Thou callest us ; the players through whom the music of Thy Heavens is to be interpreted ; the singers through whom the harmonies of Zion are to be proclaimed for Thee[7].

---

[1] *Mount Moriah or the Divine Kingdom, the Mountain of the Divine Love and Wisdom whereon Abraham was said to have offered up Isaac.*

[2] *The Christhood, which is built upon the foundations of Sacrifice.*

[3] *The Gates of Zion were the Twelve Labours of the Soul upon the Spiritual Heavens, through which, and by means of passing through each even unto perfect realisation of their meaning, the Soul attained unto the Estate of Christhood.*

[4] *Those whose life is found in the ways of the world-life, who make the world Babylon, and its ways those of Rahab the destroyer.*

[5] *The Order of the Christhood.*

[6] *One who has known Christhood.*

[7] *Those who have known Christhood are to be the Interpreters and Manifestors of the Divine.*

SOME LAY TESTIMONIES AGAINST VIVISECTION.*

APPENDIX II.

THE LATE LORD CHIEF JUSTICE COLERIDGE.

"WHAT would our Lord have said, what looks would He have bent upon a chamber filled with the 'un-offending creatures which He loves,' dying under torture deliberately and intentionally inflicted ? . . . A wrong to the creature is, moreover, an insult to its Creator, and a double insult when we bow to that Creator as a ' God of Love,' whose 'tender mercies are over *all* His works.' To perpetrate cruelty that good may come is therefore blasphemy—there is no such thing as necessary cruelty more than necessary sin."—(*Fortnightly Review*, February, 1882).

BISHOP BARRY, D.D., D.C.L., *Canon of Windsor, Late Primate of Australia.*

" For humanity at large to seek its own supposed good at all hazard of wrong-doing and cruelty to the weaker creatures of God, is surely of the very essence of selfishness. To hold that the increase of physical comfort, the removal of physical pain, the prolongation of physical life, are the supreme objects, for the sake of which we may demoralize our higher humanity, is simply a worship of the flesh, unworthy of a true man, impossible to a true Christian. To sin for these purposes against God's creatures, bound up with ourselves in the great chain of organic being, and committed to us as made in His image and having a delegation of His Sovereignty, is a pros-titution of God-given power which is almost a sacrilege." —(Church Congress, Folkestone, 1892.)

THE BISHOP OF DURHAM (DR. WESTCOTT.)

" If He who made us made all other creatures also, and if they find a place in His Providential plan, if His tender mercies reach to them, and this we Christians most certainly believe—then I find it absolutely inconceivable

---

* "Why I condemn Vivisection," by Robert H. Perks, M.D., F.R.C.S. *Vide* advertisement pages.

that He should have so arranged the avenues of knowledge that we can attain to truths, that it is His will which we should master, only through the unutterable agonies of beings which trust in us."—(Sermon in Westminster Abbey, August 13th, 1899.)

THE LATE COLONEL INGERSOLL.

"Vivisection is the inquisition—the hell—of science. All the cruelty which the human—or rather the inhuman —heart is capable of inflicting is in this one word. Below this there is no depth. . . . It is not necessary for a man to be a specialist in order to have and express his opinion as to the right or wrong of vivisection. It is not necessary to be a scientist or a naturalist to detest cruelty and to love mercy. Above all the discoveries of thinkers, above all the inventions of the ingenious, above all the victories of fields of intellectual conflict, rise human sympathy and a sense of justice."—(From the *Chronicle of St. George*, U.S.A., May, 1891.)

MRS. BESANT.

"We still find people in the astounding condition of incapacity to see the wickedness of vivisection, even after they have learned from the writings of vivisectors that it is not a question of giving a few drugs to animals rather than to men, when the quality of the drugs is unknown, but a question of submitting animals to prolonged torture in the hope of adding a fragment of new knowledge to the store already accumulated. . . . It may be that public opinion will not take alarm until some members of the ruling races are seized by the blood-stained hand of the grim tormentors, and are done to death in quest of some obscure disease. The approval of vivisection is so distinctly a selfish passion, a clutching at a possible chance of gain for man at any cost to others, that it seems but too probable that what the public calls its conscience will not be aroused until its own members are within measurable distance of the torture trough. . . . The black sorcery of savage magic has no horrors so terrible as those of the vivisectors."—(From the *Theosophical Review*, December, 1897.)

VICTOR HUGO.

" Vivisection is a crime.   The human race will repudiate these barbarities."—Reply to Pres. French A. V. Society.

GEORGE MACDONALD, LL.D.

" May my God give me grace to prefer a hundred deaths to a life gained by the sufferings of one simplest creature. He holds his life as *I* hold mine, by finding himself where I find myself.   Shall I quiet my heart with the throbs of another heart ?   soothe my nerves with the agonised tension of a system ?   live a few days longer by a century of shrieking deaths ?   It were a hellish wrong—a selfish, hateful, violent injustice.   It is true we are above the creatures, but not to keep them down ; they are for our use and service, but neither to be trodden under foot of pride, or misused as ministers, at their worst cost of suffering, to our inordinate desires of ease."—(From " Paul Faber, Surgeon.")

CARDINAL MANNING.

" I take the first opportunity that has been offered to me to renew publicly my firm determination, so long as life is granted me, to assist in putting an end to that which I believe to be a detestable practice without scientific result, and immoral in itself. . . .   I believe the time has come, and I only wish we had the power legally, to prohibit altogether the practice of vivisection. . . .   Nothing can justify, no claim of science, no conjectural result, no hope for discovery, such horrors as these.   Also it must be remembered that whereas these torments, refined and indescribable, are certain, the result is altogether conjectural—everything about the result is uncertain but *the certain infraction of the first laws of mercy and humanity*."—Speech, June 21st, 1882

CARDINAL NEWMAN.

" Does it not sometimes make us shudder to hear tell of them (*cruel experiments on animals*) ? . . . It is the cold-blooded and calculating act of men of science, who make experiments on brute animals, perhaps merely from a sort of curiosity. . . .   Now what is it moves our very heart, and sickens us so much at cruelty shown to poor brutes ? I suppose this first, that they have done us no harm ; next that they have no power whatever of resistance ; it is *the cowardice and tyranny* of which they are the victims which makes their sufferings so especially touching ; . . . there is something so very dreadful, so *Satanic in tormenting those who never have harmed us*, and who cannot defend themselves, who are utterly in our power," etc.—(" Parochial and Plain Sermons," Rivingtons, 1878.)

JOHN RUSKIN.

" These scientific pursuits were now defiantly, provokingly, insultingly separated from the science of religion ; they were all carried on in defiance of what had been hitherto held to be compassion and pity, and of the great link which bound together the whole Creation from its Maker to the lowest creature."—(Speech at Oxford, December 9th, 1884.)

(Ruskin resigned his chair as Slade Professor of Fine Arts, in the University of Oxford, as a protest against the inclusion of vivisection among its methods of teaching.)

CANON WILBERFORCE.

". . . We say that what is called vivisection is morally indefensible ; we believe it is also absolutely scientifically unsound, and we are also more and more convinced that it is one of the very greatest possible evils to the human race."—(From speech in St. James' Hall, May 9th, 1899.)

EDWARD MAITLAND, B.A.

" The practice of vivisection involves the reversal of every principle, by following which man develops those higher planes of consciousness which raise him above the animals. It means abandonment of all our moral gains, and a return to the rudiments of existence. If vivisection be right then has the world existed and mankind striven and suffered in vain. If the sacrifice of others to self is to be the rule for ever, let us at once declare might to be right, and vivisect our women and

children—any who are unable to protect themselves."—
(From letter to *Examiner*, July 17th, 1876.)

***

APPENDIX III.

THE following Extracts show the attitude of the
Medical Press in reference to Vivisection at the
time of its general introduction into England, about the
middle of the last century, and will serve to indicate the
degree to which, in these days, their ethical standard has
been lowered by the influence of those who practise it.

" MEDICAL TIMES AND GAZETTE."

September, 1858.

" . . . We are inclined to believe that the question
will some day be asked, *whether any excuse can make them*
(vivisectional experiments) *justifiable ?*"

October, 1860.

"We are sure that the profession at large will fully agree
with us in condemning experiments which are made simply
to demonstrate physiological or other facts which have
been received as settled points and are beyond all controversy."

March 2nd, 1861 (Editorial).

"We think that the repetition of experiments before
students . . . is to be condemned."

August, 1862.

"When the result of an experiment has been fully
obtained and confirmed *its repetition is indefensible.*"

" LANCET."

Aug. 11th, 1860 ; Oct. 29th, 1860 ; Aug. 22nd, 1863.

The Editor condemns the repetition of vivisectional
experiments in language similar to above.

August 29th, 1863 (Editorial) speaking of the " rather
reckless expenditure of the lives and feelings of cold-
blooded creatures," has the following :—

" The reckless way in which we have seen this poor
creature (the frog) cut, thrown and kicked about, has
been sometimes sickening. . . We cannot help feeling
there is both a *bad moral discipline for the man as well as. . .*

"BRITISH MEDICAL JOURNAL."

May 11th, 1861 (Editorial).

"*It has never appeared clear to us that we are justified in destroying animals for mere experimental research under any circumstances ;* but now that we possess the means of removing sensation during experiments, the man who puts an animal to torture, ought, in our opinion, to be prosecuted."

May 2nd, 1863 ; quoted from editorial in "L'Union Medicale," of Paris.

". . . I would gladly petition the Senate to forbid its performance on every animal which is useful to and a friend of Man."

August 22nd, 1863 (Editorial).

"We are very glad to find that the French medical journals are entering protests against the cruel abuse which is made of Vivisection in France.

L'Abeille Medicale says :—

". . . Let no one tell us that vivisections are necessary for a knowledge of physiology. . . . If the present ways, habits and customs are continued, the future physician will become marked by his cold and implacable insensibility. Let there be no mistake about it ; *the man who habituates himself to the shedding of blood, and who is insensible to the sufferings of animals is led on into the path of baseness.*"

October 10th, 1863 (Editorial) referring to a speech by M. Dubois at the Academy of Medicine, Paris : —

"M. Dubois showed to demonstration that . . . physiological demonstrations on living animals in the public (Medical) schools *are utterly unjustifiable and a scandal to humanity. In all this, we most thoroughly agree with him.*"

June 11th, 1864 (Editorial).

"Far be it from us to patronize or palliate the infamous practices, the unjustifiable practices committed in French veterinary schools, and in many French Medical Schools, in the matter of vivisection. We repudiate as brutal and cruel all surgical operations performed on living animals.

We repudiate the repetition of all experiments on animals for the demonstration of any already well-determined physiological questions."

(I have to acknowledge my indebtedness to Dr. Leffingwell's pamphlet " The Rise of the Vivisection Controversy," published by the American Humane Association, for these references).

Italics not in original editorials.

ROBERT H. PECKS, M.D., F.R.C.S.

ANSWERS TO CORRESPONDENTS.

(1) *Do you think the Magnetic Pole of the Earth is the real Pole ? If so, will it become the real Pole again ?*

The Magnetic Pole is the real Pole. What are now termed the Earth's Poles are only the Axes (North and South) of the outermost sphere upon which the Earth turns in its daily rotation.

(2) *Is there any explanation why the physical body of Jesus was taken from the Jewish people who were so materialistic, and not from the less materialistic Eastern Races ?*

The parents of the man, or rather of His body, were beautiful Souls who had attained the Redeemed Life and Spiritual Christhood. They were of the race of the true Hebrews, who were the teachers and prophets of the Nation. These were found amongst all the Eastern Nations and were of the Illuminati in those days.

(3) *Do you think the present physical upheavals may be the outer reflection of the Planet-Soul's efforts to restore harmony on its Planes ?*

The various physical phenomena resulting from what is known as Seismic disturbances are doubtless the outcome of the changes wrought in the various spheres of the Planet-Soul in its labour to regain its true equilibrium and its ancient estate as a perfect spiritul system.

(4) *May the clouds coming between our vision and the Sun and Moon be taken as illustrations of the clouds arising between the lower mind and the Soul, and formed by the lack of purity in living ?*

The clouds which obscure the Sun and Moon are atmospheric, and are the result of the Planetary Conditions. And the clouds which arise within the mind and obscure the Soul's Vision, are generated through the spiritual conditions within and around the life. The purer the ways of life, the clearer will be the Soul's Vision.

THE EDITOR.

THE HERALD OF THE CROSS.

Vol. v. New Series. August, 1909. No. 8.

SOME PRECIOUS SAYINGS.

Come, ye blessed of the Heavenly Father, inherit the Kingdom prepared for you before the foundation of this world.

For when the Christ-Soul was an hungered, ye gave Him meat ;

When He was athirst, ye gave Him wherewith to drink ;

When He was afflicted and grew sick with sorrow and anguish, ye ministered unto Him ;

When He was cast into the prison-houses where he anguished with all who were bound, ye did visit to comfort and deliver Him ;

When His garments were rent and blood-stained as He trod the wine-press of sorrow in His Travail through the Kingdoms of the Creatures and Man, ye did clothe Him afresh with fine raiment.

For in the afflictions of all Creatures and all Souls, was He afflicted ; in the least may His life be found.

As ye have ministered unto one of these least in the day of their affliction, ye have ministered unto Him.

VIVISECTION SEEN FROM THE SPIRITUAL WORLD.

IN considering this most important aspect of a great and serious question, it will aid us in an understanding of it if we also understand what the Spiritual World is, and how it is possible to look out from that world along planes to which so many seem strangers. It will take our thoughts into a region where the multitudes do not follow, to spheres high above the mundane activities which engross the thoughts and energies of men and women. It will carry us to a world whose presence within each of us is yet but dimly apprehended, whose true part in the great service on behalf of the Creatures is yet little understood, but whose potencies are great. It will lift us up to a world whose planes intersect our own truest life, a world with which we are most intimately bound up in both life and service, and by which we are overshadowed.

WHAT IS THE SPIRITUAL WORLD ?

Of what nature then is that world ? Where is it located ? How may we find it and come into the possession of the knowledge which it has to impart, and the Visions which it enables us to behold ?

To those who do not understand from experience and inward realization what that world is and what it does for us, these questions are natural. And in endeavouring to answer them we have to go up into the spiritual spheres of our own life ; to withdraw, as it were, in thought, feeling and vision, from the mundane experiences to find the true centre of our life ; to pass, so to speak, from the outermost courts of the temple of life to the innermost Sanctuary where dwell those powers whose presence testifies of the Divinity of our nature, the reality of the Spiritual World and the still more blessed reality of the Divine Presence within the Sanctuary of our being. For the Spiritual World is that world within us which corresponds to the Spiritual Heavens. In its inherent nature it is like the Heavens, pure and beautiful, and illumined with the Light of the Divine. Within it are reflected the things of the Spiritual Heavens; and in that way is it a Microcosm of the Spiritual Macrocosm. By means of that correspondence are the Spiritual Heavens able to communicate direct with the Soul, to advise and instruct, and reveal many things which could not otherwise be known. And when we are in the true condition necessary for the Spiritual Heavens to communicate unto us, we are like those who, standing within a Sphere at its very centre, are able to take in the whole sphere in one vision, from the central point to the outermost circumference. We look from the within to the things without, beholding the life upon the various planes between the innermost and the outermost; and witnessing the meaning of the phenomena made manifest upon the physical and semi-physical spheres. And the way to that centre of our own spiritual system, where we can come into direct touch with the Spiritual Heavens and receive from them those knowledges and visions which can come to us only from those Heavens, is by living the Redeemed Life—the life whose ways are pure, and whose whole spirit is one of beautiful love, manifesting itself in immeasurable compassion unto all Souls, and unfailing pity unto all the Creatures. For the Spiritual World within us must correspond in all its attributes to the World of the Divine Love by which we know we are overshadowed. It must not only be potentially Spiritual and Divine, but it must always be so in its aspirations and motives, and in its endeavours after perfect realization. And when such a life is sought after by the Soul, and the individual follows with earnest endeavour the path along which it is to be found, then that individual will not only be able to come into contact with the Spiritual World and have communications from it, but will likewise be able to hear and see upon its planes.

How Things are Beheld There.

When things are viewed from the Spiritual World they seem so very different from their appearance upon the outer spheres. The phenomena witnessed by men and

women are also beheld from those Heavens ; but along
with the phenomena upon the outermost sphere there
are beheld other phenomena of a spiritual order which
cannot be materially visualized, and which can only be
understood from the spiritual planes. We mean that
in all the various spheres of Human experience the
primary forces were and are spiritual in their nature ;
that the manifestations beheld within the various orders
of life found in the Creature Kingdom have their springs
in spiritual potentialities, though the direction of them
might at times appear .to be antagonistic to anything
spiritual ; that even the powers latent in the Vegetable
Kingdom whose manifestations may be witnessed in the
manifoldness, in form and colour and fruits, of the
various orders of life, are all spiritual when seen from
the world of the Soul. From that world the phenomenal
world is not the reality, but a manifestation under great
limitations of the reality ; and a manifestation only
upon the outermost objective sphere. For the reality
is found in the spiritual in every kingdom, just as the
real individual is not the outer form, but the inner life.
Nay, in the case of a human life the phenomena observed
upon the outermost spheres sometimes would seem to
contradict the life of the real individual, and probably
would be so interpreted by one standing upon the outer
spheres and judging from the observed phenomena ;
whereas from the Spiritual Spheres the real life becomes
known, and all the phenomena, even those which appear
to be contradictory, are understood.

VIVISECTION AS TO ITS NATURE.

Now, when we have to tell what is seen concerning
the works and workers within the Physiological Laboratories, we must needs seek grace to enable us to tell it
in language and feelings restrained and dignified. For
the things witnessed from the Spiritual Heavens—
deeds wrought in the name of true culture, knowledge
and Humanity—are too terrible and horrible to describe.
They are beheld there in their true light. The real
purpose for which the dark deeds are wrought are known

there ; and it is not such a purpose as any humane and
noble Soul would care to be consciously identified with.
The real meaning of Vivisection is not Scientific. It is
not the true progress of knowledge. It is not even the
healing of the Human Race of its self-generated diseases.
But it is the very Inquisition itself, that which the
Inquisition stood for on the Human sphere—the oppression of the defenceless, the affliction of those who were
weak in that they could not defend themselves against
the powers which the Inquisition represented, the wresting
from the life of the individual the secrets which no one
has the right to extract against the individual's will.
Vivisection is the very apotheosis of evil ; scientifically
the deification of that which is furthest removed from
the Ever Blessed and Eternal One whose Name is Love,
whose Love is manifest in His Compassion, and whose
compassion is so evident to all who are able to behold
and understand it as it breaks upon this world of distraught life in unfailing Pity. Using the term in its
derivative sense, it implies that which is furthest from
God ; and Vivisection is that in its nature. It is the
negation of love : it knows none. It is outside the
circle of Compassionate manifestations : it has no pity.
The poor, poor dumb mouths of the lacerated Creatures,
the suppressed agony and anguish told through the
eyes of the helpless victims of its power, appeal in vain
to its devotees for the manifestation of the least degree
of pity. It has its fell purpose set before it—to wring
from the Creatures some secret which Science demands
for its enlightenment ; and so it is deaf to all entreaty.
There is no humanity in it. Were there the least glint
or gleaming in its spirit of what constitutes a true
Humanity, then the sufferings of those whom it oppresses
and tortures would move it to cease from its infamous
works. For the true knowledge which it professes to
seek, it gives only agony and anguish. For the true
healing of disease which it professes to accomplish, it
only brings all manner of ailments upon Humanity, and
of a kind which Science cannot diagnose. For a true
Pathology it takes its followers into avenues whose

ending is not only hell to the Creatures suffering the anguish-fires imposed upon them by the Inquisitors, but the outer darkness for all who pursue the inhuman course.

WITHIN THE LABORATORIES.

Let us now look within the Laboratories that we may behold what Vivisection means for the Creature. The outward phenomena must be terrible to witness even by those who are students ; for though the Creatures are so well strapped down and gagged upon the operating tables that they cannot make any sign of their pain and anguish, yet the very opening of the nerve centres should be sufficient to impress eye-witnesses of the sufferings endured in the process. For the whole question of anesthetics is negatived by the admission on the part of the chief operators that complete anesthesia would defeat the purpose of the experiments. Those who have passed through these centres of experimentation can testify to the feelings with which they have had to witness the phenomena. The authors of " The Shambles of Science," and " Scientific Research—a View from within," and many others, have told what they witnessed and felt. And they found language too inadequate to enable them to express the awful things which they beheld. They saw the poor afflicted Creatures under conditions which could only be described as most diabolical. They saw in the operators and demonstrators an utter lack of pity towards the victims. They witnessed a human callousness almost inconceivable. And they felt the atmosphere to be that of the Greek Tartarus—charged with those conditions which make hell within and without.

Yet all the phenomena beheld by them, and all that may be witnessed upon the outer spheres, are only the physical manifestations of unseen powers ; the moving shadows, so to speak, of the active forces lying behind the visible ; the outer pulses of great feelings and sufferings which can only be known from the Spiritual Spheres. To witness from these Spheres what takes place within the Physiological Laboratories, is not only to witness the phenomena on the outermost sphere, but the phenomena upon the Astral Kingdom arising out of the experimentations, the phenomena upon the magnetic plane of the life of the Creatures who suffer, the phenomena upon the magnetic plane of the life of those who perform the experiments, and the effect of them all upon the individual Soul and the Planet as a Spiritual System.

Oh, the anguish within those infernos ! How unspeakable it is. Oh, the agony of many of the victims ! How indescribable to human ears. Oh, those tears unshed before human eyes, and those prayers unheard upon the outer planes of the Earth ! Who shall count them and tell of them upon Earth ? Do they feel pain as Human beings do when they have been severely wounded ? Do they agonise through a deep consciousness of their sufferings ? Are they capable of passing through experiences which make them anguish ? So do those ironically enquire who understand them not in their inner life, who look upon them as mere physical organisms. So do not those believe who view them as mere goods and chattels to be bartered for and made use of as they may deem desirable.

But from the Spiritual World the suppressed anguish and cries are seen and heard through the fearful conditions generated by the traffic in their lives. The very Heavens are bowed down with anguish because of their sufferings. The very angels weep, expressive of the compassion of the Divine, that any Creature could be made to suffer such pain and anguish.

THINGS WHICH HAVE BEEN EXPERIENCED.

In this connection it might be well first of all to refer to some of the experiences which came to two of the most consecrated workers on behalf of the Creatures. I refer to the late Dr. Anna Kingsford and Edward Maitland, B.A. Both of them came into very close touch with the Spiritual Spheres by which we are overshadowed, and they saw much and heard many things concerning the awful tragedies enacted within the Vivisectional Laboratories. Let me quote to you one incident experienced by Anna Kingsford—

" I went . . . . . last night from one torture-chamber to another in the underground vaults of a vivisector's labora-tory, and in all were men at work lacerating, dissecting, and burning the living flesh of their victims. But these were no longer mere horses or dogs or rabbits ; for in each I saw a human shape, the shape of a man, with limbs and lineaments resembling those of their tor-mentors, hidden within the outward form. And so, when they bound down a horse, and, gathering round him, cut into him with knives, I saw the human shape within him writhe and moan. . . . And I cried aloud, 'Wretches ! you are torturing an unborn man !' But they only laughed at me, for with *their* eyes they could not see that which I saw. Then they brought a rabbit and thrust its eyes through with hot irons. And the rabbit seemed to me, as I gazed, like the tiniest infant, with human face, and hands which stretched appealingly towards me, and lips which tried to cry for help in human accents. And again I cried to them; 'O blind ! blind ! Do ye not see that your victim is of your own kind, a child that is human ?' But they only laughed and jeered at me, and in the agony of my distress, I awoke."

That this was no solitary experience in their work will be learnt from the history of it written by Edward Maitland ; for they had visions and communications many and varied. And that the visions were real and the communications concerning what took place within the Creature forms were true, we have evidence which is even better than the outward history which was written with a view to the awakening of true Souls to the reality of the fearful system. We have the evidence which comes through experience. We have not only beheld the agony of the Creatures, but we have been permitted to experience the unspeakable agonies thrust upon them and the awful anguish they pass through. We have beheld them after they have passed out of their tor-mentors' hands, though not out of their anguish. We have beheld the effects of their wounding in the expres-sions of great dread upon their countenances. We have felt even as they felt when they were the victims of the Scientific Inquisition. And to adequately tell what they suffer is impossible ; but it is terrible in its reality. So terrible was the suffering, so unspeakable the agonies, so profound the anguish that, as we passed through them, we felt that even that beautiful Love in whom we had always trusted had forsaken us.

THE SPIRITUAL NATURE OF THE CREATURES.

Even as Humanity is viewed as spiritual in nature, so will the Creatures have to be. It is a beautiful thought, though not one generally accepted, especially in the Western World. For the West is yet too grossly material through its materialization of everything spiritual, and its degradation of many of the holiest and most sublime things, to apprehend the inner meaning of the lives of the Creatures. Indeed it does not yet see the inner meaning of Human Life, so blinded is it by the gods of this world—Mammon, Moloch and Beelzebub. But many are awakening to the reality ; and some are even now ready for the larger message of the continuity of *all true* Life, and the spiritual nature of the Creatures. That they are not mere physical organisms, but Creatures who persist after the outer form has had to be put away, many can testify through having seen what is sometimes spoken of as the Astral form. That many of them are more than the Creatures they seem to be has likewise been testified to by those who have been able to rise on to the Spiritual Heavens. And that they are all spiritual beings in various stages of unfoldment, we have the sure and certain knowledge given us from that world through communication, Soul-vision, and profound and sorrowful experience. And it is because they are spiritual beings in various planes of consciousness that they are capable of intense feeling and suffering. In the case of those who are upon planes of spiritual consciousness not far removed from the lower plane of the Human Kingdom, there is the capacity for enduring even a degree of sorrow and anguish. The sorrow of a dog or horse at the loss of its friend is a well known trait in these orders of the Creatures.

The surprising thing is that the people do not seem to recognise in these traits strongly marked character which has its foundations in spiritual being, traits which are essentially of the best human manifestations of fidelity and affection, traits which are indeed of the Divine potencies within the Soul. And it is a sad testimony to the great limitations of the present Human Vision, and shows how great is the spiritual darkness prevailing, that the Creatures should be shut out of the great spiritual family of the world and viewed as mere forms of organized matter with certain well-defined instincts, and only fit to be used as goods of merchandise for the increase of personal material increment, or as chattels for uses such as are required within a Physiological Laboratory. That the spiritual view of their nature, and of their past and future history, is needed even amongst the workers who are seeking to deliver them from the hands of their oppressors, is evident, judging from the views expressed in many of the anti-vivisection and humane journals. And we believe (and we have every reason for doing so when we remember the past history of the beautiful movement for the accomplishment of the·total abolition of vivisection) that the spiritual view of the nature and history, past and future, of all the Creatures is the only one by means of which true men and women will be awakened to behold the awful thing which has been wrought in the name of true Science and on behalf of the best interests of Humanity, and by which they will be most truly inspired to arise in the strength of their own manhood and womanhood to accomplish the final defeat and overthrow of all the powers lying behind the whole Vivisection movement.

THE EFFECT OF IT ALL UPON HUMANITY.

The view which is seen from the Spiritual Heavens is not circumscribed by the awful sufferings of the Creatures, but takes in the indescribable effects upon those who operate and the far-reaching influences upon the whole of Humanity. The conditions set up upon the Astral Kingdom are such as to cause many grievous afflictions to fall upon mankind in general, and to bring upon those who are most sensitive to the spiritual conditions of their environment strange experiences which no Medical Science is able to account for. Many of the most spiritually sensitive Souls are smitten with afflictions which, whilst they bring to the body pain as if it had some disease, are not of a physical order. And they oppress the mind, sometimes so greatly that the sufferers act as if they were mentally afflicted, and, indeed, are judged to be so by those who observe them. Nor is that all. Those who are so sensitive in their spiritual nature that they feel all the conditions which are set up as the result of the perpetrations within the laboratories, are liable to feel just as the Creatures feel when they are passing through these chambers of anguish, to suffer with the Creatures, and to even feel as if God were withdrawn from this world. It is terrible to think that so many sensitive Souls may suffer in this way; but it is more terrible to know that they do so suffer, and to see them passing through such great pain and anguish as the outcome of the Vivisector's work.

The day is with us in the which the Vivisector's works will all be overthrown, the conditions which he has generated entirely changed, the deliverance of all the Creatures from their terrible sufferings and false place in the world's life accomplished, and the regnancy of the Divine be realized.   J. TODD FERRIER.

O Eternal and ever Blessed One! It hath pleased Thee to make manifest unto us the sufferings within the prison-houses of all the Creatures who have been made to pass through them, and the anguish of the Souls who have imposed upon them burdens most grievous and terrible to bear. Be pleased to graciously grant unto us such a fulness of Thy glorious Love, that we shall be for Thee true servants in our service, full of tenderness and gentleness, patience and endurance as we seek to accomplish Thy Holy Will in the Deliverance of all the Creatures. Amen and Amen.

PSALM VIII.

(A NEW READING.)

O Lord, the Excellent[1] of the Earth in the day when her inhabitants all know Thee as their Lord!

Thy glory hast Thou set in the Heavens above us to shine upon the Heavens[2] within us.

Thou hast laid the foundations of our strength in our childhood to Thee; though even babes and sucklings we may still praise Thee.

When we consider the works of Thy Hands, the Heavens above us and the Heavens within us, the Moon[3] whose shining illumines our night in this world, and the Stars[4] whose light marks the path of the Heavens above and within us, because Thou didst ordain them so to shine;

We wonder at Thy marvellous works and inquire as those who would understand that Holy Love and Wisdom through which they have all been founded;

We inquire in the childhood of our life, and even when the ages have shown us Thy glory, what is Man? Thou art so mindful of Him! Who is the Son of Man[5] in whom Thou dost visit him?

Though a little lower than the Angels Thou didst fashion him, yet didst Thou make him to be crowned with Glory and exalted to Thy right hand.[6]

---

[1] *i.e., When the Divine Vision is universally realized, just as the Divine is the Supreme Life within the Soul.*

[2] *The Heavens within are the microcosm of the Spiritual Heavens.*

[3] *The Moon refers to the reflective power of the Spiritual Mind whose light is received from the Spiritual Heavens, and by which alone the Soul can have true guidance.*

[4] *The Stars are the signs within the Soul of its progress towards the Divine realization. They are the various lights begotten within the Heavens of the Soul as the result of its attainments.*

[5] *The Christ-Soul who made manifest the Christhood, thus interpreting the Divine Love and showing forth the Divine Wisdom. It was always through the Christ-Soul that the Divine was made manifest in the ages prior to the Christhood of the Sublime Master.*

[6] *The chief end of the fashioning of the Soul is the attainment by it of the image of the Divine, the true Crown of Glory by which the Soul is able to take unto itself attributes of a Divine order, so that it is said to be exalted to the right hand of the Divine.*

It is manifest that to be successful in the treatment of diseases it is necessary above all that we should recognise and deal directly with the primary causes of which they are the effects. Now we find that the great majority of diseases from which mankind suffers may be arranged as to such causes in the following groups :—

(a) Those due to violation or neglect of hygiene, public or personal, including such as are caused by overcrowding, dangerous trades, food adulteration, etc.

(b) Those due to dietetic errors, *viz.*, overfeeding and gluttony, the excessive use of flesh foods, alcohol, narcotics, etc.

(c) Those due to the premature exhaustion of vital force or nervous energy, the result of the haste to be rich, and the too strenuous struggle for purely egoistic ends which characterizes our modern civilization, aided by the depleting effects of the passions hate, envy, greed, sensuality, etc.—which find full play therein ; or to the conditions of hopeless struggle, worry and fear, which together with grinding poverty and semi-starvation are the lot of the many, and which are very largely due to the action of our ruthless competitive commercial system, accentuated by the injustice of many of our social laws.

In the light afforded by this classification we see disease clearly as the result of mistaken (in that he hopes thereby to attain greater happiness) or wrong doing on the part of man, and consequently that they are the result of the violation of Law—physical, ethical, and spiritual. In other words, it is plain that in the last analysis we find that it is to the neglect or violation of the Divine Law of Love that the diseases from the causes given are due ; that selfishness and self-seeking, manifested either positively as in the pursuit of pure self-gratification and the spoliation and oppression of the neighbour, or negatively in an indifference to or total neglect of his needs, is the evil and prolific soil from which they spring. And we may note that this conclusion is in complete harmony with the advice given by The Christ to one whom He had healed—"to go and sin no more, lest a worse thing happen" to him, therein clearly implying that disease was the result of the violation of Divine Law, and could only be escaped by the following of the Good Life.

And that this is no occult or esoteric law hidden from the mass of mankind is manifest from the fact that with reference to the causes of disease tabulated above, even the comparatively unintelligent will freely admit that if only (if, "ah! there's the rub") man were to repent him in the true sense of the word, ceasing to do evil and striving to do well in these respects, earnestly setting about amending his ways as regards himself and his fellows individually and collectively on all planes of his being, that by far the greater number of those ills which afflict him would speedily disappear as these causes ceased to be operative, and be unknown in the course of a generation or two as the hereditary taint became finally eliminated ; and that the consequent enhancement of his vigour and restoration of stamina would most probably render him immune to the remainder, thus demonstrating a life of purity and altruistic works to be the real panacea for disease. And here we may remark that by such a measure of reform not only would disease be swept away, but even evil itself in all its forms and results, and a veritable restoration of the Golden Age would be effected.

Until we have put this method fairly to the test I maintain that no one has the least right to assert that vivisectional methods are in the *least degree necessary* in the fight with disease. Rather, on the contrary, seeing that vivisection, with its endeavour to obtain possible good for oneself, no matter at what cost to others, is pure and undisguised selfishness in one of its worst forms, we should expect that, so far from helping to destroy disease, its teachings would at the best be quite useless for that end, and would rather tend to the darkening and confusion of knowledge on the subject ; and that that is really the case we have ample evidence.

The reason why the method we have referred to—the only radical, rational, and wholly successful one, in that it strikes at the very root and origin of disease—is almost neglected (except in very limited and special directions), and why we find the path of vivisection lauded as the only hopeful one, is, that the love of self still unhappily dominates the mass of mankind, and that such reform as that spoken of above would involve *self-sacrifice*. And rather than face this alternative man prefers to retain his luxuries, vices and follies, and to follow what is to him the infinitely more easy and agreeable course advocated by the vivisectors, to attempt to wring from the involuntary sufferings of *others* the knowledge that he hopes may save him from the disease and death which are the inevitable results of his own transgressions. Truly this is a veritable and literal appeal to Beelzebub to cast out himself and his works ; for, in the words of the late Dr. Anna Kingsford, " it is black or evil magic which in order to cure a patient first transfers his complaint to an innocent victim. Whilst the true magic is that of the Pure Life, which heals without blood and gives health without disease." It is this which indeed we truly need, and it is the condition of disregard for that life which is so marked a characteristic of this ultra-materialistic age that constitutes the real difficulty to the establishment of the reform we are striving for, and the final victory of our cause. This being so, let us never forget that our propaganda can only find an abiding foundation in the spiritual realm, or, to put it in another form, that it is all important for us as anti-vivisectors to remember that whilst using strenuous efforts in exposing the theories of this science, " falsely so called," and in condemning its methods, and whilst earnestly appealing to the humane sentiments and better nature of our fellows, endeavouring to show them that there are means no end can justify, our supreme effort should be directed to the awakening of their spiritual perception, so that they may be led to see the real beauty and power of the Pure Life, and, realizing this, that they may be enabled thereby to fully understand the false principle upon which vivisection rests, the true diabolism of its practice, and that it is necessarily the very antithesis and, indeed, negation of all that is of the divine. For the day that sees such an awakening when men so aspire as to realize these things will assuredly see vivisection and all its kindred evils and effects overthrown and made to vanish into the darkness of the past.

ROBERT H. PERKS, M.D., F.R.C.S.

PSALM LXXXII.

(A NEW READING.)

The Lord is in the congregation of the Mighty Ones[1] : He is the Eternal Judge among the Gods.[2]

How long will men judge unjustly that they may screen the persons of those who do wickedness ?[3]

Judge ye for the poor and the orphaned heart ; seek justice for the afflicted and needy ones.[4]

Deliver the helpless and suffering ones out of the hands of the wicked oppressors.[5]

They know not the truth, neither will they understand ; they continue in the darkness, and their evil deeds move even the foundations of the Earth.[6]

The Lord called unto the Gods and unto all the children of the Most High, that they should now execute just judgment upon the Earth for the Deliverance of all who are in bondage and tribulation.

---

[1] *The Congregation of the Christ-Souls.*

[2] *The Celestial Hierarchy spoken of as the Gods.*

[3] *The way judgment has so long been given.*

[4] *The defenceless have always suffered through the false judgments given by men.*

[5] *The Inquisition, Ecclesiastical, Scientific and Social.*

[6] *The effect of evil upon the Planet.*

EDITORIAL NOTES.

THE ANTI-
VIVISECTION
CONGRESS.

The Congress held from July 6th to 10th was most memorable. It embraced in its scope every aspect of Humane Endeavour, though the dominating note was one of complete deliverance for the Creatures from the power of the Vivisector. It sought to bring together all the workers within the various sections of the Humane Movement, and it was crowned with great success. For though there were those who could not agree with the broad basis of the Congress, and who consequently stood aloof, yet every section was well represented, and all were in their hearts workers for the total abolition of the awful work done within the Physiological Laboratories. The whole atmosphere bespoke serious and earnest endeavour to overthrow the powers of evil lying behind Vivisection. One great purpose seemed to move the hearts of all present, namely, how best to accomplish the Deliverance of the Creatures. Even the question of Vivisection did not occupy the whole platform, for the broader aspects of Humaneness were fully dealt with in many papers. The taking of the lives of the Creatures for purposes of food and clothing was shown to be equally cruel, and opposed to a true Humaneness. Even within the Medical section was this aspect ably presented, and the fallacies of those who argue for the necessity of taking the life of the Creatures for food and clothing fully exposed.

*　　*

THE WONDERFUL
UNANIMITY
OF AIM.

The Congress was memorable in many ways. It was memorable for the unanimity of spirit which prevailed upon the great issues before it. The spirit of international brotherhood was most evident. It was indeed beautiful to witness so much true harmony amongst such a diversity of tongues, such an unanimity of thought and feeling in the midst of such a variety of mind and national sentiment. It revealed anew the great and beautiful truth that all Souls are one in their true nature and life, that where the spiritual rules diversity never leads to difference and separation, and that the same Divine Spirit pulses in all hearts, even amid the diversity of mind, national sentiment and racial feeling. It was indeed good to feel how true all those Souls were who came to the Congress, how deeply imbued they were with the one great spirit of universal kindredship in which even the Creatures had a place. And it augurs well for the future work of the various societies associated with the Congress. For the whole effect of the gatherings must be to bind together more closely in the bonds of most sacred service all who had the privilege of attending them, and to inspire them and strengthen them in their work at home.

*   *   *

THE MEDICAL
SECTION AND
ITS WORK.

The Congress was likewise memorable for the number of Medical men and women who read papers against the practice of Vivisection. In a profession whose whole practice ought to be founded upon the most Humane principles and carried out as a Spiritual Science, it has meant much for those who have truly sought to follow a sane pathology and to work from a spiritual hypothesis and basis, because the whole profession has lost what spiritual genius it had, followed the path of a false science, and bowed the knee to Baal in their worship of a system whose every method is wholly materialistic and the negation of true spiritual being and experience. It has meant much for those who have found the true path to stand up against the system, to refuse to accept their panaceas built up out of the supposed excellent and truly enlightening and benefiting results of the experimentations within the Physiological Laboratories, to affirm the knowledge of the truer way and repudiate what they believed to be false, and to throw the strength of their influence and the value of their knowledge and experience into the effort to accomplish the perfect deliverance of all the Creatures. It has meant much to them in the Profession where the false system is so ardently believed in and followed ; but this very fact has revealed the true spirit within them, and the noble heroism of their conduct. It reveals them to be true lovers and helpers of Humanity, Souls who desire to be true Physicians. It was indeed good to meet and hear so many of the Profession plead

for a true Science, Human and Spiritual, pure in all its
ways and compassionate in its methods, humane in its
feelings and Divine in all its purposes.

* * *

QUESTIONS OF
FOOD AND
ADORNMENT.

The Congress was likewise memorable
for the introduction into its deliberations of the other aspects of the
Humane Movement. It has not
always been easy to introduce at
gatherings of Anti-vivisectionists the questions of food and
adornment without friction. Even amongst those who
have been most strenuously opposed to the whole system
of Vivisection have these questions, equally relevant and
urgent, been opposed. Vivisection has been denounced
with all the energy at their command, and its cruel nature
exposed ; but the equal cruelty of taking the lives of
the Creatures for their beautiful coverings as articles of
raiment and adornment, and their flesh for food, has been
not only left untouched, but refused a place in the deliberations. Nay, the questions have not only been
refused a place, but the practices have been viewed as
quite legitimate and even necessary, and the cruelties
associated with them as something quite distinct from
those arising out of the practice of Vivisection. But in
the Congress these questions occupied as large a place
as that of Vivisection, and were generally viewed as other
forms of the like evil, and as necessary to be opposed as
Vivisection. Adornment at the expense of the Creatures
was shown to be as great a cruelty to the Creatures, and
a practice just as lacking in Humaneness as Vivisection
itself. So strongly indeed was the case put that there
were present those who felt that to wear the coverings
of the Creatures was a degradation, and that they would
no longer do so. It was indeed a joy to observe how
well the papers were received which pleaded for a Humaneness full-rounded, touching every side, leading the life
to simplicity and purity of adornment which left no evil
in its path and brought no suffering to the Creatures,
teaching that Humane Life which would scorn to make
use of the Creatures in any way that would impose pain,
hardship and anguish upon them. And in this the
promoters of the Congress accomplished a great work ;
for it led many of its members to the larger vision of the

mission by which the Deliverance of the Creatures is to
be accomplished.

*   *   *

THE MOST
MEMORABLE
SPIRITUAL
FEELING.

The Congress was also memorable
for the profound spiritual feeling which
pervaded it. The whole atmosphere
was electric with a spirit other than
that which usually is found at such
gatherings. It was "religious" in
the truest and most beautiful sense. Ecclesiastical
signs were not present ; ostentatious display was absent ;
but the Divine Spirit was present, and so the gatherings
were full of Soullic force and power. The inner life
was not forgotten in the deliberations. The true religious feeling was appealed to, quickened and strengthened. The very highest ideals were set before the
members and visitors ; the Christ-life was upheld as the
sublimest aim in life, the Christ-service unto all creatures
and races, as the most beautiful and fruitful and God-like.
The Congress has only been held, but the issues of it will
be more fully witnessed after many days. Its sessions
have closed, but its influences have gone out into many
lands. The deliberations of its members have ended,
but its noble spirit and endeavours still live, and will
continue to live and find new embodiments and manifestations. It will have become unto many the instrument of power through which there may be effectually
voiced the truest and noblest desires and purposes
of the heart towards all the Creatures, as well as the
rallying ground where all Nations may meet in the
spirit of brotherhood, and all true workers find their
inspiration for a service so full-rounded that it will touch
every aspect of the Humane question and so every sphere
of human experience. Thus will the Golden Age be
made more and more possible, and the reign of the Christhood realized.

ANSWERS TO CORRESPONDENTS.

*Is not God responsible for the Fall, whether of the individual
Soul or the Planet, seeing that He fashioned both, and must
have known their limitations and have foreseen the rising of the
conditions by which the Fall was brought about?*

This is one of the most profound mysteries which the Soul
has to face. It is one of those mysteries which belong alone

to the Divine and which cannot be explained in terms understandable to the general public. It is a mystery whichever way it may be viewed, whether as something which God permitted to take place in the history of both the Planet and her children for some hidden but glorious purpose, or something which He purposed as a part of the spiritual evolution of both Soul and Planet. But to take the latter view and postulate the Fall with all its attendant evils as an integral part of the Divine Purpose in the evolution of Planet and Soul, is to make the Divine the direct author of all the evil in the world, so that evil even in its worst forms would be a good in itself not to be condemned in its manifestations nor too readily eliminated from life. It would also make all human endeavour to eradicate evil, to be either a labour which was in opposition to the Divine Purpose, or an exaltation of the human ideal at the expense of the Divine. Yet even those who accept such a hypothesis would shrink from the very thought of supposing that their inner sense of good was superior to that of the Divine, or that their earnest endeavours to change all evil conditions were to be compared to the vast spiritual forces set in motion from the Divine Kingdom with a view to the final overthrow of all evil.

The other hypothesis is less difficult to follow, because it does not involve the Divine Love and make evil the offspring of that Love. It is less difficult to follow because we may find experiences in our life which may be taken to be analogous to the relationship of the Soul to the Divine. It may seem difficult to realise that the Divine Love in fashioning the Soul gives unto it as a Spiritual Individuation whose nature is potentially Divine, the inherent power to choose for itself the path along which it will go. What was true of the individual Soul was also true of the whole system of Souls upon this Planet, and even of the Planet-Soul. It is of the very nature of the Divine Love that it imparts its own Nature to all its children, whether Planet or individual Soul ; and it is an essential element of that Love that there must ever be perfect freedom of action so that all the children may grow up in their own distinctive way. And it was this freedom of action on the part of both the Planet-Soul and the Human Soul which made the Fall possible. The Fall of the Planet as a system was occasioned through the changing of the elemental kingdoms, and the fall of the Human Races was brought about through the influences of these kingdoms upon them.

THE EDITOR.

THE WORK OF THE LATE
ANNA KINGSFORD, M.D., AND EDWARD
MAITLAND, B.A.*

THE work accomplished by the late Dr. Anna (Bonus) Kingsford and Edward Maitland is not one which is easily estimated. Indeed, we question whether anything like an adequate estimate could be given, so comprehensive was the scope of their work, and far-reaching in its influences. We might even question whether their real work has been understood by those who might be spoken of as their fellow-labourers in the great field of service, whether the great purpose of their mission has not been lost sight of because of giving unto it too narrow a scope or a meaning which is altogether inadequate. Such things as they accomplished could not be numerically stated ; nor is the greatness of their mission to be weighed by any phenomenal results upon the outer planes. Because their work was more than any outward plane mission could be. Whilst it took the work upon the physical spheres within its scope, it extended beyond them into the spiritual. It embraced the objective fields, but its foundations and inspiration were in the subjective. It dealt with the phenomenal effects, but also with the causes which it discovered through contact with the Spiritual Spheres. They both saw the manifestations which we all witness ; but they were also led to witness the subjective effects. They beheld the Creatures writhing within the Physiological Laboratories, as they passed through the fearful ordeals imposed upon them in the name of Science and Humanity ; but they were at last led to also behold who the Creatures were who so suffered, and to understand the nature and origin of the dreadful conditions which had brought about all their sufferings. Nay, they even saw the inner meaning of the insane pursuit of knowledge along the lines of Material Science as expounded by the leaders of Vivisection, beheld the forces which lay behind many

---

* Read at the International Anti-vivisection and Animal Protection Congress, Caxton Hall, July 6-10th.

of the chief apostles of the monstrous heresy in their conduct within the Laboratories, and had given unto them the knowledge of the unspeakable issues of that conduct.

When Anna Kingsford set out on her beautiful mission, whose purpose was to pass through the Physiological Schools which were then open to women so as to know from experience what those schools were in their nature and ways, and to be able to demonstrate how it was possible to acquire sufficient knowledge of Physiology and Medicine so as to take the Medical Degree without having the knowledge gained through the unspeakable demonstrations made upon the Creatures who anguish within the prison-houses, she little imagined what experiences lay before her, and how she and Edward Maitland would be called upon by the Powers of the Invisible World to give to the Western world a view of Vivisection which would at last bring about such a change in the field of Medical Research that the practice of Vivisection would not only be looked upon as a mistaken Pathology arising out of ignorance of the true laws of life on the part of the profession, but an actual crime against the whole of the Human Race. She did not then foresee all that would arise out of her mission ; whither the path she had taken would lead her ; the fearful sufferings which must needs accompany her along that path and arise out of her walking in it ; the strange and, what has appeared to some people to be, inexplicable experiences which would become her portion ; the profound meaning of the terrible evil which, with her colleague, she was called to expose both as to its nature and issues. She did not then anticipate all the revelations which afterwards came to her concerning the more than material phenomena which always accompany the work of experimentation within the Laboratories, and the spiritual consequences which follow these dark deeds. For though she knew that it was to be part of her mission to effect the deliverance of the Creatures from the tyranny of the worshippers at the shrine of this modern Moloch, yet did she not then realize all that the inner meaning of her mission implied, nor its relation to the fuller and more perfect deliverance and redemption of all the Creatures from their sad and ofttimes painful limitations through the upliftment, the ennoblement and complete Redemption of the various branches of the Human Race. It was not until she and her colleague seemed to be almost withdrawn from the special work of dealing with Vivisection upon the physical spheres, that the real nature of the mission came to her. For she had to be withdrawn from the more outward spheres of activity in order that she and her colleague might be able to carry out a work whose nature was such that it led them into experiences which took them more and more away from the outer spheres of service, and were the means of causing nearly all those who formerly had been their friends to forsake them. They were both led to see that the whole question of Vivisection belonged to the spiritual realm and not merely to the physical, and that it was but part of the manifestation of deep-seated evils whose nature no one could have imagined unless shown to them from the Spiritual World. They were called very especially to a work for which their strange experiences fitted them, to carry out which they had often to leave the ordinary paths of service and follow one which brought upon them much sorrow and anguish of heart, and upon their fair names obloquy and scorn. For they had to be the Apostles of the new vision that was to be given unto the soul by means of which the whole materialistic systems —Scientific, Ecclesiastical and Theological—should at last be overthrown—systems of which Vivisection is the most satanic exposition. They were called to be the Apostles of that new vision wherein the true nature of Man and Creature is made obvious, by means of which life is to be lifted far above the planes of mere organic matter and shown to be entirely spiritual in its nature ; to touch with its magic wand the Creature Kingdom and make all its inhabitants appear in their *real life* as spiritual organisms rather than material, as elementary Human Souls on their way to the Human Kingdom ; and to throw such light upon the Human experience as to give unto both the past and the future history of the Soul certain knowledge which testified to the spiritual origin and nature of all true life, and the high destiny unto which it was called when first created. They had not only to contend against a Science which affirmed the necessity of Vivisectional practices for the healing of disease, but to lay sure foundations for the overthrow of the whole system upon which any such doctrine could be built up. They had not only to expose the falsity of the position taken up by Physical Science, and the horrible nature of the phenomena of the evil, with the awful results unto the Creatures ; but very specially they had to make clear the real nature of the Materialistic Systems out of which such beliefs could grow into experimentation.

And in following the path along which they must needs go in order to accomplish their mission, they became subject to experiences of the saddest kind, experiences which caused them to be misunderstood by their intimate friends, and even to be cast off and repudiated by many of them. Whilst they were wholly consecrated to the work of receiving for Humanity a higher and truer vision of all life, both as to its origin and its destiny, they were maligned by those who were at heart enemies of the beautiful mission in which they were engaged ; and by their previous friends the profound spiritual import of their work was so misapprehended and grossly misrepresented that for many years a dark cloud was cast over the Divine work accomplished through them. For their work's sake they were made to pass through fires of trial which imposed upon them sufferings beyond the power of tongue or pen to portray ; and these terrible trials were intensified by the attitude of those who should have been able to apprehend the sublime nature and purpose of their work, to enter into real sympathy with them in their most difficult task and support them by their loving thoughts and co-operation, and to defend both them and their mission against the calumniators who were only too anxious to injure them and to make their mission ineffectual.

It is one thing to now look at their work, to behold it in its manifoldness and discern its high and holy and all-embracing nature, and to turn to them with thoughts of admiration and gratitude for their splendid and noble heroism on behalf of truth and righteousness; but how very differently were they dealt with when they were doing the great service on behalf of the Creatures and the whole Human Race? It is now one thing to recognise the meaning of their work as expounded in " The Perfect Way or the Finding of Christ," and " Clothed with the Sun," but it was verily another thing to be of them when they were proclaimed by not a few to be *the Apostles of Antichrist*. In these days they are being hailed by many as belonging to the world's Illuminati; they are being crowned with the laurels given to Prophets and Sages; they are being called Apostles of the Christhood that is to adorn this distraught earth soon and turn its planes into scenes of beautiful Redeemed Life wherein all things are pure and good; and all life finds help to enable it to grow and find its perfect fulfilment. Would that something of that appreciation had been bestowed upon them in their lives! It would have helped to dry up their tears of anguish and ease their pain. Verily they passed through the valley of Baca (or Weeping) where were the pools full of Soul-tears. But they passed through even in their anguish as those who were more than conquerors, though no cornet sounded the jubilation of their triumph. They were of the world's noblest heroes, though no acclamation of the world's approval greeted them. They were Deliverers and Redeemers, though their lives were turned into Gethsemane and Calvary. Out of their experiences were born those new visions of all life in its inherent properties, the purpose for which Life was fashioned and individuated, and the high and glorious destiny unto which it is to attain through the deliverance of all who are in bondage (Man and Creature), and the redemption of every one unto the true ways of life, the ways of perfect purity, perfect service, through perfect love.

It might be well to present in a brief and succinct

form the work specially accomplished by both of them, lest it should appear to some as if our paper were more a plea for their recognition as true Reformers and Seers than a presentation of the work done by them.

1st. It should be borne in remembrance that Anna Kingsford demonstrated to the whole Medical Faculty that woman was capable of taking her true place by the side of man in the service of life, and that in order that a student should qualify for the degree of M.D. it was not necessary for him or her to pass through the Physiological Laboratories. This was a work of no small importance, accomplished in the very environment of one of the worst centres of vivisectional experimentation ; and to all students who are humane in their sympathies, and who desire to escape the unspeakable tragedies wrought within the demonstration classes, it should be an example full of encouragement to them to follow the same path.

2nd. She likewise exposed the whole system of modern Therapeutics as fallacious because built up upon wrong principles. For she showed by her keen perception that the origin of disease is not upon the physical plane of life—that is, the plane of phenomenal effects, but within the mind ; that all organic disease is spiritual in its nature and can be truly eradicated from the system only through the purification of the mind ; and that the true physician is he who knows these things and who heals in that way. She thus lifted, or rather, she sought to lift, the whole Medical Profession out of their materialism, and make their beautiful mission to Humanity something infinitely higher than the earth-bound perfunctory service now alas ! too often rendered by those who have taken upon themselves the Sign of the Healer.

3rd. By the visions vouchsafed to her she saw the terrible effects upon the Astral Kingdom of not only the monstrous heresy of Vivisection, but of the whole system of the traffic in blood pursued and gloried in by the Western World. She beheld that kingdom which should have been pure and helpful to the true evolution

and culture of the Soul, turned into one of blood, so that
the Planet was girdled with a dark belt whose density
was so great and whose elements were so impure, that the
beautiful spiritual magnetic relationship between the
Soul and the Spiritual Heavens was interrupted to such
an extent that, though the Heavens encircled the Planet,
the spiritual life of Humanity languished. And so she
gave to the world a new and true reason for the lack of
true spirituality which has been so characteristic of the
whole Western World even under the profession and
supposed reign of the Christhood, and showed that the
way to return unto true spiritual conditions and realizations was through putting away the whole system of the
traffic in blood, and making manifest true compassion
and love unto all Souls, Human and Creature—a truth
which is now being realized through the new spiritual
conditions springing up everywhere as the outcome of the
purer ways which so many are following in relation to
diet, clothing, and their attitude towards the Creatures
—a truth the fuller realization of which by all compassionate Souls will at last effect the complete deliverance
of all the Creatures, not only from the shameful ordeals
of the Physiological Laboratories, but also from those
of the Abattoirs and Shambles.

4th. Then when we turn to what we may term *the
inner aspects of the mission of herself and her colleague*, we
find that they arrived at the hitherto unknown meaning
of the influences by which Vivisectors are led to pursue
their unspeakable calling. For unto them was it shown
that many of those who practise Vivisection are under
the influence of what may even in these days of greater
spiritual perception and realization be spoken of as demons
—*i.e.*, elemental powers whose magnetic conditions are
in opposition to the true ways of life. It was shown
unto them that not only was Vivisection the embodiment
of the very worst form of the materialistic sacrificial
system, but that its high priests were under the influence
of the very spirit out of which all evil grows, and that
all the terrible things done by them in the Physiological

Laboratories were the manifestations of that diabolical power. And thus they gave a view of Vivisection which is self-interpretive, since it explains by inference how it is that men who should be truly humane, who should understand the true meaning of compassion and pity, and who should be expected to make these beautiful feelings manifest, can pursue a line of conduct whose ways are cruel and whose works are Satanic.

5th. In their experiences it was given unto them also to know that the Creatures were often other than they seemed ; that they were not mere physical organisms with nothing more than animal instincts, but Souls who were on their way to the true Human Kingdom, some of them indeed Souls who had missed their way after arriving upon the Human Kingdom and who had to return into the Creature forms for purposes of purification. It was even given unto them to see the Human Soul looking out through some of the Creature forms, and anguishing within the Physiological Laboratories. And in this beautiful, if in some respects sad, truth they brought into the newer and higher vision of the Life of the World the true meaning of the wonderful intelligence of many of the Creatures, the truly Human affection and devotion which ofttimes may be witnessed in the Creatures, and the reality of their powers to endure suffering and even anguish like human lives. And they thus showed that the Creatures were parts of the organic whole, the little children within the household, the elementary Human Souls within the great Spiritual System of the world who were to be cared for as those who were to attain with ourselves the fulness of Soul-life before the Divine, the crown of spiritual manhood and womanhood, even the Life of the Divine consciously realized.

6th. And then all these things were crowned by the yet larger work of being the instruments through whom the falsity of the entire sacrificial system was to be exposed ; how that system, Scientific, Scholastic and Ecclesiastic, had arisen and the terrible evils which had always followed in its path ; how it blighted the aspirations of the Soul and prevented its true evolution ; and how Humanity had been dwarfed by it and robbed of the Divine birthright which was to have been and shall yet be the heritage of all Souls, *viz.*, the Christhood Estate. And in this they were the heralds of the Coming Christhood ; the harbingers of the restored Golden Age when all the world should be once more young and its Kingdoms, Planes and Spheres know evil no more ; the prophets through whom the Divine once more spake, and the wisdom of the Ancients was once more recovered.

J. TODD FERRIER.

TRUTHS WHICH SHOULD BE KNOWN.

Are not two sparrows bought for one farthing ? Yet the Heavenly Father taketh notice of them.

Of how much more value is a man than a sheep ? Yet the Heavenly Father careth for the lambs of the fold.

The ox knoweth the crib wherein its owner hath placed it, though the owner knoweth not unto what end the ox was fashioned : but in the day wherein the owner of the ox understandeth why it was fashioned, he who killeth the ox shall be as one who slayeth a man.

The horse is a useful creature. He hath understanding, though he is held and guided by bit and bridle : but do those who use him know that when he looketh at them, he doeth so with the eyes of a man-child ?

The dog is a faithful companion. How great is his affection and beautiful his devotion ! When he respondeth to his master's call he doeth so with the impulse of a child, for he is a little man-child.

Hurt not therefore one of these little ones for whom the Heavenly Father careth.

The Herald of the Cross.

Vol. v.   New Series.   September, 1909.   No. 9.

THE BESTOWAL OF GIFTS.

The Lord, when He ascended on high, gave gifts unto all who were able to receive them.

For He who ascended was He who also first descended into the lower states upon the Earth that He might lead away from captivity all who were bound.

For He took unto Himself the forms of sinful men that He might know, by passing through them, the depth of our humiliation and the bitterness of our sin.

Through bodies like unto that of our humiliation did He come to taste the anguish of all Souls within the hells who cry by reason of their bondage and suffering.

For in His humiliation He descended even unto the lowest hell, that He might deliver those who were held fast by the chains of evil.

But now that He hath ascended from these states, and risen unto the Heavens, once more hath He poured forth the gifts of His love that through them all who are yet bound may find deliverance.

SOME OF THE MASTER'S WORKS.

THE way that the Blessed Master wrought the great works attributed to Him in the Gospel Records, was not that so frequently represented. He has been thought of as one who controlled the Laws of Nature at will and made the elements obey His command. And this power in Him has been taken as the sure sign of His Christhood, the evidence of His Divine Nature, the testimony of His Divine mission. The fact that there have been many workers of signs and wonders in Nature, many who have controlled the elements at will and made them do their bidding long before the manifestation of the Christhood as well as in these days, seems to be overlooked by them. For many have wrought great things with the elements in past ages who knew nothing of the beautiful state known as Christhood. There were many who knew the nature of the elements through having watched them, and who arrived at the knowledge of how to make use of them. There were even some who gained the knowledge of the inherent magnetic properties of many of the elements and who applied that knowledge in working wonders with them. They wrought marvellous things by means of their knowledge, things not always wise or good, indeed ofttimes things which were hurtful and which became the instruments of great evil. If the past history of this Planet could be seen and understood by those who set such store upon what they call the "miraculous," they would see a history whose events were often of the most miraculous order. When the true meaning of the history of many of the works of those periods covered by the Druidical circles, is known, much that is now wondered at and viewed with astonishment because of its greatness, will be explained. The Druidical Circles with their enormous monumental stones, not to speak of the work of such piles as the Great Pryamids with their stupendous blocks, will have new light thrown upon them, both as to their purpose and the means by which they were raised. Often has it been conjectured that they were raised by some power now not known. They were the outcome of a power over the forces and elements of Nature which, if known and applied to-day, would by many still be accounted as miraculous. But they were not raised in an age of great spiritual power and attainment. They were the works of purely Occult power, not the manifestations of the genius of Christhood. For, whilst Occult knowledge and power may be great, it need not necessarily be spiritual ; whereas the power of the Christhood is always spiritual in its nature and manifestations. And whilst Occult powers may be used, and have been used in the past ages, to overcome the natural laws of the Planet and to turn them to other uses, the powers of a Christhood could not be put to any use other than those in harmony with the true laws of the Planet. For it is of the very nature of a Christhood to restore to their original nature and purpose the elements of the Planet, and cause to become truly equilibriated all the magnetic forces within the various spheres. And when we closely examine the works wrought by the Master, we find that they were all of the kind which brought into harmony upon the various spheres upon which the work was accomplished, *the laws of true being.* They were works by means of which the spiritual within the sufferer was restored, the disorganized life brought into a state of true equilibrium, and the suspended true laws of being made to fulfil their functions. Let us look at some of the works of the Master, that we may witness what actually took place.

THE HEALING OF THE LEPER.

It is recorded that a leper came to Him with the words upon his lips, " Master, if Thou wilt, Thou canst make me clean." To which request it is said the Master replied, " I will, be thou made whole."

The narrative would give any reader the impression that the mere word of the Master healed the afflicted one immediately. And many have been thus misled and have believed that it only required the word of the Master to be spoken in order to effect the healing of any

disease. Had such a thing been possible, we can well
conceive of a Galilee and Judea and even Samaria without
a sick home or life, so great was His love that He would
gladly have healed all in those parts. But in all that
He did as well as said, there had to be the right conditions.
There were times, it is recorded, when He could not do
any mighty works because of their unbelief.

The conditions essential were two-fold. They were
the right condition of mind of the recipient, and the
right life to be lived by the recipient. The right condition
of mind implied perfect trust in the Divine Love, and
perfect sincerity in the request. The right condition of
life meant the following of *the true path* whose ways were
all pure, the laying aside of all ways which were not pure,
so that mind and body would be able to cast off from
them the injurious elements and influences from which
the affliction had sprung. Without these conditions no
affliction could be truly healed. When we say *truly
healed*, we mean, the *perfect* healing of the whole man.
To merely remove the outward manifestations for a time
must not be mistaken for true healing. When the healing
which the Master gave took place, the entire manhood
or womanhood was equilibriated. And to have that
accomplished was to not only heal the sufferer of the
disease from which he was suffering, but to lift all his
powers out of the wrong conditions out of which his sickness or illness was generated, and to bring them into a
state of perfect harmony.

When, therefore, the leper appealed to the Master to
heal him, we may readily understand that there were
things said which are not recorded, and that the event
had a profounder significance than appears in the record.
To heal leprosy was not simply to remove the superficial
sore which was the manifestation of a deep-seated evil,
but to so change all the spiritual conditions within the
mind of the sufferer that new spiritual forces would flow
from the Spiritual Heavens into the Soul conveying that
Divine magnetism by means of which perfect life would
be realized. And through the change of conditions in
the mind and the inflowing of the Divine magnetism to

the Soul, the entire life in all its ways and aims would become changed and the outward man be renewed through the renewal of the inward man. And the process would be comparatively quick or slow in proportion to the inward state, the quickness or otherwise of the unfoldment of the new life. And when it is said that the Master replied to the leper, saying, " I will, be thou made whole," we must understand that the healing was of a Divine order and not merely physiological, that it was Spiritual and not simply material, that it was first *inward* and then outward, the outward being only the phenomenal results of the interior change. The power which was in the Master was the power of the Divine Love and Wisdom, and the magnetism which flowed from Him to aid the person afflicted, was the Divine magnetism.

But that magnetism could only flow towards the one who attracted it through the innermost life longing for its help. The Master willed through the Divine Love in Him, to make all the children of the Heavenly Father whole, to heal them even unto the uttermost, just as the ever Blessed One longs to make His children perfect; but the conditions had to be provided, as without these there could be no true healing. And these new conditions the Master could only aid to bring about within and around the leper. From the Christ-presence there will ever flow beautiful healing influences; but only when there are present, and in proportion to the strength of, the inward desires of the sufferer for such spiritual healing as He has to impart. Wherever the Divine Presence is, there may complete restoration take place; but it must always have the right conditions both within and around the one to be healed. For the Divine Healing is no mere suspension for a time of outward manifestations such as may be accomplished through what is known as mesmeric and hypnotic powers; it is such a healing as will restore the individual to that condition of life within in which all the powers of the Soul are equilibriated, and will make the life upon every sphere immune to disease of any kind. It is true healing; for the individual is *made whole.* Harmony is restored within the various spheres. The magnetic forces of Heaven flow into the Soul, and from the Soul outward, purifying and perfecting every sphere.

When the Master was on His way to the City of Jerusalem, there came to Him to be healed one who was a leper.

The afflicted one had long desired healing, but knew not how to get it ; for the physicians were powerless to help him.

Then he heard from some kind friend of the beautiful works of the Master, how the afflicted found in Him unfailing compassion and healing, no earnest seeker being turned away without blessing ;

And how that the Master was approaching the City, and would pass near to the place where he dwelt.

Therefore, when the Master drew near to his dwelling-place, the leper came out and entreated Him that He would help him and take away the loathsome disease.

He spake unto the Master, saying unto Him, " If Thou wilt Thou can'st make me whole."

And the Master approached him, beholding how greatly the sufferer longed for healing, and how his life was inwardly changed, said unto him, " Be Thou made whole from this hour."

And the leprosy left him, and he was made whole.

*   *   *

A PROFOUND ALLEGORY.

Let us now look at a work of a different order in which the Master was not asked for the manifestation of His healing power in restoring health to one who had been long afflicted, but who nevertheless was healed by Him through simply touching His garment. It is recorded that when the Master was surrounded by a throng of people, of whom many pressed upon Him, one of them, an afflicted woman, made her way through the throng to touch the hem of His garment, believing that by so doing she would be healed. And it is said that when the Master felt her touch He asked who it was who had done so, as He perceived that power had gone from Him.

The incident is based upon a truth of the most profound nature. It was truly a miracle, but not such a miracle as is generally supposed. What could the meaning be of power going from the Master, and as the result of one specially touching Him out of many who were around Him ? To lose power meant that a great change had taken place in Him as the result of having been touched by the afflicted one. Of course, in the incident it is taken to mean that the woman only touched the hem of His garment, and that spiritual power went out from Him to heal her. But something far more profound in its meaning happened. The whole incident, far from being a merely outward event, was one relating to the tragic and unspeakably sad experiences of the Sin-offering. The loss of power by the Christ was the loss unto Him of the Estate. With that loss power went from Him. And it went from Him through His raiment having been touched, *i.e.*, through the garment of Christhood which was spotless having been laid aside in order that He might stoop to effect the Redemption of the Planet through changing and purifying its Astral Kingdom. And the woman who was said to have pressed upon Him in the throng, knowing well in her heart that to touch the hem of His garment meant healing for her, was in very deed the Soul itself.

It was a true miracle, a restoration of the laws of the Soul's true being which had long been out of harmony, through the touching of the hem of the garment of the Christhood Estate, and which was made possible through the Sublime Christ-Soul passing through the thronged Astral Kingdom in His wonderful ministry of Redemption. Power went forth from Him to heal. He gave up His life for that purpose. He laid it *down* to accomplish that beautiful end. He passed from His Christhood to tread the path which the Soul had taken, and through touching Him in the path the Soul was healed.

Here, then, is a sublime truth concerning an inward
spiritual and profound experience effected through the
Soul finding the Christhood, touching only the hem of
the garment of that wonderful Divine Estate, in the full
assurance that in doing so all evil would depart from
life and perfect restoration to spiritual equilibrium
would be effected. The outward history has obscured
the inward meaning. Beautiful indeed to think of the
afflicted one being healed through just touching the hem
of the Master's garment amid the throng ; but more
beautiful to know that the healing was that of the Soul as
the outcome of the great love of the Christ-Soul entering
into its very conditions, bearing the burden of its affliction,
and so redeeming it through the Divine Power or Virtue
that went from Him for its healing

*The Master when speaking unto those friends who
were of the innermost group of the disciples concerning all that must happen unto Him when He
left them, presented one of the terrible experiences
which would come to Him in His Office as Redeemer
as He bore the burden of the Ransom, by illustrating
it with the story of one who had been healed of an
affliction which drew upon the sufferer's life so much
that no physician could heal the affliction.*

*" A certain woman had an affliction for thirty
years.*

*To try and rid herself of it she spent all that she
had possessed, but no physician could heal her of
her infirmity.*

*But one day she heard of a healer who was passing
through the Country in which she dwelt, whose
wonderful power to heal had become known in many
cities.*

*It had likewise been told her that if only she could
touch the hem of his garment she would find the
healing she sought.*

So she eagerly set out to find the Healer.

*But when she found him, to approach him was
most difficult, so hidden was he by the people who*

thronged about him ; and only by pushing her way through the throng was she able to reach Him.

And she kept saying unto herself, ' If only I may but touch the hem of his garment I shall be healed.'

And when she reached him so that the hem of his garment could be touched, the affliction was healed.

But the healer was conscious amid the throng that he had been specially touched by some one, for there had gone forth from him the power which he possessed.

So he inquired of those immediately about him who it was who had touched him.

But they, perceiving not, neither knowing what manner of woman it was who had pressed through the throng to touch him, wondered that he should inquire.

Then did she who had been so greatly afflicted, and whose touch had not only brought healing to herself but impoverishment of power unto him, come to tell him what she had done and how the touching of the hem of his garment had healed her.

And she was troubled and fearful at what she had done.

But he said unto her, ' Daughter, be of good cheer ! Thy faith hath saved thee.' "

*   *   *

TALITHA CUMI.

Let us look at yet another incident which, according to the Records, and in the judgment of most readers of the Records, is viewed as still more wonderful. We refer to the raising from the dead of Jairus' daughter. It has been made use of by many writers in order to prove that the Master had power over what is known as physical death so as to raise anyone from the dead at will. And as the result of that interpretation many have gone to sleep peaceably, believing that He would some day raise them up also in the body of flesh. But if that were the true interpretation of the incident we cannot but wonder that he did not abolish death at once ; for it cannot be imagined by any one who truly believes in the reality of His great love, that death to Him was not the cause of great grief, and that, had He been able, He would gladly have made it impossible. It is quite true that He came to abolish death ; but it was by overthrowing him who had the power to impose it, *viz.*, The Astral Kingdom. He came to change the power within that Kingdom from one which was inimical to the life upon every sphere, to be one which would become an instrument by means of which perfect Redemption would be wrought for the whole Human Race. For when the Astral Kingdom within and around Humanity is purified, and so redeemed, what is now known as death will no more have any place. There will be change as the Soul passes on to higher conditions, but it will be more like a transmutation than a dissolution.

The incident given in the Records is not so difficult to understand as would appear from the manner of its presentation. Indeed, even in the Records it is stated that the blessed Master said that the little maid was not dead but asleep. To the friends present she must have appeared to have left them ; but when the Master saw her He knew that she had not, but that she was in a state of deep sleep outwardly, because the Soul was elsewhere. So few seem to realize that the Divine Love giveth unto His Beloved Ones in sleep, giveth unto them visions of the night wherein the Soul receiveth much Heavenly Wisdom. They take for granted that whilst the body rests the whole life is asleep, not knowing that the hours of physical rest are not infrequently those of real spiritual education wherein the interior life is illumined from the Spiritual Heavens. And there are times when the Soul appears to leave the outward form, so calm and peaceful are the conditions that they might easily be mistaken for the passing away of the life. For when the Soul is receiving inward knowledges, all the powers of life seem to be indrawn. And it happens at times that the experiences are of such a nature (not peaceful and beautiful as we have instanced in many cases, but such as to fill the mind with troubled thoughts) that even apparent illnesses are the accompanying phenomena, illnesses which none but a truly Spiritual Physician like the Master could diagnose.

It is in this light that the incident in the Ruler's home should be viewed, a light which illumines the incident in all its parts and gives to it a meaning at once beautiful in its spiritual significance, and so reasonable that the mind does not feel demands made upon it to accept and believe that the incident was the local manifestation of the power which the blessed Master exercised over what is known as physical death. For had it actually been such a rising from the dead as is believed by those who view the story in the Records as literal history, it would be most difficult to conceive that the Master who was universal in His nature, love and compassion, would have only given a few local manifestations of His wonderful power, leaving the vast world of life to go on suffering the darkness, pain and anguish which physical death brings in its train.

The blessed Master when He saw the maid, at once knew her state. He knew that hers was not any ordinary illness issuing in physical dissolution, but was the outcome of spiritual conditions. He beheld her in the deep sleep of one who is receiving Angelic ministration, because He beheld what none other could behold ; not as an ordinary Clairvoyante beholds, but as the Christ. He knew that what was mistaken for the passing away of the Soul, was the placid state associated with the Soul rising on to the Spiritual Heavens, in which the body at times becomes so passive that the ordinary observer might think that what is known as death had taken place. He was therefore able to say, " Give place ; for the maid is not dead, but sleepeth." And though there were those who laughed at Him scornfully, He was soon able to make manifest that what He had said to them was the truth ; for He counselled the return of the Soul and the arising of the maid from her couch.

Such was the miracle, wonderful and beautiful in its spiritual significance, too wonderful for the non-spiritual to understand, too spiritual for the literalist to apprehend ; a miracle which should have been a common

experience, but which could not be because of the Astral
conditions.   But the miracle will now often be repeated ;
for the Astral Kingdom has been greatly changed through
the wonderful redemptive ministry of the Christ-Soul
as He travailed, bearing the burden of the Sin-offering ;
and now the Soul may rise on to the Spiritual Heavens
and always function there.

*There dwelt upon the shores of the Sea of Genesaret
one who was a Ruler in a Synagogue, a man just
and kind whom the people honoured and loved.*

*The same had a little daughter who was subject
at times to illness which made her appear as if she
were suffering from an Eastern fever.*

*On one of these occasions she became so ill,
apparently, that the parents grew most anxious
concerning her and sent for the Master to come to
them.*

*The Master knew the Ruler and at once went to
his home to minister unto his child.   But whilst the
Master was on His way a message was sent to Him
that He was not to trouble to come as the child had
passed away.*

*But the Master nevertheless went to the home.
And when he entered the room where the child lay,
He found both the parents and the friends mourning
for the loss that had come to them.*

*Then said He unto them, " The child is not dead ;
she only sleepeth."   And those who had come to
mourn, scornfully laughed at Him.*

*But the Master beheld the Soul of the child and
spake unto her, saying, " Talitha Cumi " ;   and
she arose from her couch.*

*   *   *

POWER OVER THE ELEMENTS.

One more illustration would we here give of the materialization of the sacred work of the Master, and the consequent loss to the Soul of the inner meaning.   It is
that of the story of the calming of the storm on the
Sea of Galilee.   The incident as it is presented in the

Records is full of dramatic interest. The situations arrest the attention of the reader so much that the obscuration of the meaning of the story is effectually accomplished. The situations are placed upon the physical spheres, and the reader is left to associate them with events upon those spheres, so that their allegorical spiritual significance is lost.

It is said that the disciples took a boat to cross the Sea of Galilee, and that the Christ went with them ; that a storm arose and was so tempestuous that the disciples feared for the safety of the little ship ; that to the amazement of the disciples the Master lay fast asleep in the stern of the boat ; that in their fear they awoke Him asking Him if he did not care lest they should all perish, that He in reply rebuked their faithlessness, and then commanded the tempestuous waters to be still ; and that, as the result of His word, a great calm fell upon the lake.

The story is taken as an instance and illustration of the power of the Master over the elements. It is made use of as a testimony to the Divine power resident in Him. It is sometimes made use of as the foundation of an argument showing forth the power of the Christ over the elements to be a necessary attribute of Christhood, though it is well known that there have been many, especially in the East, who have manifested remarkable power over the elements without possessing the true attributes of a Christhood. Indeed, as we have said, in the greatest Occult ages, those ages in which the powers of the elements were well understood and miraculous things done with them, the ages in which some of the historic stones and monuments were fashioned and raised, the elements were often controlled, though there was an absence of Christhood from the land. For in the great Occult ages marvellous things were accomplished by those who had learned the secrets of Nature.

But the story of the storm on the Sea of Galilee is not of that order, though in the Records it seemeth so to be. It is rather a dramatic setting of one of the most profound experiences through which the Soul passes in its Spiritual

history. It is an epitome of the condition in which the
Soul finds itself now in this cosmos as it makes its passage
over the sea of life.   The little ship was a picture of the
Soul with all its attributes represented by the various
disciples.   The Sea of Galilee was the Spiritual Mind
upon whose waters the Soul, so to speak, is borne.   The
storm-swept waters were all the powers of the Mind
so disturbed by the opposing elemental conditions until
life's experiences were such that they might be most
fittingly described as tempestuous.   The fearful disciples
were the powers of the Spiritual Mind which should
ever be calm, aroused to a sense of spiritual danger
through the adverse conditions overwhelming them.
The Christ who was asleep at the stern of the ship was
the Christ who is potentially in every Soul, the Divine
within the Sanctuary.

The Christ is not absent from the Soul during the
stress and anxiety due to the stormy conditions amid
which the Soul now lives its life, though He is only
potentially in all those Souls who have not yet
arrived at the consciousness of the Divine Presence within
them.   But in all those who had arrived at that blessed
consciousness in past ages, but who again lost the consciousness of the inward Presence, and so of the Christhood which once they knew, the Christ may be said to
be asleep in the stern of the ship amid the tempestuous
seas of life.   Nor are life's storms turned into a great
calm, the Spiritual Mind filled with a beautiful Divine
Peace, and the whole being lifted up into the regions of
true Faith or the Vision of Divine things, until the
sleeping Christ is awakened.   But when He is awakened
then is the miracle wrought within the Mind ; all its
fears generated by the effects of the storm-swept elemental
kingdoms are allayed ; all its beautiful attributes are
revivified from the Divine Presence, and all its powers
restored.

*When the blessed Master found an hour of quiet
with His immediate friends, He spake thus unto them
concerning the experiences through which the Soul
passes when it is beset with conditions which try it—*

"*The Soul is like a ship upon the open Sea when all its attributes are out of true harmony ; it is tossed about upon the tempestuous waves, and is in danger of becoming overwhelmed.*

The mind of the Soul which should be always calm and clear like pellucid waters, is then filled with disturbing elements, so that it cannot reflect unto the Soul the Heavens of its Lord.

Even the powers of the mind itself are so troubled that they fill it with the fear of a great dread, and make it cry out like those who are in dire distress.

For as I have said unto you, the mind of the Soul is the Sea of Galilee ; and the sacred little ship upon it is the Soul, the sacred Ark within which the Divine Presence abides."

In order that they might the better remember and understand the significance of the things of which He had spoken, He told them the allegory of the Stilling of the Storm on the Sea of Galilee.

"*A great Teacher who was sent from the Heavenly Father entered into a little ship with His disciples, and launched into the Deep.*

When in the midst of the Deep, a storm arose and grew tempestuous more and more until it was so great as to almost overwhelm the boat ; and fear laid hold of the disciples.

But the Master was asleep in the hinderpart of the Ship.

Then the disciples came unto Him in great distress and called unto Him to save them.

And when the Master was awakened He asked them why they were so fearful, and how it was that their Spiritual Vision was so easily obscured, and said unto them, ' O ye whose faith is not little ! Wherefore, do ye doubt ? '

And the Master arose and spake unto the storm-tossed waters, saying unto them, ' Peace ! Let there be stillness.' And there was the Great Silence in which the winds and the waves grew calm."

J. TODD FERRIER.

THE COUNSEL OF PERFECTION.[1]

I DREAMED that I was in a large room, and that there were in it seven persons, all men, sitting at one long table ; and each of them had before him a scroll, some having books also ; and all were grayheaded and bent with age save one, and this was a youth of about twenty without hair on his face. One of the aged men, who had his finger on a place in a book open before him, said :

" This spirit, who is of our order, writes in this book, ' Be ye perfect, therefore, as your Father in heaven is perfect.' How shall we understand this word perfection ? " And another of the old men looking up answered, " It must mean Wisdom, for wisdom is the sum of perfection." And another old man said, " That cannot be ; for no creature can be wise as God is wise. Where is he among us who could attain to such a state ? That which is part only, cannot comprehend the whole. To bid a creature to be as wise as God is wise would be mockery."

Then a fourth old man said, " It must be truth that is intended. For truth only is perfection." But he who sat next the last speaker answered, " Truth also is partial ; for where is he among us who shall be able to see as God sees ? "

And the sixth said, " It must surely be Justice ; for this is the whole of righteousness." And the old man who had spoken first, answered him : " Not so ! for Justice comprehends vengeance, and it is written that vengeance is the Lord's alone."

---

[1] DREAMS AND DREAM-STORIES, by the late Dr. Anna (Bonus) Kingsford. Edited by the late Edward Maitland, B.A. This Edition with Preface and Notes by Samuel Hopgood Hart. (See advertisement page).

The little book from which this and the following Dream are taken, contains many Dreams given as " visions in the night " to Mrs. Kingsford, some of which were burdened with a meaning for her that she could not at the time fully apprehend. And it is only in the light of the work accomplished through her that some of them can be fully understood. But even to the general reader, all the Dreams will be found deeply interesting ; and in the Dream-Stories they will find a charm, and much food for thought. (Editor H. of the C.).

Then the young man stood up with an open book in his hand and said : " I have here another record of one who likewise heard these words. Let us see whether his rendering of them can help us to the knowledge we seek." And he found a place in the book and read aloud :

" Be ye merciful, even as your Father is merciful." And all of them closed their books and fixed their eyes on me.*

THE PERFECT WAY WITH ANIMALS.

I SAW in my sleep a carthorse[1] who, coming to me, conversed with me in what seemed a perfectly simple and natural manner, for it caused me no surprise that he should speak. And this is what he said :—

" Kindness to animals of the gentler orders is the very foundation of civilization. For it is the cruelty and the harshness of men towards the animals under their protection which is the cause of the present low standard of humanity itself. Brutal usage creates brutes ; and the ranks of mankind are constantly recruited from spirits already hardened and depraved by a long course of ill-treatment. Nothing develops the spirit so much as sympathy. Nothing cultivates, refines and aids it in its progress towards perfection so much as kind and gentle treatment. On the contrary, the brutal usage and want of sympathy with which we meet at the hands of men, stunt our development and reverse all the currents of our nature. We grow coarse with coarseness, vile with

---

* Anna Kingsford regarded this dream with especial delight " as affording high recognition and encouragement of her labours on behalf of the animals," and Edward Maitland considered that it was " a complete answer to the allegation that the Gospels are silent on the subject of man's treatment of the animals." (Life of A. K., vol. i., p. 172 ; The Story of A. K. and E. M., pp. 134-5). S.H.H., Ed. of 3rd Ed. of last named.

[1] Edward Maitland says : " Whether it was really the spirit of a carthorse, or some other who assumed that aspect, was not stated. We were, however, given to understand that, though animals are rudimentary men, it is a great mistake to limit the intelligence of the spirit in them to that implied by their external forms, upon which their power of expression depends." (Life of A.K., vol. i., pp. 328-9).

reviling, and brutal with the brutality of those who surround us. And when we pass out of this stage we enter
on the next depraved and hardened, and with the bent
of our dispositions such that we are ready by our nature
to do in our turn that which has been done to us. The
greater number of us, indeed, know no other or better
way. For the spirit learns by experience and imitation,
and inclines necessarily to do those things which it has
been in the habit of seeing done. Humanity will never
become perfected until this doctrine is understood and
received and made the rule of conduct."

THE VOICE OF WISDOM.

*Wisdom crieth without. She uttereth her words
of warning in the streets ;*

*She crieth in the chief thoroughfares among the
gatherings of the people ;*

*She openeth all her Gates to the dwellers within
the City, and proclaimeth the Goodness of the Lord.*

*How long will men remain deaf to her crying and
scorn the message which she proclaims ? How long
will their ways be foolish, and they themselves refuse
to seek knowledge and simplicity ?*

*I have called and ye have refused saith the Lord ;
I have stretched forth My hand but ye have
regarded it not ; all My counsel have ye set at naught
and murmured at reproof.*

PSALM CXLVIII.

(A NEW READING)

Praise ye the Lord!

Praise ye the Lord from the high places; praise Him all ye in the Heavens.

Praise ye Him ye who are His Angels and His Heavenly Hosts.

Praise ye Him ye dwellers within the Sun, and ye who are the children of the Moon.

Praise Him all ye dwellers upon the Stars, ye Sons of the Eternal Light.

Praise Him ye Heavens of His Glory, and ye Waters of the Great Deep wherein His Holy Spirit moveth.

Let all praise His Holy Name who spake them into being.

By Him were they established for ever and ever; and His decree will not pass unfulfilled.

Praise the Lord all ye dwellers upon the Earth, ye powers of the heights and the depths:

Ye Mountains whose heights reach the Heavens; and all ye hills with fruitful trees, whose fruits are from the Lord;

Ye who are yet Creatures, the cattle in the valleys and the birds on the wing;

Ye Kings of the Earth amongst the people, ye Princes who execute just judgment;

Young Men and Maidens, the Sires and little Children;

Let all praise the Holy Name, for the Lord alone is the excellent glory of all the Earth and the Heavens.

Let the powers of the Earth become exalted, and the praise of His Saints be raised.

Praise ye the Lord!

EDITORIAL NOTES.

QUESTIONS OF
GRAVE MOMENT. The questions of the hour which are of the most vital moment for the Human Race, are those concerning the attitude of the people to the whole of the Creatures. For until these questions are understood and answered in the right way, the true forward movement of the Human Race will be retarded and its full upliftment made impossible. It is indeed sad to think that the multitudes seem to care for none of these things ; but it is even sadder that so many who should be true workers for the realization of the highest and noblest life in the Individual, the Community and the Nation, should seem to know so little of the real nature of the Creatures and the close relation which they sustain to the Human Race. Men and women take for granted that there is a great and impassable gulf between the Creatures and the Human Kingdom, and this notwithstanding all that Science has to say concerning the evolution of the human form. They are accustomed to think of the Creatures as having a very different kind of life lying behind their forms from that which they themselves possess. They think of them as quite distinct in any real experiences which may come to them, not knowing that *all true life is one*, and that what differentiates the Creatures from the Human is not the *kind* of life, but the limitations under which it makes itself manifest.

*   *   *

WHAT THE PEOPLE
THINK OF THE
CREATURES. How few of those who have to deal with the Creatures behold in them anything more than the physical organism through which the life lying behind expresses itself ? How very few regard them as highly organized sentient lives, capable of feeling and suffering keenly, in some instances feeling deeply and suffering acutely, even apparently more than many human beings ? How very limited is the number of those who truly know what the life is in those Creatures, whose affection, fidelity and devotion might well often put to shame those of the Human Race in whom a true devotion, fidelity and genuine affection have been strangely lacking ? The multitudes have been taught to regard

even the most highly organized Creatures as only so many goods and chattels, things for merchandise and such uses as men and women may wish to put them. They have been long taught to regard their lives as of no value, something of which they have the right to deprive them whenever it seemeth good to them. The taking of their lives in order to provide flesh-foods for the home whose threshold should ever be pure and free from all blood-guiltiness, they have been taught to regard as a necessity in the economy of Nature, and as a Divine provision, and one sanctioned and practised by even the blessed Master. The innumerable Abattoirs within which the lives of the Creatures are shed, and the multitude of Shambles where their poor mutilated forms are exposed for sale in the most disgraceful and shameless way, abundantly testify to the effectiveness of the teaching which the people have received.

*   *   *

THE EFFECTS OF THE FALSE VIEW.

Nor is that all the tragedy. The long ages of such teachings and practices have had a most injurious effect upon both the body and mind of men and women, and upon the whole Animal Kingdom. It has generated in those who have to carry on the business of the Abattoirs and the Shambles an almost inconceivable and inhuman callousness. It has dulled the finer feelings and prevented the outflowing of the noblest emotions in the people, and filled them with a spirit of indifference towards the Creatures even when they know of the sufferings imposed upon them. It has made them the ready dupes of any false system which has demanded the sacrifice of the Creatures, and made them so dull in their innermost senses that though they have had ears to hear and eyes to see, yet have they not heard the groaning of the Creatures as they suffered, nor seen the iniquity of the traffic in their lives. Their spiritual blindness and dullness has enabled those who make merchandise of the lives of the Creatures, to continue the awful traffic in their flesh —a traffic which is one of the most appalling pursuits for men and women to be engaged in ; or to encourage by their own tastes, a traffic which is not only a blot on the escutcheon of modern civilization, the antithesis of the religious ideals professed by the West, but is in its very nature the negation of the divinity of our nature. Many of the terrible conditions of Humanity to-day are at once the issues of the effects of the system upon the physical and spiritual nature of the people, and the adumbrations upon which may be traced something of the past history of the Human Race.

*   *   *

EVILS RESULTING
FROM WRONG
TREATMENT OF
THE CREATURES.

Had the awful system of the traffic in the flesh of the Creatures never been known, then many of the ills to which it is commonly said that " flesh is heir " would never have been known. There would have been a very different history written by the Western World. The health of the Nations, physically, mentally and morally, would not have been what it is to-day. The false pathological processes which to-day prevail in our midst would not have been known. The *Serum* delusions would not have been generated. The iniquity known as Vivisection would have found no place. There would have been no room nor need for the Therapeutics of the present Medical Profession ; for the Physicians would have been healers of another order, who would not have believed in the blood and anguish-bought panaceas with which the Physiological Laboratories furnish them to-day. The people would have been free from many of the afflictions which are their lot now. Their physical constitution would have been purer and nobler, and their bodies would have been more responsive to their minds ; their minds would not have been so dull to understand spiritual things, for the conditions within and around them would have been so much purer and nobler that they would have reflected the light which broke upon them from the Heavens ; and so their spiritual life would have been both beautiful and strong, the manifestation of the Divinity within them, and the interpretation and realization of their true life. For the building up of the body upon the lives and flesh of the sentient Creatures has made that body more and more responsive to those feelings and desires which are animal and are at variance with a true Humanity; it has made the the mind duller and duller, and less able to fulfil its true functions of reflecting the light of the Soul, but more susceptible to every kind of animal influence ; and it has dried up the springs of real Divine Goodness which is natural to the Human Soul in its true and original state, and prevented the outflowing of true and full compassion and pity towards all lowly things. It has likewise taken away the true and beautiful Divine Vision which the Soul once beheld, wherein all Life was seen to be One in various orders and degrees of manifestation, having the same basis as parts of an organic whole ; and the highly organized sentient Creatures were known to be as the little children within the system on their way up to the Human Kingdom, many of them human in their feelings and devotion, so that they were regarded with compassion and treated with unfailing gentleness.

* * *

THE TRAGIC RESULTS OF INHUMANITY.

Perhaps the most tragic part of the awful tragedy is the view of the Divine Compassion and Love which it has led men and women to accept. They gradually came to associate their own attitude towards the Creatures with the Divine Love, to accept it as the true attitude approved by Him. The conception of His beautiful Nature which dominated them for untold ages found its expression in the animal and even human sacrifices which they offered unto Him in the name of faith, devotion and service. Their teachers and priests affirmed that He demanded such offerings and that they must be made. And so the vision of the Divine Compassion unto all Souls and Pity towards all the Creatures gradually passed away as there grew up in its stead that most terrible image of the Divine Nature found associated with the sacrificial systems, wherein the Ever Blessed One is represented as demanding and delighting in the blood-offerings made by the priests. In the light of that history it is not difficult to understand how it came about that the true Seers and Teachers died out of the land, and the spiritual vision of the people gradually perished.

And then when the blessed Master lived His beautiful life in order to show unto all who were yet able to understand the kind of life which the Heavenly Father desired all His children to live, and restored in the Teachings

which He gave the long-lost vision within the Soul of the
Divine Love and Wisdom, those who professed to have
an intimate acquaintance with His life, but who knew
Him not, represented Him as one who ate flesh and drank
wine, even whilst He preached purity and compassion.
They presented pictures of Him which could not possibly
have been true. They would have made His beautiful
life one blemished with blood-guiltiness, and have made
His wonderful Christhood impossible. They so presented
Him in the Records which they wrote and scattered
abroad that the vision of the Redeemed Life which He
gave to His disciples, and which He said all Souls must
live in order to find their true childhood to the Heavenly
Father, was not a life of beautiful compassion and purity
in all its ways ; for it encouraged the use of flesh as an
article of diet, and the making of the Creatures mere
goods of merchandise. It associated the partaking of
flesh with one of the most profound spiritual mysteries,
and related the efforts of the Soul (as the blessed Master
illustrated these) to the catching of fish by the disciples
on the Sea of Genesaret. Over the horror of the Shambles
and the tragedies of the Abattoirs it threw its protection,
as may be found in the second part of the third Record.

And so they set forth an image of the blessed Master
which was not His image, a picture of the nature of the
Redeemed Life which contradicted that life, a vision of
Christhood whose path was stained with the footprints
of blood-guiltiness ; and they asked all Souls to look
at it, to worship it, and to follow it. And the whole
Western World has done so with the most startling
results.

*　　*　　*

HOW THE
DIVINE VISION
WAS OBSCURED.

When we look at the Western
World to-day and witness the conditions which prevail, notwithstanding all the beautiful efforts which
have been put forth to lift that
world into the truer and nobler ways of life, we may
behold the effects of the false view which it has had of
the Redeemed Life and the meaning of a Christhood.
It has interpreted the Christhood as something merely
personal. It has thought of the Master's Christhood
just as we think of any one whose name we know. It

has been to that world merely a name, rather than a beautiful and sublime Estate, with the result that the profound and far-reaching meaning of the Master's Christhood .has remained unknown. Even the Churches where the Christhood is professed have missed the inward meaning of the Master's Christhood. They have made use of it to designate the Master in His personal life, through having failed to apprehend its spiritual and Divine significance for Him. They confounded the vehicle with the wonderful Estate, and in this way did they fail to understand its nature and purpose. Had they understood the meaning of a Christhood, they would likewise have understood the meaning of the Redeemed Life ; and they would have known that the first step towards that life was the putting away from the path of their life every evil thing, to cleanse their ways from everything savouring of blood-guiltiness, to cultivate and make manifest true pity for the Creatures and genuine compassion towards all Souls. *They would have come to understand the Oneness of all true Life, who the Creatures are, and what their place once was in the economy of this Planet as a Spiritual System.*

THE LORD REGARDETH ALL CREATURES.

The Lord delighteth not in the sacrifice of bullocks, nor taketh pleasure in the slaughter of the sheep and lambs.

He heareth the crying of the oxen in their distress, and the bleating of those which are made to lay down their lives.

Of those who take them from the fold for the Sacrifices unto Mammon and Moloch will He require their lives ; for the Lord loveth all things, great and small, weak and strong. His compassion is unto all Creatures, and His pity unto the ends of the Earth. He is just in His ways ; His kindness is unfailing.

DID THE MASTER EAT FLESH?

IT is becoming more and more important to have a true view before the mind of the nature of the life which the blessed Master lived. It is absolutely essential to the Soul that the nature of that life should be understood, otherwise the true growth Godward of the Human Race will be not only retarded, but the life unto which the blessed Master called the Soul will be missed. And in these days is it specially necessary to have the nature of the life which He lived presented to all who truly desire to realize that life within themselves, since many are the false or imperfect views of the nature of the Redeemed Life which He so fully and beautifully manifested, and the Christhood which He interpreted. The "higher life" unto which so many are now feeling called, must itself be understood if it is to be perfectly realized. It must be a *higher life on every sphere of experience*, and not simply on those spheres usually denoted spiritual. So often do we find that life sought for only upon the spiritual spheres, without the Aspirants also seeking for its true and beautiful manifestations upon the lower and more outward spheres. And the divorcement upon the outer spheres can only be accounted for by the fact that those who are seeking the higher life and yet fail to recognise its relationship to the life to be lived, upon even the outermost spheres of experience, must have a wrong conception of the nature and manifestations of that life.

THE CAUSE OF MISAPPREHENSION.

It seems to us that the failure of so many truly beautiful Souls to apprehend the meaning of the higher life in its application to the outermost spheres, has arisen from their misconception of the beautiful Redeemed Life of the Master, and their failure to understand the sublime and exalted nature of the Christhood. For the Records wherein His wonderful history is supposed to be recorded are so imperfect and so mixed that the nature of the Christhood is obscured, and the Redeemed

Life misrepresented ; and the readers who have truly
desired to follow the Master unto the realization of the
Redeemed Life and the understanding of the Christhood,
have not only been unable to see the true path along which
they must needs walk in order to attain that knowledge
and Life, but the way in which the Master in His own life
is presented, has led them from the true path into one
whose ways are full of " blood-guiltiness." The amazing
thing is not that the Western multitudes do not recognise the error, but that the Christian Churches have
failed to see it, and that their chief teachers should
continue to proclaim a Christhood marred and stained
with blood-guiltiness. For the Churches believe in a
Christ who could not only partake of flesh in His daily
diet, but who could and did encourage by example and
precept the taking of life for that purpose. They do not
believe in the sacrifice of animals as oblations to Deity,
but they do believe in them as necessary and legitimate
sacrifices upon the altars of their own physical desires
and tastes. And, strangest of all, they apparently quite
sincerely believe that they have the example of the
blessed Master in doing these things.

What a tragedy it is that the beautiful purpose of the
blessed Master's life should have been defeated for so
many ages through the false presentation of the meaning
of His Christhood and the nature of the Redeemed Life !
Who, having known Him in that life, could have imagined
that such a mirage would have been presented in His
name wherein His truly wonderful purity, goodness,
compassion and love would have garments put upon
them bearing the signs of blood-guiltiness ?

THE TRUE NEOPHYTE KNOWS.

So long as the Churches believe that the presentation
of the Christhood and the nature of the Redeemed Life
found in the Records is the true one, so long will it be
found difficult to answer to their satisfaction the question,
Did the Master eat flesh ? But where the Soul is seeking
only for the truth, and seeks beyond all earthly records
to know the path wherein it should walk, even at the

Source of all Heavenly Knowledge, that Soul will come to understand what was done to the life-story of the sublime Master by those who wrote the Records upon which the Churches base their existence to-day. And that Soul will come to know the meaning of the Redeemed Life, and to understand how utterly impossible it was for the Master to show any sympathy whatever towards a practice whose every step was stained with the blood of the beautiful Creatures whose lives are demanded to provide the food so much desired.

That the blessed Master did not and could not partake of flesh as diet will be known unto all who find the Redeemed Life unto its realization upon every sphere of experience. They will know that His beautiful compassion would not have permitted Him to take the life of the Creatures for any purpose whatever. They will also know that to have done so would have polluted His wonderfully pure form, and dimmed the Divine Vision ever so clear and great within Him.

J. TODD FERRIER.

SOME FORGOTTEN LOGIA.

Not that which entereth through the eye or the ear, defileth a man, but that which proceedeth from the heart when its desires are impure ;

For out of the heart are the issues of good and evil.

To eat the bread of this world with unwashen hands, defileth no man ; but to eat of the Bread of Heaven with unwashen hands is not only to defile himself, but also the sacred bread which he eateth.

For when the hands are unwashen, the ways of the man's life are impure ; his heart seeketh only those things found in the paths of evil, and his hands do them.

But when the hands of a man have been made clean, then are his ways those of compassion and pity, goodness and righteousness.

THE GIFT OF MARY.

THERE is a story told in the fourth Gospel Record concerning the anointing of the Master by Mary of Bethany, which, whilst it is not outward history, is yet full of beautiful pathos, exquisite in its tenderness and profound in its loving devotion. It is usually taken to be an actual incident in the life of the Master upon the physical planes, rather than a beautiful spiritual experience ; and because it is so understood its innermost meanings are lost and its real inspiration and value are missed. As an outward incident in the life of the Master, it may appeal to many : indeed, we know that it has drawn many on to love Mary for her devotion to the Master ; but the appeal is not of the highest order, since the love bestowed is upon the mere outward form and person, and the gift becomes material in its expression. That there is a charm in the story as the act of a woman to the great Teacher whom she loved, need not be questioned ; for it has arrested the thoughts of many. But we must not permit any outward charm, however delightful it may be, to deprive us of the innermost meaning of some of the most wonderful experiences of the Soul. We should not rest content with the mere form in which the truth is cast in order to be presented upon the outer spheres, but ever strive to discover even to the full understanding of it, the innermost meaning of the Soul. For the innermost meaning is the real one, whereas the outward story has only an apparent meaning.

Its Meaning for the Soul.

Now this beautiful story is full of the most profound significance for the Soul, first as an act of the Soul herself whereby she makes her supreme choice, and secondly, as an embodiment of one of the most sacred and momentous experiences through which the Christ passed. It is a picture of the Soul having arrived at the Vision of the meaning of Christhood, and pouring out its own love in devotion unto that Vision and the wonderful life unto which it calls. For the term Mary means the Soul when it has once known Christhood. It was the term used in the most ancient times to indicate that a Soul had risen up through the various spheres of experience and reached that sphere where Christhood became a possession. And the anointing at Bethany in the House of Mary was the Christhood Estate being realized by the Soul as the outcome of pure and beautiful love in which devotion to the truth, devotion to goodness, devotion to the manifestation of the spiritual and divine love-principle in all things, were the chief features. For Bethany is the House of the Christhood; that is, it is the state of experience which precedes the coming of the Christhood as a possession, the state in which the Soul arrives at the Vision of the meaning of Christhood. And the very precious ointment of spikenard poured over the Christ, is the precious Soul-love used in the divine service. For there is nothing so precious as Soul-love born from the consciousness of the Divine Presence within the Soul's Sanctuary. What in the whole world is so beautiful as love in which the purity, goodness, gentleness, compassion and pity of the Divine are imaged ? What is so exquisite in its magnetic healing power as such love ? It knows only the purest and highest devotion. It seeks only the noblest and sublimest realizations. Its gentleness is unfailing, its compassion and pity uncircumscribed. Its ministry is even as the Divine. Though Judas Iscariot, Simon's son, may use his influence against such an apparent waste of power and devotion upon the Christhood and all the wonderful life and experiences implied in it, yet the Soul so full of love is never turned from the path of pure and beautiful service to the Divine. For who is Judas Iscariot but the betraying condition of mind which ever regards the material things as the chief things of life, and values every power, even those of the spiritual world within us, according to their material uses, and would sell even the most precious possession of the Soul (the Divine Love within it) for so much earthly gain ? Truly Judas is the betrayer who carries the bag ; the son of Simon—the mind when it becomes engrossed with the affairs of the world, and regards not the spiritual and Divine except in a material sense.

ITS RELATION TO THE CHRIST.

But the story has also another meaning. Its signification for all Souls is truly beautiful, and the exquisite pathos should appeal to us all and draw us on to not only seek the Vision of the Christhood, but to pour out in its fulness all the love which wells up within us as the outcome of our consciousness of the Divine Presence. But it has also a signification at once sublimely pathetic and tragic, for it presents to us a scene which actually took place on the Spiritual Heavens prior to the descent of the beautiful Christ-Soul into the depths of anguish which came to Him when He left this world as the Christ and became the Sin-offering. It is a presentation of the anointing of the Master upon the Spiritual Heavens, the pouring forth upon Him of the Divine Love, the most precious and costly spikenard, by the Adonai who had always overshadowed Him, the Divine Maria who was the embodiment and manifestation unto the whole Heavens of the Ever Blessed and Eternal One. He it always was who spake through the Master as "the only Begotten of the Father." And it was He as the Divine Maria who anointed the Christ-Soul unto His burial—by which is to be understood the spiritual impoverishment unto which the Master descended when He left behind Him the beautiful Christhood Estate, and took upon Himself a body like unto that of our deep humiliation. He was buried indeed when He descended into the conditions upon the Astral Kingdom which prevailed against the Soul, preventing all who would fain rise to the sublime heights of the realizations which He Himself knew, from doing so. And the beautiful incident in the Record was the picture drawn by the one who was the witness upon the Spiritual Heavens of the event. It was first embodied in the Logia of St. John, from which it was taken when the other Records which now form the Gospel Stories were built together. None knew of its innermost meaning but those who had belonged to the innermost group of the Master's friends. Only they knew anything of the inner meanings belonging to all the Logia relating to the sad Sin-offering.

The Gift of Mary was one of the most wonderful gifts ever bestowed.

J. TODD FERRIER.

THE GRACE OF THE LORD.

Know ye the Grace of the Lord made manifest in Christ Jesus, who, though He was rich with all the riches of God, yet for our sakes stooped unto our low estate, and knew our impoverishment, that we might become enriched.

For it became Him through whom we all were fashioned, and for whose purpose all the things in the Worlds were made, that, in bringing again unto the state of Salvation all who went down into bondage to the elemental Kingdoms, He should know suffering, even the anguish of the Cross as He bore the burden of us all.

For unto this end was Christ Jesus made manifest that He might destroy him who had the power of spiritual death, even the Devil and Satan, with all his principalities, visible and invisible ; and thus work out the deliverance of all those who fell from their first estate and became subject to the powers of the air, and Redeem the whole House of Israel from the darkness which overtook them, and Judah from the thraldom of her oppressors.

The Herald of the Cross.

Vol. v. New Series. October, 1909. No. 10.

THE MEASURING OF THE TEMPLE.

The Lord spake unto His Servant, saying unto him, " Son of Man,[1] arise and measure the Temple[2] of the Lord, its length and its breadth, its depth and its height, with the Measuring Rod[3] which I will give unto thee ; for the hour is now come when the House of the Lord must be shown unto the Children of Israel that it may become their heritage, and that they may know the beauty of holiness and behold the Glory of the Lord."

And the Servant of the Lord took the Measuring Rod and measured the Temple therewith, and found that its length and breadth, its depth and height were equal.[4]

And He found that the Temple was Four-fold, and that each square of its dimension was as a cube within a cube, and that within the innermost was to be found the true Beauty of Holiness, even the Divine Presence whose Glory filleth the Temple.[5]

---

[1] The Christ-Soul.
[2] The Soul-System spoken of Divinely.
[3] The Christhood Estate by which life is measured.
[4] The Perfect Man.
[5] The Divine Presence unto the Consciousness of which the true evolution of the Soul leads.

THE MINISTRY OF HEAVEN.*

" Hereafter ye shall see the Heavens open, and the Angels of God ascending from the Earth with the Son of Man, even as they descended with Him."—John I., 51.

MY address to you this morning has been suggested through the absence of the outward presence of many who once were with us here, and who loved Heaven's ministry within this earthly sanctuary. And its purpose is not to fill us with the sad thoughts which cast long shadows upon life's ways, but rather to bring to us all a great and beautiful hope. Nay, even more ; to bring that world into which they have passed, so near, that its reality may become a most blessed Realization unto all. For the ministry of Heaven is a real ministry which may be felt and seen by us, if we seek in the true way.

Heaven with its beautiful Angelic ministry seems so far away to most people, that its sublime, healing and comforting atmosphere is never known to them. They think that they truly believe in its reality, yet fail to know it as such. To them it is a dream which remains a dream, because the dreamers never become Seers.

Therein is the sadness of it all, and the great loss of wonderful faith within the Church ; for faith is the vision of the Soul, that Vision which sees beyond the outward garb of life in its manifold manifestations, to the *real* life lying hidden from the outward vision ; which transcends all earthly limitations and knows no bounds, but rises upward, ever upward, penetrating that world where the Angels are said to dwell and minister, even until the Soul beholds the Glory of the Lord.

Its Blessed Reality.

The Angelic ministry is very real unto all who are able to behold with the Vision of the Soul. To them it is as real as the outward life is unto all men and women. With them it is not a mere believe, but a seeing that which others only believe. Unto them it is not simply a hope ; it is a blessed realization. They behold the

---

* An address given by the writer in Park Green Congregational Church, Macclesfield, on Sunday morning, August 29th.

substance of those things for which so many only hope with such sad uncertainty, and have the sure evidence of the Unseen and Eternal. When they withdraw themselves from the thronging things and duties of the outward life and seek the silence without and the Divine Presence within, the ministry of the Spiritual World becomes as real to them as are the ministries upon the outward spheres. They see and hear those things which cannot be seen and heard upon the outer spheres, and come to know of the reality of that life which is to so many only a vague dream or uncertain hope.

It is very difficult for many to understand such an experience. So accustomed have they become to the world in which they seem to pass all their days and spend all their energies, the world of phenomena with its spheres of merely material effects, that they have lost the inner consciousness of the Spiritual World until they now think that it is impossible for any one whilst yet upon the outer spheres to pass upward within their own spiritual system and reach that world where the Angelic ministry takes place. The common belief is that such an experience is impossible. And even by those who might believe that it was a possible thing to do, the experience is comfounded with what is known as the phenomena of Spiritualism. For it is not of that nature, though many of the phenomena of Spiritualism are quite true. But these phenomena are not often from the Spiritual World of which we speak; nor are they often concerned with that world; nor with the Angelic life and ministry unto which all Souls are called by the Ever Blessed One. So these things should not be confounded by any one. For the Angelic World is a very different world from that looked into by the ordinary Clairvoyant. Its nature is entirely spiritual, and all its visions, messages and teachings are spiritual. They are related to the Soul; to the life to be lived and the path to be pursued in living the life; to the true way of service and the Divine Light essential to it; to the true history of the Soul and its sublime destiny; to the meaning of our way of life here and the interpretation of all our sorrows and afflictions.

The Visions which come from the Angelic World concern themselves not with material gain or worldly ambitions ; they show forth the glory of the Divine Love. The messages which break upon the Soul from the Divine are not of a sensuous nature ; they are concerned only with the things of the Soul in its upward march towards the Divine. The teachings which are given to the Soul from that world are of the profoundest nature, and can only be understood by those in whom the Light of the Divine shines, those whose Souls are as Lamps lit from the Lord.

WHAT THE MASTER MEANT.

The promise of the blessed Master unto Nathanael was, therefore, no vague thing : it was burdened with meanings the holiest and most sublime. It was so definite that there could be no mistaking what the Master meant, *viz.*, that he would see the ascension and descension of the Angels of God upon the Son of Man. The Angelic World was to be seen and the Angelic ministry understood. It was the promise of a Divine blessing coming to Nathanael as the outcome of his own spiritual growth. He was an Israelite, indeed ; one in whom was found no guile *or that way of men in the world by which they deceive both others and themselves.* His Soul was beautiful, for his motives and purposes were pure. He was an Israelite, indeed—one who was as a prince with God, because he had prevailed over all the earthward and sensuous tendencies of the lower nature. His Lamp had been kindled from the Lord : the Divine Light burned within him. He was at the point of inward spiritual experience when he was able to recognise the sublime vision interpreted in the Christhood of the blessed Master. He was in that stage of unfoldment when it was possible for him to receive the Angelic Vision implied in the words of the Master. The promise was, therefore, fraught with blessings unspeakable for him.

THE GUILELESS HEART.

Nathanael is but a type. He represents the Soul who is seeking along true spiritual lines for the vision of the

Christhood and the realization of the true Redeemed Life. He stands as the picture of the disciple who has purified all his ways through overcoming evil with good. He is not a weak man, though he would have scorned to do anything ignoble ; for he was strong in his purity, and gentle in his judgment. He was the embodiment of the purified heart—of all those who, through seeking the true Redeemed Life and living it, are ready for the Vision of the Lord. He is the type of the Soul who has so far attained the victory over the world that he or she is ready for the true Vision of the Christhood with its profound and sublime meanings, and the ascending and descending of the Angels of the Lord upon the Son of Man. For the Vision of the Christhood means far more than the vision of the personal Master. Indeed, it has no such personal meaning. The Vision of the Christhood is the Soul arriving at the true meaning of the wonderful Life and Teachings shown forth and interpreted by the blessed Master. It is the Vision of Him which came to the innermost circle of His friends ; not that which the public saw, but that which the multitudes could not understand. For the Christhood, whether of the blessed Master or another, is not a personal attribute which comes with birth into this world, but a Spiritual and Divine Estate or inheritance and possession with which the Soul is endowed.

When the Soul sees that Vision it acts as Nathanael did : it acknowledges it as the true Christhood, and follows the Vision whither it leads. There can be no hesitation ; to follow it unto the attainment of it, even unto all its sublime fulness, becomes a glorious spiritual necessity. For in the possession of the Christhood is " The Holy Grail " to be found by the Soul—*the consciousness of the Divine Presence within the Soul*, a consciousness which the Soul once knew but which it lost. For " the Holy Grail " sought for by the true Knight of the Cross, was and is the Divine Presence. And the Vision of that Presence within the Soul with all its unspeakably beautiful sublime meanings, can only be realized and seen in and through the realization or attainment of Christhood by the Soul. For that Estate known as Christhood is always and ever shall be the Way to the true knowledge of the Father, the Truth or exposition of the Divine Purpose concerning the Soul, and the Life of the Divine interpreted and made manifest, the attainment of the real Crown of Life.

The way to the realization of that wonderful vision and experience may be known as " the Spiral Staircase " whose every step leads the Soul higher and higher, upward, ever upward, that Spiral Staircase whose steps are trod by the Saints of God—all those who are truly seeking for the Divine Life as a Vision and Realization. It is indeed a steep ascent, but it is a blessed one. It is trying often-times, but it is glorious in its issues. To not a few it is a wearisome way, but it leads to such a rest in the Divine Love as this world never dreams of. To all Souls it means the pursuit of purity, goodness and love immeasurable, and its gain is the Crown of the Immortals.

THE SON OF MAN A TYPE.

As Nathanael stands as the type of the disciple seeking for the Vision of the Christhood, and one who is ready to receive and understand that Vision when it is presented to the Soul ; so is the term Son of Man to be understood as the type of that life unto which the Divine is ever calling all His children. For the Christhood of the Master was the Archetype of all Souls, the embodiment of the Life unto which in their spiritual evolution they were to attain. The Son of Man was not a term applied to the personal Master, but to the state of experience in which He was as the Christ. And just as it was made use of in the prophetic days to indicate a Life whose ways are pure and whose Lamp is lit from the Lord so that the light which shines within the Soul is the Divine Light, so was it to be applied unto the Soul in the days when the Christhood should be restored amongst the people—the days of the coming of the Son of Man or the life of Christhood realized by many Souls, the Redeemed Life whose every way is pure, whose every thought is full of tender love, whose every purpose is to heal and redeem, and whose inward light is from the Lord whose Holy Presence fills the Sanctuary of the Soul.

That is the true coming of the Son of Man, the *real* appearing of the Christ in the Christhood of all who are able to find the " Holy Grail," to ascend the " Spiral Staircase," to rise up into the realization of the beautiful life and service signified by the term Son of Man.

What a sublime thought it is that is presented to us in the message contained in the Master's words ! How beautiful is the life unto which it calls all Souls ! How profound are the experiences of which it speaks !

It presents to us *the reality* of the Spiritual World where the Angels minister for the Divine. It affirms *the reality* of the ministry of that world unto the Soul. It promises *as a reality* the Angelic Vision unto all who are of guileless heart, and who have sought after that Redeemed Life whose ways are pure and guileless.

To be pure, to be good, to be gentle and kind, to be compassionate and pitiful, to be Souls whose chief desire is to know the Divine Love and to be the Interpreters of that Love, is the way, the only way, to the sublime Realization of all that the words of the Master mean.

J. TODD FERRIER.

ON WHOM THE SPIRIT ABIDETH.

And I, John, saw the Heavens open and the Spirit of the Lord descending, even as a Dove desends in her flight, to rest upon Him.

And when it rested upon Him I heard a voice saying unto me, " Behold the Lamb of God ! for He it is who taketh away the sin of the world."

He who spake unto me bare record that the One on whom I should see the Spirit of the Lord descending, the same was the Christ.

And I beheld, and now bear record, that He was and ever is the Son of God.

In Him is Life, and that Life is the Light for Men.

A VISION OF SACRIFICE.

The Heavens were opened unto me in the Day of the Lord, so that I beheld the Glory of the Lord resting upon the Holy Place within the Sanctuary of the Most High.[1]

Over the Altar of the Lord[2] *was there One beheld like unto the Son of God,*[3] *who ministered unto all the House of Israel as their High Priest before the Lord.*

His raiment was pure as the most purified wool, glistening in its whiteness and reflecting the glory of the whole Heavens.

Upon His breast He bore the twelve signs[4] *of Israel set within the Urim and Thumim ; and He was crowned with the crowns of both Israel and Judah,*[5] *for He was Judah's High Priest and King as well as Israel's.*

And upon the Altar there was laid an offering unto the Lord, even the Lamb of God,[6] *for a whole burnt offering on behalf of both Judah and Israel, for the taking away of the sin of the people and the purification of their Sanctuaries, and for the restoration unto them of the Kingdoms which the oppressor had taken away from them when they went down into the land of captivity and bondage.*

And I beheld that as the offering was made upon the Altar the whole Heavens were moved like a Temple when its foundations are shaken and its supports are moved out of place ; for the Heavens were bound down in anguish, because the Lamb of God had to carry away the sin of the people.

---

[1] Whether of the Soul or the Planet, the Divine Abiding-place.
[2] The Soul in its sacrificial attitude.
[3] The Adonai.
[4] The Christ-Souls and the Planet-Soul.
[5] The Spiritual and Celestial Estates of the Christ-Souls.
[6] The Divine Love sacrificially manifested within the Soul, that it may be purified, and its Kingdoms of Christhood may be restored.

THE PHENOMENA OF SPIRITUALISM.

THE phenomena which are associated with the modern spiritualistic movement, are not new. They were known long ages ago when the conditions upon this world were very different to those which prevail now. Originally the phenomena were of an entirely spiritual order, having for their beautiful purpose the spiritual education of the Human Race. For when the whole of the conditions upon the Planet were pure and all the children of the Heavenly Father were yet unfallen, it was as if the Angels of God ascended and descended in loving ministry before the Divine. The Planet was the theatre of the most wonderful spiritual activities. The drama of the Soul knew no evil, nor the darkness and bitterness born from evil. There were no tragedies in those ages within any of the kingdoms of the Planet, for all her spheres were in beautiful order, and harmony reigned in all the elements. There was no difficulty found by those who ministered for the Divine Love in approaching the outer spheres of the Planet. They were able to descend without danger to their own spiritual magnetism, and to easily ascend again when they had completed their mission.

And the work accomplished by them was one not unlike that accomplished by the phenomena of modern spiritualism, though most of it had a very different purpose and was of a higher order. The Soul was taught, when it reached the Human Kingdom, by means of objective manifestations from the Angelic World ; but the entire purpose of these phenomena was to lift the Soul up on to the Spiritual World by educating it in things Spiritual and Divine, and preparing it in this way to rise from sphere to sphere until it was able to function entirely upon the Angelic Kingdom and behold the wonderful manifestations of the Divine Life and ministry which are to be found there.

These were true spiritual phenomena, objective without being sensuous, tangible to the vision of the Soul

without being material. They were truly spiritual in
every way. They were generated by those who were
beautiful in their own life and service, and whose only
purpose was that of the education and illumination of
the Soul. They were spiritual in their nature ; for they
were magnetic visions thrown upon the then pure magnetic
plane of the Soul, generated amid the most beautiful
spiritual conditions, and having only truly spiritual
influences upon the Soul. If they spake to the Soul
concerning those things which most people now view
as only material, it was always unto great spiritual and
Divine ends. When what is now known as Nature was
spoken of, it was that the Soul might be instructed in
the mysteries of all the wonderful life beheld in the
Vegetable Kingdom, the inner meanings of the beautiful
forms and colours which then much more than now
adorned that Kingdom. When the teachings were in
relation to the Creature-Kingdom, they had for their
purpose the education of the Soul into the knowledge
of the purpose and meaning of the Creature-Kingdom.
And when the teachings were concerning the life to be
lived upon the outer spheres, their purpose was never
mere earthly knowledge for gain and pleasure, but
knowledge to aid the Soul in its path, so that all its experiences might be rightly interpreted.

Thus will it be seen that all the phenomena beheld
by the Soul, and all the ministry unto it from the Spiritual
World had a beautiful educational purpose, and that in
those ages the Soul sought the aid of the phenomena
only that it might become stronger towards the Divine,
and be enriched with spiritual knowledge. And all
those who were the venues of the communications and
the generators of the phenomena, were pure and beautiful
in all the ways of their life and the motives which bore
them along in their wonderful ministry. The work
which they did was of a very different nature to that
now accomplished through most of the mediums who
are supposed to be the venues of the phenomena of the
modern Spiritualistic Movement. Every one who knows

anything of that beautiful time when the Angels of God descended to commune with the Human Race, feels that, whilst the phenomena of modern spiritualism is true, it is not of the highest order ; that whilst the aim of the phenomena made manifest is ostensibly to demonstrate the reality of the Spiritual World, the phenomena frequently have little to do with that world, and are generally merely Astral in their character. Were they from that world, they would be of an order far above the material plane. They would not be circumscribed, as they mostly now are, by the material and sensuous spheres. Instead of bringing down all those things which were always meant to be purely spiritual, to the outermost plane, and there changing their nature and meaning, the Soul would have been gradually drawn above the outermost plane to witness the phenomena upon the spiritual magnetic plane, and thus taught and strengthened until it could transcend the limitations of its environment and function upon those Spiritual Heavens whence all true illumination and spiritual vision come.

It must surely strike a truly earnest spiritual aspirant, one who longs to rise above the material influences of life and find the true Spiritual World, to discover that the communications given through most of the mediums who profess to receive illumination from that world, are so very largely taken up with the things of this life, the merely sensuous experiences. Such an inquirer will not fail to observe how frequently what was meant to be a message for the Soul-life is turned into one for the physical life ; that truths which were meant to be understood spiritually, are taken to mean the things of sense ; how nearly all the visions described by the Clairvoyants have relation to earth-forms, and mostly to the more recently departed. If he should attend the Séances of the Clairvoyants and a truly spiritual vision and message be given, he will soon witness the change in the conditions of the audience ; either they will be lifted up into more spiritual spheres through the heavenly conditions around them, or the Medium will be drawn down again to the outer spheres through the failure of those present to respond to the new environment. For even though the Medium may only desire a true spiritual vision and message, the atmosphere generated by those present will either prevent the Medium from rising to receive such help from the Spiritual World, or cause the message to become changed in its nature as it comes to the Medium, unless the prevailing conditions are entirely of a pure order.

The phenomena of a purified Spiritualism would have an educational power, an uplifting and redeeming ministry for the Soul, were only the conditions made pure through the purified life of the Medium in the first place, and the pure intentions of all who sought the aid to be rendered through such a ministry. For the phenomena of modern Spiritualism are the signs of the new times in which we are living, the testimonies to the profound cravings of the Soul for the realization of the Spiritual World. And the order of the phenomena observed is the sign of the great requirement in the heart of the Spiritualistic Movement, the need for pure conditions, the necessity for pure living on the part of the Mediums in order that they may be able to rise up out of the earthly or sensuous conditions and receive from the Angelic World those beautiful messages whose teaching is so essential to the guidance and culture of those Souls who are not yet able to rise up into those heavenly spheres. For if all the Mediums lived the Redeemed Life ; if they purified all their ways ; if they nourished their bodies upon the pure fruits of the Earth instead of the flesh-foods which most of them take ; if they kept both body and mind pure, their hearts full of a very real compassion and pity towards all Souls—Human and Creature ; if they sought only true spiritual vision and message, and never prostituted their gifts to mere astral purposes, then would the message of Spiritualism in this age become a very real one, a spiritual message for the Soul, a message glowing with the glory of a light born from the Divine. Then would the phenomona of Spiritualism be of an order wholly spiritual ; for they would be lifted high above the Astral conditions which now prevail where they are sought after and made manifest. Then would the phenomena have a real mission, and not, as at present, one which frequently so misleads both Medium and seeker that they follow a wrong path in life ; for the phenomena would not simply bear testimony to the persistency of the Soul after it has passed over from the outer spheres, but also become the sure evidence to the Soul of the approach of the Spiritual Heavens, because of their heavenly nature and teaching.

J. TODD FERRIER.

THE VISION OF ARIES.

In the day in which I beheld the descent of the Constellations Scorpio and Cancer from the Celestial Heavens, and heard a voice proclaiming the coming of the Lord, I likewise beheld the Constellation Aries passing downwards until it overshadowed the planes of the Earth, and heard a voice proclaiming that the Lamb of God would take away the sin of the world.

And I beheld that the whole Heavens marvelled at the graciousness of the Divine towards His Children, and sang Praises unto His Name, saying, " Great and marvellous are Thy works, O Lord of Hosts ! Who is to be likened unto Thee ? For Thou redeemest all Thy Children who have gone away from Thee, even those in the uttermost parts of the Earth, and dost heal them of their diseases and purify them from their sins through the out-flowing of Thy gracious Love, even the Blood of the Lamb of God."

And through the descent of the Heavenly Sign, even Aries, I beheld the whole world become purified and transformed, and restored to her ancient greatness and glory ; for the Blood of the Lamb maketh all things new upon the Earth.

THE SPIRITUALISTIC MOVEMENT.

SIGNS OF A NEW AGE.

THE Religious Movement known as Spiritualism is one of those signs which were expected to accompany "the coming of the Son of Man." There were to be signs in the "heavens above" as well as in "the depths of the Earth" at the appearing of the Son of Man. The phenomena in the depths of the Earth have been manifest not only in the physical realm but in that of Humanity. For the upheavals in the Nations from East to West and North to South ; the remarkable arising of down-trodden Races to assert their humanity and claim the right to be thought of as part of the organic whole ; the supreme efforts of many Peoples to throw off the yoke of those who have long oppressed them ; the noble endeavours of some Peoples to set their own Nation in order, to relieve the oppressed, to execute only righteous judgment in removing from the paths of life the causes of so much human failure, to abolish customs whose whole tendency has been to bring to the individual and the family life sorrow and shame, to so change the conditions of society that it will be less difficult to do right and be pure, so that the Nation shall become more and more a Community of men and women whose great aim will be to realize the meaning of Brotherhood. These are indeed signs and wonders in the depths of the Earth, great social upheavals having spiritual meanings, National earthquakes whose seismic forces are born from conditions other than physical, the phenomena of invisible powers within Humanity as the spiritual foundations of men and women are moved to finer issues.

And along with these signs of the coming of the Son of Man to awaken from the dead all the Nations, Races and Peoples, and set up just judgment upon the Earth through the overthrow of every form of evil and the establishment of righteousness, there were to be signs in the Heavens. Nor were these signs to be merely of a planetary order as some have supposed. Indeed, they were not to be physical in their nature, but of purely spiritual character. Even if great stellar phenomena have also played a part in the heavenly signs of the coming of the Son of Man, yet is the meaning purely spiritual ; for originally the influences exercised over the Earth by the Celestial objects, were all spiritual. But the wonderful signs predicted were those which belong to the Soul and its Kingdom. They were to be of an Angelic nature, and made manifest from the Angelic World. They were to be so evident unto all that the hearts of many would be filled with fear. And they were to issue in the Sign of the Son of Man appearing in the Heavens.

MISREADING THE HEAVENLY SIGNS.

The phenomena of the modern Spiritualistic Movement should have been the sure signs and tokens of the Coming of the Son of Man. They were originally so meant to be. And they would have been had the conditions been provided by the Mediums, and the people who have sought their aid. Those who were to have been the mediums and venues of the Angelic messages failed to recognise the meaning of " the opening of the Heavens " to the Soul. They failed to apprehend the inner meaning of the messages at first given unto them, so that they began to not only misinterpret the messages for the Soul, but likewise to give to them a purely sensuous and material signification. So much did they misapprehend the inner signification of the messages sent unto them concerning the necessary conditions to be observed by them in their ministry, that they utterly failed to recognise the true path shown them, the path which they were to walk in, and by following which they would alone be able to rise on to the Spiritual Heavens to receive direct from the Angelic Kingdom. They not only missed the way themselves in failing to respond to the heavenly counsel to purify their ways in life, nourish themselves on only the purest fruits of the Earth and make manifest the Redeemed Life as one of true and beautiful purity, compassion and pity ; but they gave a wrong direction to the whole of the new spiritual awakening. They mistook the visions which came as the result of their seeing along the Astral plane for true spiritual vision ; and confounded the instruments who were sent down through the Astral spheres to them, with a true Angelic ministry. They changed the beautiful office of their ministry into one whose work is now almost exclusively Astral in its character, and thus reduced the spiritual function to one that was Astral ; from being one that was the venue of messages for the Soul, to be the instrument by which men and women sought to gain earthly things. And it was in this way that the new movement known as Spiritualism was misdirected, and how it became so sensuous and materialistic. It was in this way that its beautiful spiritual meanings were lost, and its appeals made to the sensuous and super-sensuous realms in men and women rather than to the Spiritual World and the Divine Presence within them. It was in this way that unto all who sought the aid of those who should have been true mediums for the Divine, the Spirit World which comprises every degree of soul-experience from the lowest spiritual forms to the highest, was confounded with that *Spiritual World* which is the true Kingdom of the Soul, and that Angelic World from which alone trustworthy messages reach the Soul.

THE OFFICE OF MEDIUMSHIP.

True Mediumship is a Divine Office. It is an office of the Soul and not of the lower mind. It is an office that comes through spiritual realization alone, the true and, therefore, natural unfolding of the Divine powers within the Soul. It cannot be cultivated by any occult means, though a degree of ordinary Clairvoyance may be so acquired. It is not such as is generally understood by the term Clairvoyance, though the vision is most real to the Soul ; for it is entirely spiritual, and deals not with material things as such, because, when it speaks of the latter, it is always concerning their spiritual purpose and the heavenly uses to which they should be put. It can take in its vision the spiritual forms of all things ; see the wonderful reflections of the Vegetable Kingdom on the spiritual magnetic plane ; see into the world of shades and reflects where those things associated with the personal and material life are to be beheld ; witness the tragedies (should it be necessary to do so for some heavenly purpose) enacted within the spheres occupied by all who have gone wrong upon the outer planes through the worship of and service to the false gods of mammon and unrighteousness ; see into the beautiful Angelic World with its manifold ministries, and interpret these ministries unto the Soul ; and even rise so high in inward Soul experience as to know by realization the Divine, and behold the Vision of the Ever Blessed One as He is made manifest within the Holy Place or innermost Sanctuary of the Soul.

True Mediumship is, therefore, something more than Clairvoyance or Clairaudience. It is far higher than what is understood generally in the Spiritualistic Movement as Mediumship. And it can be acquired and retained only by truly spiritual means. As it is the outcome of true Soul culture, the unfoldment of all the Spiritual and Divine potentialities of the Soul, so it can be retained as a Divine Office only through the means by which it was acquired, *viz.*, *the way of the Redeemed Life*. The life of true purity must be lived. The body must be nourished only upon those things which are pure. The mind must seek above all things the Kingdom of God and His righteousness—that Kingdom of pure spiritual being through which the Divine Love is made manifest. The heart must become as a fountain of love which is born within it from the Divine, loving only the highest, breaking in wonderful compassion unto all Souls without distinction of Creed or Race or Nation, and in a pity whose fulness and tenderness know no limitations in its manifestation towards all the Creatures.

J. TODD FERRIER.

THE CONSTELLATION GEMINI.

When I beheld the Constellation Aries descending from the Celestial Heavens to overshadow the Earth, I likewise saw what had the appearance of two forms, chaste and exquisite, whose garments were glorious because of the light that shone upon them from the Divine.

They were the Heavenly Twins who serve before the Lord in the Sanctuary of the Heavens, ministering unto all who are able to understand the deeper mysteries of His wonderful works.

These two Messengers who send forth the Light from the Divine Sanctuary concerning the unsearchable riches of the Grace of the Lord, beheld I approaching the planes of the Earth; and, as they drew near, they poured forth the effulgence of the Glory of the Lord, that all who were able to receive it might become instructed in the ways of the Divine Love and Divine Wisdom.

And when they had filled the whole Earth with the Light which they had to administer, I saw how the World became glorious to look upon. Her planes were flooded with a light whose spectrum reflected the wonderful Glory of the Lord, whilst the Planet became like an emerald whose facets were so pure as to be transparent, so that the Planet was clothed in a garment of radiance wonderful to behold.

For the Constellation Gemini represents the Divine Love and the Divine Wisdom, the Heavenly Twins who find expression for the Soul in the realization of the Divine Life and Light.

SPIRITUALISM A NEW CHURCH.

WHEN the New Age was heralded by the signs and wonders in the depths of the Earth and in the Heavens, the Divine Purpose was not understood. The meaning of the signs and wonders in the depths of the Earth was misinterpreted by the Churches, because these latter were unable to perceive the heavenly signification of the great National, Racial and Social upheavals. And when the signs of the approaching advent of the Son of Man were given in the new view of the Redeemed Life which was presented in the reformed ways of living which broke upon the Western World, and which is now generally known as the Vegetarian Movement, all the Churches failed to recognise in the new spirit a testimony to the *real* awakening of the Soul to the need for a Redemption which took in every sphere of its experience, and made *all the ways of life pure.* Indeed they did then what they have continued to do since, they repudiated the whole movement as a hurtful and evil influence. Even those religious Communities which were raised upon teachings supposed to be the most spiritual and profound in their interior mystical sense, took the like action towards the new movement, utterly failing to perceive, notwithstanding their mystical knowledge of the doctrine of " correspondences " and " uses," that the only way to enter into the understanding of the interior sense of all things is through purity within all the spheres of the System of the Soul.

How Spiritualism was Received.

And then when the signs appeared in the Heavens through which the new movement known as Spiritualism arose, all the Churches from the ultra-rationalistic to the most professedly spiritual, looked with dismay at them, and came to think and speak of them as the signs of the working of the forces of evil. They spoke often against the supposed phenomena without having beheld them, or having tried to understand their nature, or even to enquire whether they had any meaning for the Soul.

They condemned and repudiated those things which they had not even tried to understand, and looked with some degree of horror upon those who were believers in the reality and heavenly character of the phenomena. And thus they drove out of their several Communities those who had come under the influence of the new Spiritual awakening brought about as the result of the phenomena ; and these latter created new Societies in the name of the New Movement, and became simply another Church amongst the many.

This was one great fallacy in the movement. It should have remained free from the materializing conditions generally associated with the Churches. It should never have organized itself as a separate religious movement, seeking to gather into its circles all sorts and conditions of men and women, without respect to their fitness to witness any truly spiritual phenomena or receive spiritual messages. The new Spiritualism was meant to have been a beautiful influence finding its way into the Churches, recalling these Communities to a more spiritual view of the things which they professed to believe, bringing the Spiritual World with its beautiful Angelic Ministry unto them that they might know its sublime reality, awakening within the Soul the long-lost knowledge of the Divine Nature and Presence, and restoring unto it all those gifts, powers and attributes which were once the possession of every Soul who had arrived at the knowledge of the Divine Love. And had the Churches understood the signs, then might they have received a great deliverance from the bondage of their limitations, the darkness within their Sanctuaries concerning the Heavenly realities, the meaning of the Spiritual World with its wonderful Angelic Ministry, the interpretation of the history of the Soul in its evolution before the Divine Love, the true history of this Planet, with the explanation of all the apparent contradictions in Nature, the Creature Kingdom, and the Human experience. They would thus not only have enlightened their own Sanctuaries and found again the Vision of the Divine, but they would have saved that which was meant to be a beautiful spiritual influence for the upliftment of Humanity from becoming merely another Church within which the new movement is ostensibly preserved, but is in reality brought down and materialized.

MATERIALIZATIONS OF THINGS SPIRITUAL.

The New Movement having been organized into a distinctive religious community, and become ecclesiastically like many of the Churches, like them also it has set great limitations upon its followers through materializing those sacred things which are and were always meant to be wholly spiritual. It has repudiated many most beautiful and sacred teachings because those who have come under the materializing influence of its various Communities have failed to behold the inner meaning of these sublime truths even as the other Communities failed before them. It has, indeed, professed to come into such a knowledge of the Unseen World as the other Churches have not known—that knowledge of Divine Life in the Beyond, concerning which the other Communities have only spoken with uncertain voice—but it has put great limitations upon the knowledge which has come through the various venues ; for most of the things which have been given have been so sadly materialized that they have lost their spiritual significations. And so the disaster which overtook the other Churches as they rose, has very largely overtaken the new movement known as Spiritualism. The like materializing spirit has dominated the whole movement. Things have become inverted. The signs which come through to testify to the reality of the persistence of life beyond the physical planes, the symbols of great spiritual verities whose inner meanings are of the Divine and relate to the Soul, have their beautiful significations limited. For the Heavens into which the Mediums look are taken by most of the adherents of the new movement to be the Spiritual Heavens, full of Angelic Ministry, and the Ministry and Visions they behold are mistaken for the Visions and Ministry of those Heavens ; whereas most of the Mediums only see along the Astral plane. Even the ministry rendered them is misunderstood; for it is invariably related to the material life and the things associated with the physical planes. There is so little real Soul upliftment as the outcome of the knowledge which comes through and the Visions which are seen. The phenomena are eagerly sought after, *the inner meanings* of the phenomena are at a discount. The crowd is attracted by the phenomena, the very few desire only the Soul upliftment which the approach of the conditions brought from the Spiritual Heavens always should give and were meant to give. It is the signs and wonders of the supersensuous spheres which are craved for by most of those who are attracted to the new movement, not the wonderful things to which they point, and of which they are only semi-material expressions : for the real signs and wonders which testify of the Divine Love and Wisdom are within the Soul and are experienced there ; but the very few, even in the new movement ostensibly so spiritual, seek these.

What may be said of all the various Religious Communities may be most truly said of Spiritualism : they have all missed the inner spiritual meanings of the things they have believed, and so has the new movement. They have materialized the sacred mysteries concerning the Soul, the Planet and the Divine Love and Wisdom ; and Spiritualism has done so with the Spiritual Vision and Angelic Ministry. They have all put their own limitations upon the possible Divine Realizations by the Soul whilst still a denizen of the outer planes by denying to the Soul who had reached the spiritual state, when it was able to rise up out of the conditions of the Earth and function upon the Angelic Heavens, the power and the right to assume the office of one who was both Seer and Prophet ; and Spiritualism has put its own limitations upon the knowledge that may be given from the Spiritual Heavens, for its adherents deny much that is known to have been communicated from the Angelic Kingdom.

J. TODD FERRIER.

SPIRITUALISM,

ITS POSSIBILITIES AND RESPONSIBILITIES.

THAT the possibilities of the new movement, known under the designation " Spiritualism," are great, must be obvious to everyone who knows the meaning of the manifestations out of which it was born.   If it had given to it a right direction and purified avenues, what might it not accomplish for the Human Race ! It contains within itself all the powers by which the Heavens are opened unto the Soul and the Angelic Ministry unto this world is seen and understood, and possesses the means whereby that Ministry could be made *a reality* unto Humanity.   It has the first instalment, but requires to pass upwards from the alphabetic spheres to learn to read with the Spiritual Understanding the Angelic Signs and Messages, and apply them for the accomplishment of the real Redemption of the people.   It has paused at the Kindergarten department of the glorious spiritual education which the new movement was meant to bring, and even failed to understand many of the lessons given through the simple signs and forms.   It is yet in its childhood, though surely the time has come when it should make progress and grow into the fulfilment of the wonderful possibilities which are latent, but as yet unfolded.   If only all its leaders and mediums would recognise the true meaning of the purified life, *the true Redeemed Life*, the life whose ways are ways of purity upon every sphere—in meats and drinks, in life's surroundings, however humble, in all the outward relationships as well as the inward and spiritual—what an impetus would be given to the movement !   And what an upliftment it would receive !   How very different would the conditions be from those which now surround it, how true the spiritual communications, how beautiful the Angelic Visions, how glorious the inspiration that would come upon all earnest seekers !

The possibilities implied in the Spiritualistic Movement have never been accurately estimated by those within the movement. They have apprehended its first meaning, but missed the vision of its larger message. They have found in it the answer to the Soul's yearning for the close approach of the Spiritual World, but as yet have failed to discern whither it would lead the Soul if its messages were rightly understood and followed. The glorious possibilities latent in the new experiences resulting from the approach of the Spiritual World they have not only failed to behold, but through that failure they have affirmed practically the limits of the knowledges to be gained from those who are sent from the Angelic Kingdom. They glory in the elementary things associated with the movement, just as all the Churches have done with their distinctive movements, but refuse to see those higher and deeper aspects which lead the Soul up into the various spheres to be illuminated and taught in all the sacred Spiritual and Divine Mysteries, even whilst it is a denizen of the outer spheres in the sense that its experience and ministry are found there. They accept the messages which come through the average Medium as real communications from the Spiritual World, but reject those messages given unto other Mediums whose meanings are of the highest order. The elements of Spiritualism, however materialized, they will accept ; the more inward spiritual revelations and visions they refuse to believe. _ They can accept the visions which the Mediums see upon the Astral Kingdom, but not those visions which the Soul sees upon the Angelic Heavens. To them the possibilities of Spiritualism lie more in the universal recognition of the elementary conditions, the attestation of the persistency of the Soul, and the possibility of growth and progress in the Spiritual World, rather than in the inward Divine drama of the Soul, the approach of the Angelic World to the Soul as the result of the purified conditions, the inward illumination of the Soul as the result of its having attained the purified life, the true Redeemed Life, the Christ-spirit and Christ-love.

The possibilities of the Spiritualistic Movement will never be understood, nor its real mission to the Churches, Religious Hierarchies, Institutions and Communities be beheld, until the day arrives when the whole movement will be lifted right up out of its present sordid conditions, freed from the extreme limitations of "the beggarly elements" by which it is now circumscribed and even held in bondage, purified through the purification of all its channels, *made a real Spiritualism* through the realization within the Souls of all its adherents of the consciousness and meaning of the Divine Love, when the Spiritual World shall be sought for within the Soul.

When those things are accomplished within the movement, then will it become a real redeeming and enlightening power in the world. It will have a real message for all Souls, and become the channel of a blessed enlightenment unto all peoples. It will make manifest unto all the Churches the meaning of a true "Communion of Saints," and bring unto them the World in which they have only blindly believed, with its heavenly visions and Angelic messages. It will restore unto the Churches the Prophetic Office, and interpret for them the meaning of true Mediumship. It will give unto them the meaning of "the gift of tongues," and the power to Heal, and show them how the Divine illumines the Soul.

If the possibilities of the Spiritualistic Movement be so great, how great then are the responsibilities of all its Leaders and Mediums !   J. TODD FERRIER.

THE CONSTELLATION PISCES.

The Vision of the Mystery of the Constellation known as Pisces was given unto me in the day when the Constellations Aries and Gemini approached the Earth to overshadow her planes and accomplish her Redemption and Regeneration.

I beheld the Constellation descending from the Celestial Heavens and approaching the planes of the Earth ; and as it drew near the Mystery of its sign became clear to me, for it spake of the Great Deep out from which all the Mysteries of the Soul have come.

I saw it encompassing the Earth in its twofold meaning, pouring out, as it were, the Waters of Life from its fulness and giving unto all Souls the wonders of its depths.

And when its Waters of Life had fallen upon the the planes of the Earth, there arose a new race upon her planes, unto whom it was given to understand the Mystery of the Divine Nature and Unity.

The Mystery of the Divine Nature was shown unto me to be the Mystery of all true Life, since all proceedeth from the Divine ; and the Mystery of the Divine Unity is the Mystery of the Unity in all true Life.

For the Mystery of Life is the Mystery whose meaning can be known only when the Soul has become even as the Divine ; and the Mystery of the Divine Unity is the two-foldness of all true Life—the positive and negative forces which are expressed in the terms, masculine and feminine, fatherhood and motherhood.

It is the Mystery of the Father-Motherhood of the Eternal One.

THE THREE KINGS.*

THE time was drawing towards dawn in a wild and desolate region. And I stood with my genius at the foot of a mountain the summit of which was hidden in mist. At a few paces from me stood three persons, clad in splendid robes and wearing crowns on their heads. Each personage carried a casket and a key : the three caskets differed from one another, but the keys were all alike. And my genius said to me, " These are the three kings of the East, and they journey hither over the river that is dried up, to go up into the mountain of Sion and rebuild the Temple of the Lord God." Then I looked more closely at the three royalties, and I saw that the one that stood nearest to me on the left hand was a man, and the colour of his skin was dark like that of an Indian. And the second was in form like a woman, and her complexion was fair : and the third had the wings of an Angel, and carried a staff of gold.[1] And I heard them say one to another. " Brother, what hast thou in thy casket ? " And the first answered, " I am the Stone-layer, and I carry the implements of my craft ; also a bundle of myrrh for thee and for me." And the king who bore the aspect of a woman answered, " I am the Carpenter, and I bear the implements of my craft ; also a box of frankincense for thee and for me." And the Angel-king answered, " I am the Measurer, and I carry the secrets of the living God, and the rod of gold to measure your work withal." Then the first said, " Therefore let us go up into the hill of the Lord and build the walls of Jerusalem." And they turned to ascend the mountain. But they had not taken the first step when the king whose name was Stonelayer, said to him who was called the Carpenter, " Give me first the implements of thy craft, and the plan of thy building, that I may

---

* Dreams and Dream Stories, by the late Dr. Anna (Bonus) Kingsford. (See advertisement on Cover).

[1] " The angel king is, of course, Hermes, the Spirit of Understanding, who with his rod of gold, the Symbol of Knowledge, measures the Holy City of the Apocalypse." (E.M. The Life of A.K., Vol. ii., p. 78).

know after what sort thou buildest, and may fashion thereto my masonry." And the other asked him, "What buildest thou, brother?" And he answered "I build the Outer Court." Then the Carpenter unlocked his casket and gave him a scroll written over in silver, and a crystal rule, and a carpenter's plane and saw, And the other took them and put them into his casket. Then the Carpenter said to the Stonelayer, "Brother, give me also the plan of thy building, and the tools of thy craft. For I build the Inner Place, and must needs fit my designing to thy foundation." But the other answered : "Nay, my brother, for I have promised the labourers. Build thou alone. It is enough that I know thy secrets ; ask not mine of me." And the Carpenter answered, "How then shall the Temple of the Lord be builded ? Are we not of three Ages, and is the Temple yet perfected ?" Then the Angel spoke, and said to the Stonelayer, "Fear not, brother : freely hast thou received ; freely give. For except thine elder brother had been first a Stonelayer, he could not now be a Carpenter. Art thou not of Solomon, and he of Christ ? Therefore he hath already handled thy tools, and is of thy craft. And I also the Measurer, I know the work of both. But now is that time when the end cometh, and that which hath been spoken in the ear in closets, the same shall be proclaimed on the housetops." Then the first king unlocked his casket, and gave to the Carpenter a scroll written in red, and a compass and a trowel. But the Carpenter answered him : "It is enough. I have seen, and I remember. For this is the writing King Solomon gave into my hands when I also was a Stonelayer, and when thou wert of the company of them that labour. For I also am thy Brother, and that thou knowest I know also." Then the third king, the Angel, spoke again and said, "Now is the knowledge perfected and the bond fulfilled. For neither can the Stonelayer build alone, nor the Carpenter construct alone apart. Therefore, until this day, is the Temple of the Lord unbuilt. But now is the time come, and Salem shall have her habitation on the Hill of the Lord."

And there came down a mist from the mountain, and out of the mist a star. And my Genius said, "Thou shalt yet see more on this wise." But I saw then only the mist, which filled the valley and moistened my hair and my dress; and so I awoke.[2]

ANNA (BONUS) KINGSFORD, M.D.

A PRAYER.

O Infinite and Ever-Blessed One! We would bless Thee. Thy praise is in all Thy works, and heard throughout the Heavens where Thy Glory is: we would have the Praise of Thee welling up in our hearts.

Thou openest the Heavens unto Thy Children that they may again behold Thy Glory and become recipients of the Angelic Ministry through which Thy great goodness is made manifest and Thy Holy Wisdom interpreted.

May we be of those who through a living faith enter into the heritage of the Angelic Life, the Crown of Life which fadeth not away, but whose lustre is from the Glory of the Lord.

May Thy Heavens within us ever be open unto the incoming of the Son of Man, that we may also become Thy true Sons. *Amen and Amen.*

---

[2] For the full comprehension of the above dream, it is necessary to be profoundly versed at once in the esoteric signification of the Scriptures and in the mysteries of Freemasonry. It was the dreamer's great regret that she neither knew, nor could know, the latter, women being excluded from initiation. E.M.

THE DEVELOPMENT OF DIVINE LOVE.*

THERE is no envy in Love.   Love is satisfaction in itself.   Not that satisfaction with personal self and its possessions and attractions, which is but vanity, but an inner satisfaction that sees good everywhere and in everybody.   It insists that all is Good, and by refusing to see anything but Good, that quality finally appears uppermost in itself and all things.   When only Good is seen and felt how can there be anything but satisfaction ?

The one who has found this inner Love, and lets it pour its healing currents into his Soul and body is fortunate beyond all description.   Instead of envying another, the desire is to show others the great joy which may be theirs, when they have opened out the flood gates of their love nature.   Truly, " Love envieth not."

Yet with all these glorious possessions, beyond the power of man to describe, " Love vaunteth not itself— is not puffed up."   Love does not brag about its demonstrations.   It simply lives the life, and lets its works speak for it.

Love does not seek its own.   It does not make external effort to get anything, not even that which intellect claims belongs to it.   It is here that Love proves itself to be the invisible magnet that draws to man whatever he needs.   But, instead of leaving this department of the work to Love, the intellect has seen what it wanted, and then, in its cumbersome way, gone about the getting. Thus the true begetting power in man has been ignored until its office has been forgotten, and its usefulness no longer recognised.

When Love, the universal magnet, is brought into action in the consciousness of our race it will change all our methods of support and supply.   It will harmonize

---

* Extract from TWELVE LESSONS IN CHIRSTIAN HEALING. by Charles Fillmore.   (Unity Tract Society, U.S.A.).   These little lectures should be of great service to many seeking earnestly the higher path of life. They insist upon taking the noblest view of life, and show that all true Healing within the individual and through the life must be based upon and find its power in a pure spiritual love. (Editor, *Herald of the Cross*).

all the forces of nature, and the discords that now infest earth and air will disappear. It will control the elements until they shall obey man, and bring forth that which will supply all his needs without the sweat of his face. This earth shall yet be made Paradise through the power of Love.

That condition will begin to set in for each of one us just as soon as we develop the love nature in ourselves.

When Love has begun its silent pulsations at our solar centre no one can keep us in want or poverty. Love itself will draw unto us in the invisible currents of the inner ether all that belongs to us ; and all belongs to us that we require to make us happy and contented.

This mighty magnet is a quality of God that is expressed through man, and it cannot be suppressed by any outside force. No environment or external condition can keep back Love when once you have firmly decided in mind to give it expression. The present unloving condition of the world is no bar to you ; in fact, it is an incentive. You will know as you begin to make Love manifest how great a sinner you have been—how far short you have fallen in making yourself the man or woman of God. This will show you by comparison how greatly you have missed the mark of high calling, which is yours in Christ.

We have all been taught the beauties of Love and its great power in the world, but no one has explained that it has a centre of action in the body that was designed by the Creator to do a specific work. The man or woman who has not developed the love centre is abnormal ; is living in partial exercise only of consciousness. The love centre has its nerves and muscles in the body, which through neglect have become atrophied in nearly the whole race. But they are just as necessary to the perfect man as the legs and arms ; and even more so, because with the love centre active one might live happily and successfully without legs or arms.

The body is the instrument of the mind and no one has ever seen his real body as it is in the sight of God, except through the mind. The body of flesh, bones and blood that the eye of sense beholds is not the true body any more than the heart of flesh is the true organ of Love.

The true body is an electrical body ; an indestructible body, and this body of flesh is the grosser vibrations which the sense-consciousness beholds. But the Spirit-body is not absent nor dead, but simply inactive. When through purification of his ideas and acceleration of his mental energies man comes into sight of the real forces of Being, this Spirit body is quickened into new life, and the body of flesh responds to its vibrations. This is done through the mind—through thinking right thoughts, and doing right things also, because man is in ultimate a unit, and the thinking and doing cannot be separated.

To develop the love centre commence by affirming, " From this time forth and for evermore I shall know no man after the flesh. I shall not see men and women as body and mortal thought. I shall always behold them with the eye of Love, which sees only perfection." Ask daily that love be made alive in you ; that she take up her abode at your magnetic centre and make it alive with her strong, steady pulsations of spiritual energy.

THE WAY OF PERFECT HEALTH.

The way of the Divine Love is the way of perfect health.

The stream of the Divine Love maketh whole the life through which it floweth.

It floweth inward to the centre of man's being, filling with its fulness the life able to receive it ; and then it floweth outward through every sphere of experience, making each sphere pure and its service beautiful.

Thus doth the Divine Love heal the whole life of man, saving all its powers from the influences which are adverse to their truest unfoldment, bringing them into a perfect state.

The Herald of the Cross.

Vol. v. New Series. November, 1909. No. 11.

THE VISION OF THE LORD.

I saw the Lord. He stood before me on the shores
Of Sacred Galilee whose calm clear waters could
Reflect the glory of the Heavens by which they were
O'ershadowed, and the Hills and Mountains which
  rose
Peak above peak, those Uplands of the Soul, the home
Of Angels, the Heights Divine whence streameth
  far God's
Glory in unclouded day, wondrous, unspeakable.
At first I knew Him not, so clouded was my
Vision, for sorrow had laid her heavy hand upon
Me, and deep grief had struck its roots into my life.
For I had sought my Lord with great desire and tear-
Stained countenance and anguishing of Soul, yet
  found
Him not ; the Night had closed about me, and the
  Stars
Were lost amid the darkness, those Angelic Lamps
Dependant from the Heavens, that I could not find.
My way back to the land of Life Immortal, that
Land of pure delight and joy unspeakable where
Saints dwell and evil is unknown, the land whose
Pastures are God's Wisdom rich and full, whose
  rivers
Flow still, calm, and deep, bearing Life's Waters for the

Soul, rivers of Love Celestial and Divine.
But when I saw His form, His well-known Counte-
    nance
Radiant with Light ineffable which made the
Darkness fade and brought in day, His Vesture
    seamless,
Pure, glorious, then knew I that it was the Lord.
And when I heard His voice so full of gentleness,
(So tender were His words), my sorrow was no more
With me, nor the deep grief which pulsèd through
    my veins,
Nor anguish overwhelming at my loss, but in
Their stead came peace and joy and comfort such
    as He
Alone could give my Soul. " As ye have naught
    to eat,
Come dine with me : Take ye this Bread of Life
    and be
Ye nourished, this Mystery of Love strengthening
And fitting you to bear your Cross, your burden,
    through
The Via Dolorosa unto Calvary's Hill,
The Pathway of the Christs, the Sons of God who bear
The burden of the world unto Redemption, and
Yield themselves in Service to their Lord, sublimely.
Lo, I am with you alway, e'en when the shadows
Fall as when the light is full, to guide you.
You I will never leave, nor forsake my Temple
Wherein I love to dwell in commune with the Soul."
Thus spake He ; and there came upon me His own
    Holy
Breath which filled me with His Peace, and made
    me joyous,
And caused the fire to burn upon my Altar night
    and day,
And lit my Lamp with His own glorious Light.

O Blessed Vision of my Soul ! My Mind is Galilee,
And there upon its shores the Lord doth walk.

                        J. TODD FERRIER.

WHAT IS A CHRISTIAN ? [1]

I.

CAN one be a true disciple of the blessed Master whilst continuing to eat the flesh of the Creatures ?

Many will think the question not only to be unnecessary, but even to be impertinent. Men and women have long been accustomed to view the taking of the lives of the Creatures for food and raiment as one which was quite in keeping with true discipleship to the blessed Master ; for all the Churches, without exception, have looked upon it not only as a necessity in the economy of Nature that the Creatures should lay down their lives to sustain the bodies of men and women, but that the Divine Love had ordained that it should be done, and that to eat flesh was to obey the Divine mandate. If therefore we were to answer the question in the negative it would seem as if we were assuming the rôle of judge, and cutting off from allegiance to the Master the tens of thousands who do truly desire to follow Him, live His life, and take part in the Divine service.

Yet are we compelled to take up this position, however hard and unjust it may appear when judged of by those who only stand upon the outer planes of life and perceive not that *all true life* must be lived from the innermost spheres, and that the outermost must be brought into perfect harmony with the innermost, otherwise the life will not be in true harmony. We are led to affirm that no one who takes the lives of the Creatures to minister unto their desires in any way can be a *true and intimate* follower and friend of the Master, because we know that the life which the Master lived and which He urged all who followed Him to live, was absolutely free from the evil of blood-guiltiness caused through sacrificing the Creatures upon the altars of the sense-life. The Christ could not violate the fundamental laws of the Divine

---

[1] This and the following articles, with an introductory chapter, will be published in booklet form suitable for distribution. We shall be glad to hear from those friends who desire to procure them.

Order, the laws of true compassion and pity; to have done so would have meant the abrogation of the beautiful Estate with all the Divine Heritage it implied. It would have been to contradict the very nature of the Christhood and degrade His Divine Mission.

Men and women do not seem to understand the meaning of a Christhood; nor do the Churches appear to apprehend the significance of the life which it implied. They like to think that the blessed Master was pure, yet they imagine that He lived as other men lived in eating and drinking. They do not behold what is meant by the beautiful purity of the Master or they would at once see how impossible it was for Him to eat flesh or encourage others to eat it. They love to think that He was Divinely compassionate, yet they can believe that He followed those ways of life whose paths run blood, even the blood of the Creatures slain in the abattoirs to meet the demands of the sense-life of thoughtless men and women. And so they naturally think that one can be truly compassionate and at the same time eat the flesh of slain Creatures; that one can know a Divine Pity and yet agree to the wholesale slaughter of the Creatures for food, and the imposition upon tens of thousands of others of tortures unnamable; that one may make of the Creatures mere goods and chattels of merchandise which men and women buy and sell to get gain, irrespective of what is to become of them—and yet retain the compassion which is said to have moved the blessed Master towards all Souls.

It is indeed sad to think that men and women who should know the true meaning of following the blessed Master could ever have had given to them such a view of the meaning of His wonderful ministry. And it is especially sad that within the Christian Churches where the true vision of His Christhood surely should have been known, a view of the meaning of the Master's Christhood prevails which is a violation of all pity, the antithesis of compassion, and the abrogation of that profound and sublime experience implied in the wonderful Christhood of the blessed Master.   J. TODD FERRIER.

WHAT IS A CHRISTIAN ?

II.

THE NATURE OF THE REDEMPTION.

THAT a follower of the blessed Master may not eat flesh will be understood when the meaning of the Master's life is understood. What was the purpose of that life ? Was it not one of Redemption ? What was the nature of the Redemption which He meant to accomplish ? Was it not the restoration to man's life of the Divine purity, love and goodness ? And how were these to be restored within man's spiritual system unless the man was to be purified upon every sphere of experience, learn the profound and all-embracing nature of the Divine Love, and the universality of the Divine Goodness in its manifestations ? And how could a man become pure whilst he defiled his body with the flesh of the sacrificed Creatures, his mind with the unlovely conduct of having the helpless slain to minister unto his low, unmanly, and even inhuman tastes, and his heart with the violation of the fundamental principles of all true compassion and pity ? How could he come to know the Divine Love without first realizing its own tender reverence for *all life* ? How could he know and understand the Divine Goodness unless he learnt to permit it to flow as a life-giving stream through his own life, expressing itself in gentleness, fellow feeling and spiritual kinship with all true forms of life ?

That this view of Redemption to a true spiritual state is not that which the Churches believe in and teach, will be admitted by all who have learnt at the shrines of these Communities. For the Churches,[1] though differing amongst themselves, nevertheless all date their origin and teaching from the Records which were supposed to have been written by those who knew the Master and understood what His Christhood meant ; and in these Records the true Redeemed Life illustrated by the

---

[1] We only know of two communities in the whole Western World which make flesh-eating an obstacle to membership—one in Manchester and another in the U.S.A.

Master is obscured so that none can tell what it really was except those unto whom it has been given to behold the erroneous presentation, to see the true picture, and to restore the long-lost vision of the Christhood. The Redemption to be accomplished by the Master is not presented in the Records as a life lifted up out of the influences of the evil conditions which prevail in the world, but rather as something to be accomplished by the Master apart from the upliftment of the Soul and its co-operation in the work. It is presented as a mysterious work wrought on behalf of the Race, the true nature of which none may fully understand. And all the Sayings in which the Redemption is spoken of have been made to relate to the personal Jesus, rather than to the Christhood which was made manifest through Him, consequently their mystic meanings were all changed, and their profound significations became lost. That happened to them which happened to the pure spiritual teachings in other ages; they were made material instead of spiritual in their meanings, and personal rather than universal in their relationships. The Redemption was thus changed from being a Divine work *within* man, to that of a Divine work apart from him; from an inward experience whose influences touched the whole realm of man's life, to be only a work wrought on his behalf, by which the attitude of the Divine Love was changed towards him. Such is the picture of the Redemption of the life presented in the Records upon which the Churches have built up their organizations and theories, so that it is not difficult to understand how it has happened in the Western World with the religion of a Christhood widely confessed, that the true Redeemed Life has not been understood by those who worship within the various Sanctuaries.

WHAT DISTINGUISHES A CHRISTIAN ?

What are those features which should distinguish a Christian from any who may not profess belief in the Christ and His Christhood ? Are they to be understood as mere intellectual differences, the results of difference of birth and environment ? Are they to be circumscribed by the assent of the mind to certain views held by the Churches, or the outward admiration of the Master and professed allegiance to Him such as the world gives to earthly potentates ? Are they to find the fulness of their manifestation in the religious fervour and ecclesiastical devotion which are characteristics of all religions ? Are not all these features to be found where no Christhood is professed, where the religious concepts and life are considered to be greatly inferior to those of the Christian ? Indeed in some of the Eastern religions there is a far higher conception of the sacredness of all life than may be found in the West. The principles underlying these religions inculcate humaneness in a way unknown within the Christian Churches. And the writings upon which these religions are founded lay stress upon true charity or love towards all the Creatures as one great essential to the right understanding of Divine things and the attainment of the Divine life.

Wherein then lie the distinguishing features of Christianity and of the man who would interpret Christianity in his life by being a Christian ? Is it not in this, that Christianity gathers up into itself every good in all the other religions, giving to them a new and higher meaning, transcending them in its vision of the purpose of the Divine Love concerning this world and all its children (Creature and Human), and giving a very real meaning to the Soul in its Evolution, Fall, Redemption and Regeneration ? And in gathering up all that is good in the other religions it could not fail to make manifest a most beautiful love towards all Souls, a compassion immeasurable in its outflowing unto all who are weak and defenceless, and a pity towards the Creatures tender and boundless. It could not fail to reveal wherever it was truly received, a life full of purity and goodness, a life whose every sphere was purified and which made manifest the Redeemed Life as the attainment of Redemption. It would not fail where the other religions had failed by simply setting forth the nature of the Redeemed Life (as in the case of Buddhism), and leaving man without a perfect embodiment of its meaning, but would give a most unmistakeable manifestation of what the Redeemed Life was, so that all men might in beholding it know the nature of the life unto which they were called. And as the crown of all other religions it would not fail to show forth the inner meaning of a Christhood, what it was in its nature, how it was to be attained, and in what sense it was the crown of the Redeemed Life ; and it would illustrate all these things in a sublime interpretation given in manifestation through one who lived the Redeemed Life and was crowned with the Christhood Estate.

An Obscure Presentation.

That the Life and Teachings of the blessed Master transcended any manifestation in earlier times would have been known unto the whole Western World had the Records which purport to portray Him as He lived and taught, contained a true and faithful portrait. But these Records do not contain a true picture of the Christ. For had they done so the path to Christhood would not have been hidden. The true way unto the Christhood Estate would have been obvious unto all who desired to enter upon it. The Redeemed Life with its *threefold path* would have been clear unto every reader. There would have been no room for doubt as to anything the Master meant when He called men and women to live the Redeemed Life. His teachings concerning the way of the Redemption would not have been obscure as they now are, so that men and women would have known that true Redemption was a thing to be accomplished within them through the Soul and all its powers seeking to realize the Divine way of life, the way of purity, goodness and love.

But that these things are obscure must be evident to any one who knows what the Redemption means. To them the Records must appear as remarkable and strange betrayers of the picture of Christhood, since they fail to direct the Soul to the threefold path of the Redeemed Life, and, instead, simply direct the mind to a personal allegiance to the Master as the true meaning of following Him.   J. Todd Ferrier.

WHAT IS A CHRISTIAN ?

III.

THE PICTURE IN THE RECORDS IS NOT THAT OF A CHRIST, NOR EVEN THAT OF A BUDDHA.

WE have seen that the Records which profess to give a true portrait of the life of the blessed Master fail in those things which some of the other great religions emphasized. The portrait is not that of a Christ, though the Master is so called in them. It is not even that of a Buddha ; for there is no direct teaching concerning the relationship which exists between the Human and the Creature Kingdoms, and the attitude which the Christian must assume towards all the Creatures. Had the portrait been truly that of the blessed Master as He was, then not only would the relationship of the Christian to the Creatures have been made clear, but it would have been also shown to have been an essential experience in the threefold path of the Soul seeking to follow the Christ. And had the Christhood been truly drawn by the writers of these Records, then all the world could by this time have come to the knowledge of the meaning of the beautiful Estate known as Christhood, and every earnest seeker who desired to understand the Divine Mysteries would have been able to follow the Teachings of the Master, arrive at the vision of the Divine Love within the Sanctuary of the Soul, and even come to know the Divine Wisdom through entering into the wonderful experiences expressed by the term Christhood. Then there would have been no need to inquire " What is a Christian ?" so manifest would the answer have been. Christianity would have been a truly living force in the world ; not as at present, but as it was meant to be. The astonishing ecclesiastical systems which have grown up in its name would have found no place ; nor would the awful conflicts between the various sections have been known. For the whole world would have had the Holy Breath upon its spheres as the outcome of the beautiful lives through whom the Christhood was made manifest and the Heavenly Wisdom interpreted. The awful burdens which are now crushing the lives of the toiling millions would have been unknown ; for the conditions out of which they have grown would have been impossible. The shameful and unspeakable systems whose ramifications have penetrated the Churches, and whose whole influence is for evil, could have found no soil in which to grow. The blighting Drink Traffic with its holocaust of victims and its indescribable influences for degradation and woeful tragedy, would have found no men and women to support it, nor Churches to shelter those who sought to impose so infamous a wrong upon the children of the Heavenly Father. The equally evil system represented by the abattoirs and shambles would have been unknown with all its cruel and shameful work ; for the people would have loved purity in their ways, and humaneness would have adorned them as a beautiful garment. The Creatures would have been cared for and loved as the little spiritual children in the great Household of the Heavenly Father. The health of all the people would have been so different, for they would have known and followed the ways of health, and the evil, cruel and inhuman work of vivisection and all it implies, would never have been conceived of by those who were the physicians and healers. Love between man and man would have triumphed ; compassion in man towards all the Creatures would have shown gloriously ; pity would have had a real dwelling-place and fulness of manifestation. The vision of the Redeemed Life would have led Souls to the realization of its purity, goodness and love. The vision of the Christhood would have led many into the vision of the Divine Love, and not a few into the vision of the Divine Wisdom which maketh all things clear unto the Soul.

The Records failed in things essential. The writers obscured the vision of Christhood, misrepresented the Redemption, and gave a false picture of the sublime Master. Behold the Western World where they are believed!

J. TODD FERRIER.

WHAT IS A CHRISTIAN?

IV.

THE THREEFOLD PATH FOR THE SOUL : SELF-DENIAL, SELF-SACRIFICE, SELF-ABANDONMENT.

THE FIRST STEP.

A CHRISTIAN is one who follows the Christ wheresoever He leadeth. He follows Him along the path which imposed upon all the desires and affections great self-denial in respect to their more outward manifestation. For that is the first path which the Soul must learn to tread. The man who would truly follow the Christ must take up his cross and bear it along the road of self-denial. The sense-life must be chastened. It must be restrained in all its outgoings and purified in all its feelings. The outer spheres of experience must be made quite pure. Nothing must enter into the outer courts of the Temple which would defile them. The tastes must be brought into perfect harmony with the innermost desires of the Soul. "If any man would follow me," said the Master, "he must take up his cross and deny himself." The following was to be along the road of purification of all the senses. "If a man will not deny himself, he cannot be my disciple," showing clearly that such a purification was absolutely essential to true discipleship. And wherein was man to deny himself were it not in those things which men and women in general seek after? What are those things most sought for by men and women but the things of the sense-life, the gratification of the sense desires, the eating of flesh and drinking of wine, and the pleasure which gratification of the senses gives?

These things a man must overcome if he would follow the Christ. He must learn to deny himself of every gratification of the sense-life wherein mere pleasure is sought. He must conquer the adversary on the outer spheres if he would attain to the glory of the inward life. He must "go forth bearing his cross" through all the outward spheres of experience, however heavy

that cross may become to him. He must cease ministering to his body except as to a precious vehicle through
which he has to make manifest his inmost purposes, and
he must nourish it upon the pure fruits of the Earth.
If he would know the Christ, he must first learn to know
Jesus. If he would follow the Christ he must first follow
Jesus. When he has followed Jesus along the path
which bringeth purification, then will he understand the
true meaning of the Jesus-life, that it is not a personal
following of the Master, but a spiritual experience which
leadeth the Soul upon all its spheres into a state of
Redemption.

To be a Christian is, therefore, to be a man who knows
the Redeemed Life.

THE SECOND STEP.

When a man has accomplished the first step through
self-denial and purification, then may he go on to know
the Christ. Having learnt the meaning of the Jesus life
he may seek for the meaning of the Christhood. But
he is met on the way by the step which leadeth unto the
Christhood path ; it is the step which imposes upon the
Soul renunciation of all things for the sake of the Christ.

It is recorded that the Master said to the disciples,
when they were contending as to which of them should
be first in the new kingdom, that the Master affirmed
that unless a man were prepared to forsake everything
in this world—goods, estate, family traditions and ways,
even those most closely related to him in the outer
spheres—he could not know the Christ.

This would appear at first sight as something contrary
to the ways of a true and beautiful love ; but when
understood as the Master meant it, there is beheld a
profound truth which all who would follow the Christ
must learn. When the Soul is following the Christ along
the second path it must needs learn that all outward
things and relationships have only an outward and
temporary value, and that their real value lies in their
uses for truly spiritual ends. No other uses are recognised
in the Heavens of the Divine Love ; nor can they be
recognised by the Soul who would follow the Master.

And so, everything of the Earth in its outward spheres must be renounced as things which are to have no value in the Soul's just estimation of life. The love for them which is so characteristic a feature of the life of men and women to-day, is opposed to the true progress of the Soul, because it draws the Soul earthwards to find satisfaction for its noblest longings in them ; and so when the Soul sets out to follow the Christ it must needs learn how to renounce all these things so that in its following it may be hindered by none of them.

How often a Soul is hindered through its social and family ties from pressing forward in the path that leads to the Christ-life. Pride of birth and heritage, love of social position, desire to hold the things of the world as valuable possessions, longing to know success as the world knows it, to have fame such as men and women see, to keep the old friendship born from the earthly conditions—all these things have to be renounced. Their power over life has to be broken. The Soul must be set free from the love of them that nothing may retard its progress in the path along which the Christ-vision draws it.

Thus is it that the experience comes to those who really love divine things, in which life is made hard for them, the path difficult, the renunciation great, when in the path, they have to forsake the old ways and affections—friends, land, goods, heritage, prestige with all the pleasures which these bring. They have not only to be pure in all their ways of life, but also spiritual in all their purposes ; for the kingdom they seek is purely spiritual, and concerns itself only with spiritual things. And so we see what a profound meaning lies couched in the term Christian, and what it implies for the Soul who would be a Christian indeed.

The Third Step.

Nor is that the full answer to the question What is a Christian ? Purity in all the spheres of life is absolutely essential. Renunciation of all earthly things and attachments is likewise a necessary experience. But in following the Christ there is one more step to ascend which leads unto the realization of Christhood itself. It is to ascend the cross of absolute abandonment to the Divine Service. It is not only to know the crucifixion of the desires of the sense-life and the renunciation of the world for things spiritual and Divine, but it is also to go wheresoever the Spirit of the Lord directeth, and bear whatsoever burden of service He may in His Holy Wisdom deem expedient to impose. It is not only to be pure in all the ways of our life, and spiritual in all its aims, but it is to have the beautiful spirit of true childhood unto the Divine Love, humble and obedient even unto the death of our most cherished hopes, willing to be even a seeming failure in the world of service, submissive to the Divine Will should that will demand that we should be crucified before the world by those who failed to understand us, and forsaken by all in whom we had trusted and loved.

The pathway of the Christian is not only one lit up with a great and glorious hope, and one full of the promise of a spiritual enrichment of the life, but it is also a pathway leading through the "Via Dolorosa" upward to "the Cross of Calvary" where the crosses of Self-denial and Renunciation meet in that yet fuller cross of perfect self-surrender or Abandonment to the Divine Service.

"Are ye indeed able to drink of the cup of which I shall drink? and to be baptized with the baptism that I shall have?" Thus did the Master inquire of two who would follow the Christ unto perfect realization of Christhood. And they replied, "We are able."

The answer is now before us ; who would follow on to be a Christian ?   J. TODD FERRIER.

A VISION OF THE MASTER.

There came to me a vision in the Night of this
World's travail, in which I saw the Master as He
Was when Nazareth was His home in Galilee.
And I must tell that vision unto you to show
How beautiful was His life, how pure in all its
Spheres. He knew no wrong nor in His ways did
*   evil ;*
He loved all Souls ; the Creatures He did shield
*   from those*

Who would oppress them ; Compassion flowed in
*   fulness*
Unto all, and bore upon its crest unfailing
Pity, which passed to the remotest states of life
Finding the wounded ones to touch and heal them all.
No Creature suffered from His look, His word, His
*   deed ;*
No life was sacrificed to meet His earthly wants ;
His lips were stainless, free from the darkening and
Polluting sin of shedding blood ; all life to Him
Was sacred ; His pathway saw no bloodmarks
*   where He*
Trod which spake of mangled forms and anguish-
*   cries of*
Helpless victims within the awful Abattoirs.
He was a Man complete, holy and true, whose
Vestures were the garments of pure life; a Man
Beneficent, upon whose brow there sat that crown
Which good men fain would merit—the Crown of
*   Good,*
Image of the Gods, resplendent with a love
God-born, boundless, free for all, knowing no limits
In its giving, nor recognising any.   To Him
All Souls were dear as unto God ; no Human kind
Nor Creature, howsoe'er remote, He passèd by
Unheeded, but gave His Benison of healing
Love, and called all Souls to follow in His Way,
The Way of Life Redeemed from bondage, sin and woe;
The Soul upraised, from evil freed, and sphered in
*   love ;*
The Life of Self-denial that would scorn to make
A Creature suffer pain, or have its days cut short
To minister to desire ; the Life that seeks
No pleasure in this world born of desire, but only
That of sacrifice, full, beautiful, Divine, that
Gives out from its own in service born of love.
Such was my vision ; now may ye behold the Man
Whose way was narrow, but which led to Life.

J. TODD FERRIER.

WHAT IS A CHRISTIAN ?

V.

WHITHER THE THREEFOLD PATH OF SELF-DENIAL, SELF-
SACRIFICE AND SELF-ABANDONMENT LEADETH.

WE have seen that the path of the Christian is three-fold, that it embraces Self-denial, Self-sacrifice and Self-abandonment, and that only through the realization of these does the Soul become a Christian in very deed, one who knows the Christ and so has entered into Christhood.

We have beheld all that Self-denial implies ; how it makes the life give up those things whose use is hurtful to the Creatures and the body, and degrading to mind and heart ; how it demands that every sphere shall be pure, that the sense-life shall learn to be dumb until every sense becomes the avenue through which the Redeemed Life is made manifest.

We have seen how the path along which the Christian travels insists upon Renunciation as the next step, how the life must learn to give up all that it has, to sacrifice every earthly interest, to forsake all worldly estate and possessions as things to be valued and loved, to know by experience the meaning of Self-sacrifice when even the most sacred ties upon the outer spheres have to loosen their hold upon the life until the Soul even walks alone.

We have also seen that the way of the Christ draws the Soul yet further from the ways of men and women when it impels it to walk through the " Via Dolorosa " and ascend the " Hill of Calvary " unto crucifixion of its most ardent hopes, however pure and beautiful they may have been ; how in the hour of crucifixion the world's scorn may be poured upon the Soul, and the deep sorrow of desertion by all whom it has loved, break upon it. And now we have to look at the result unto the Soul of all these experiences, the kind of life by which it is crowned, the realizations which come to it, and the service unto which it is called. For to be a Christian is to be as a Christ.

THE CROWN OF LIFE.

The Soul who has passed along that threefold path at last arrives at the state of spiritual experience known amongst the most ancient Hebrews (not the Jews) as Zion, and amongst the inner group of the Master's disciples as Christhood. It was said by the Hebrew Prophets and Seers to have been the ancient estate of Israel, those who had prevailed with God and had become His princes upon the Earth. And it was always unto the Holy City of Zion that Israel were counselled to return and come again to the vision of the Divine Lord within the Sanctuary. So the Soul who follows the threefold path is of the Redeemed of the Lord who return unto Zion, the Holy City of the Lord.   .

To arrive at that state is to attain unto the Vision of the Divine Presence within the Sanctuary of the Soul; and to reach that Vision is to be interiorly illumined from the Divine. It is to be baptized with the Sevenfold Spirit, the baptism of Christhood when the Soul is crowned " A Son of God." It is to be wreathed with the laurels of the conqueror, one who has overcome and risen to the Right Hand of the Majesty on High, by which is to be understood the rising up of the Soul into the blessed realization of the Divine Love, the Divine Wisdom, and the oneness of the One Divine Life.

To be a Christian, therefore, is to be a Soul who knows and lives the Redeemed Life, who understands and lives the life of Self-sacrifice, who sees and follows the Divine Will wheresoever it leadeth, until at last it is crowned with Christhood, and becomes one whose Lamp is kindled from the Lord, one whose Soul is illumined from the Divine, and who only needs to retire into the silence for communion to know from the Divine those Heavenly Things which no man can give nor the wisdom of the world impart.

J. TODD FERRIER.

WHAT IS A CHRISTIAN ?

VI.

WHAT THE CHURCH AS A COMMUNITY OF CHRISTIANS SHOULD BE.

IN the light of the things which we have written, things concerning the truth of which we have both seen and heard within spheres which are not adjacent now to this Earth, the real Spiritual World, the world of the Soul and the Divine Light, it will not be very difficult for us to also conceive of the true Church as to the life and ministry of its members. For the full answer to the question "What is a Christian ?" is likewise the answer to the question, "What is a Christian Church ?" For the Church must be the fuller, because multiplied, manifestation of all that is implied in the term Christian.

The Christian Church should be Christian in its Fellowship, its Worship, its Communion, and its Ministry unto the world. It should be composed only of men and women who know and live the Redeemed Life, men and women who have sought to purify all their ways, who have had that vision which makes purity of life a necessity unto them and fills them with compassion for all Souls and pity unto all the Creatures. They should be men and women who in their fellowship truly love the Brethren without any regard to their mere earthly estate, men and women of humble heart who desire to attain the spirit of the little child in all their ways. They should be men and women whose fellowship would be as the breath of Heaven unto the Soul, because they know the purified life, have come into direct touch with Heavenly things, have risen on to the Spiritual Heavens to behold the Angelic Life there and receive of the Angelic Wisdom from the Divine, who have themselves become recipients of Divine Illumination and true Mediums through whom the Divine communicates His Love and Wisdom unto those Souls who are not grown sufficiently towards the Divine to enable them to receive these within themselves. They should be men and women who are not only pure in all their ways and spiritual in all their aims with a love which is born from the Divine within them and which manifests itself in profound compassion for all Souls and unfailing pity unto all Creatures, but who also have within themselves the consciousness of the Divine Presence.

They should, therefore, be in this world the repositories of the Divine Presence, and be always conscious of it, and derive all their illumination and guidance through the consciousness of that Presence. When they worship it should be with "the open vision" which the consciousness of the Divine Presence within the Sanctuary of their being gives them. The spirit of the Fear or Divine Awe of the Lord should fill them and make even the earthly house of their fellowship a place whose gates are as doorways through which the breath of the Heavens is felt. It should be worship, indeed, in which all earthly things should pass out of the vision to be replaced with purely spiritual and Divine things. The whole being of each worshipper should be uplifted from the earth into the clear air of "the heavenly places" to behold with open vision upon the Heavens the Glory of the Lord as that glory is broken unto them. Their communion should be with the Divine Love and His Saints, and the Angelic World should be a beautiful reality unto them. Upon them should sit the tongues of cloven fire, the signs of their inspiration and the testimony of their Christhood.

What such a Church would become.

What a wealth of meaning is couched in the expression *A Christian Church*? And in the realization of that meaning, what wealth of spiritual riches and power for the accomplishment of the Redemption? In the manifestation of the life of such a community of Souls, what illumination would break upon the ways of life in the world to expose evil and error, and make clear the true path along which the Soul must needs walk if it would enter into the experience of the Redemption? How real would the Spiritual Heavens become unto every true seeker who desired the heavenly life, if the Church were thus Christian! The Ladder that was seen let down from the Heavens to rest upon the Earth would no longer

be a mere dream-story but a glorious reality ; for the
ministry of Angels would have become known and
realized.

What the Soul in its life and ministry must become if it
would follow the Christ, so the Christian Church *must*
become.   Great influences are sweeping over the whole
Western World as the outcome of the Soul's awakening
from its long spiritual sleep to seek for and find " the
Treasure hid in the field " of its own history and regain
once more " the Pearl of great price "—the Christhood
vision and life.   There is a great spiritual upheaval.
The foundations of the Earth are being shaken.   Old
positions are being changed, old ways of thought are being
forsaken.   The land-marks tell of the leaving of the old
heritages and the seeking for and, in some cases, the
entering into new lands with fairer life and heritage.
The " beliefs " of men and women are passing from phase
to phase, bringing the thoughtful and earnest nearer
to the true path by which the glorious goal is to be won.
The foundations of the Churches are also being moved.
There is a shaking of the dry bones amid the desert of
spiritual life, the breathing of a new vitality into institutions which have for ages been lifeless, the passing away
of the old vision of things through the Soul seeking for
something nobler, the craving after a living expression
of Christianity rather than the ecclesiastical and priestly
one.

As institutions the Churches are changing with the
times.   The claims of dogma by which they bound themselves and so prevented their spiritual growth and enlightenment, are being broken.   They are beginning to
realize the needs of Humanity and to try and meet them,
though they are yet far from understanding the true
meaning of a Christian Church.   They see how much
society requires of purification in order to accomplish
its Redemption, though they themselves are not yet in
the path of the Redeemed Life.   Indeed, the true meaning
of Redemption has not yet dawned upon them.   There
is no *open vision* with them yet, they see not the Divine
path.   They have not yet arrived at the meaning of

purity, nor the knowledge of the nature of the Soul and
the Oneness of all true life. They are still blinded by
the Gods of this world as at present constituted—Mammon whom they worship in many forms ; Moloch unto
whom they sacrifice the Creatures in unspeakable num-
bers ; Beelzebub the lover of discord and strife, whose
ways, alas ! they have not yet ceased to follow.

But the Day of Redemption for them is also at hand.
The Hand of God is upon them to make them purge
their courts, cleanse their ways, and offer upon their
altars pure oblations. The threefold vail, which has
been thrown over them almost since the day of their
foundation which was soon after the blessed Master
made manifest the Christhood, is being removed. The
idolatory of worshipping the personal Jesus in place of
the Divine is gradually ceasing throughout Christendom,
for the Soul is being recalled to the true worship of the
Ever Blessed One who makes Himself manifest within
the Soul's Sanctuary. The vail which obscured the Divine
Love through the exaltation of the personal Jesus as the
object of worship, is now being taken away in order that
the vision of the Ever Blessed One may break upon
the Soul.

But the other two vails remain, though the day breaketh
when they also must fall apart to let in the light of the
Glory of the Lord, to show forth the true way of love
and the path of Redemption, the glory of the Redeemed
Life and the diadem of Christhood. For the vail of Blood
is still over the Churches, since they slay the Creatures
in the name of the Divine Love to minister unto their
unpurified tastes and desires, knowing not that it is the
way of Moloch to make the little children (the Creatures)
in the great Household of the Heavenly Father pass
through the fires of suffering and anguish ; for such is
the whole traffic in their lives. And until that vail is
put away no vision of the Divine Love can break upon
the Soul. For there must be purity in living, humaneness
in feeling, compassion made manifest in unfailing pity.

And then the third vail must be put away, that vail by
which not only the vision of the Divine Presence within

the Sanctuary has been hidden, but also the Queen of Heaven, the feminine principle of the Soul, the Intuition. The Churches would never have gone wrong had not the Intuition of the Soul been vailed ; indeed, they would never have been founded in the manner in which they were had not the gods of this world blinded the Intuition of those who laid their foundations. Moloch they have always sacrificed unto as the Jews had done before them ; Mammon soon found a place on their altars and claimed their reverence ; and Beelzebub—the prince of darkness or the darkening one—from the beginning obscured the Soul's Vision and drove out the Seer and the Prophet.

When the Churches have put away these three vails, then will they arrive at the right understanding of what is meant by a Christian Church as to its Life, Communion and Ministry. Then will they know the Redeemed Life and teach it, and understand the Christ and make Him manifest in Christhood. Then will they know those things of which now they have but dim visions, and speak of the Divine Love and Wisdom as those who have realized them. In that day will the Heavens and the Earth be as one unto them, for they shall behold with open vision the life of that Spiritual World in which they have only in a vague way believed, and enter into the realization of those blessed Communions of Souls for which they now only falteringly hope.

J. TODD FERRIER.

WHAT IS A CHRISTIAN ?

VII.

IF THE CHURCHES WERE CHRISTIAN THERE WOULD SOON
BE A NEW CHRISTENDOM.

IF all the Churches in the Western World were truly
Christian, what a wonderful World it would be !
It would be a Christendom in very deed, Souls who were
seeking and finding Christhood. How very different
would be the policies of the various nations and the purposes of all the Communities. How changed the conditions of life would become within the Communities,
how pure and beautiful even to transparency would the
ways of men and women be. It would be a world to
make glad the life and fill the heart with unalloyed joy ;
for it would be a redeemed world, and the life of its
denizens would be the Redeemed Life. In it the things
which make life sad and sorrowful would have no place,
for the worshippers of Mammon, Moloch and Beelzebub
would cease to inherit the land, and all the graven images
of these world-gods would be thrown down. In it " the
cradle-song of the poor " would never be sung, for there
would be none who lacked nourishment. In it there
would be no such fearful tragedies as are now written by
so many lives, for all the evil pitfalls would be banished
from the land. No longer would the sounds of strife and
discord be heard in home, community or nation, for the
things which bring peace and harmony would be established, and the Divine Love would reign in every life.
The cries of anguish would no longer be heard breaking
forth from the Creature Kingdom, for the prison-houses
would be closed and the altars of sacrifice thrown down :
such a world would know neither Abattoirs nor Physiological Laboratories, for all Souls would live upon the
pure fruits of Nature and indulge in the flesh-pots of
Egypt no more. The Social and National conditions
would all be changed. The world's Princes would not be
those who were simply born so of Blood, or of the Flesh,
or of the Will of Man, but those who were Princes indeed,
Israelites in whom there was no guile, Souls who had been

crowned from the Divine as Sons of God, the Illumined
Ones through whom the Divine was made manifest and
interpreted ; There would no more be Lords many, both
temporal and spiritual, for the Divine Lord above would
possess the land and rule over it.   He whose Name is One
and whose ways are those of righteousness and truth.   The
great ones would be the servants of all, the true Kings
of the East or the Divine children whose diadem would
be Christhood.   The voice of oppression no more would
be heard, for the deliverance of all the people would be
accomplished.   The claims of bondage and slavery would
be broken, and all Souls would go forth into the glorious
freedom which the Divine Love giveth, a freedom begotten
of love and doing only the works of love.   All Souls
would walk in the true *Union of One Life*, however
diversified its manifestations in their different spiritual
states.   All Souls would live in the Light of the Divine,
for the glory of the Lord would become the heritage of
the Nations when everything crooked was made straight,
everything broken and rough was made smooth, the
low lying valleys or conditions lifted up into the sunshine
of the blessing of purity and goodness, and all the spiritual
uplands and Divine Heights up which all life is to climb,
made clear.

THE NEW LIFE SEEKING EXPRESSION.

Such is the Western World as it should be as Christendom, and what it shall be when all the Churches have
learnt the meaning of a Christian Church, and what it is
to follow the Christ.   It is the Western World as it must
become as the result of the forces which are now working
within its Nations and Communities, causing Social and
Religious upheavals, in the day when the Churches
through being truly Christian are able to show forth the
nature and meaning of the Redeemed Life through all
their members living it, and to guide all seeking Souls
into the true path of life along which alone Redemption
is found and the Christ-vision beheld.   It is what the
Churches should have long ago made the Western World,
and would have made it had they been truly Christian

in character and service. But not knowing the meaning of the Redemption of the Soul, they could not teach it; and not understanding the meaning of the Redeemed Life, they have not lived it, and so the people could not understand the meaning of purity in living. Old things are passing away, behold how all things are becoming new! The Churches are gradually changing; but even should they fail to find the meaning of the Redeemed Life and attain to it, yet shall the field of their operations be won unto the true life. For just as all the great movements for the upliftment of Humanity have begun outside of the Churches, and the new light has broken upon the Soul beyond their borders, and the Redeemed Life has become known and practised outside their communions, so shall the world be won for God without the Ecclesiastical priests and Schoolmen, and the agency of their materialized institutions and teachings. Some trust in Horses and some in Chariots—the powers of the mind and things material—but only to be disappointed; for the powers which are so born are incapable of uplifting, redeeming and illumining the Soul. Horses and Chariots are only useful when in the hands of those who are capable of rightly guiding them; and so are Churches and all their earthly powers. As mere Hierarchies they have won no world unto Christhood; as Priesthoods they have been powerless to portray the Christ and present His vision to the world; as centres of Scholasticism they have not had the light which breaketh from the Eastern Heavens of the Divine, but only that light (which so frequently is only as the darkness) which cometh through history and tradition; as Spiritual Communions they have not known the reality of the things which they believed in and so could not make manifest their meaning. But all things must and shall become new within them, and then may they indeed perform a beautiful ministry before the Lord as embodiments and manifestors of the Redeemed Life, and interpreters of His Love and Wisdom.

J. TODD FERRIER.

WHAT IS A CHRISTIAN ?

VIII.

WHAT THINK YE OF THE CHRIST ?

There is but one Lord and His Name is One.

THE New Age is breaking amid great changes. The Religious World is electrically charged, and diverse forces are making themselves manifest. The elements are being moved, and the magnetic effects are heard on every hand. The spirit of controversy is abroad, and it is breaking up ground that has long been fallow and preparing the soil for the good seed. Old themes are discussed with new vigour, and the points of view are as various as the interpretations which prevailed in the different ages. What think ye of the Christ, is being discussed with a fervour and an earnestness which can only bring good to the Churches. The old ways of answering the question are passing, though a few of the Scholars still cling to them. The magnetic attraction of the Christ is great, though the real meaning of the attraction seems to be as yet little understood. The Master draws many to inquire who He is, but few find the true answer, *so lost are they in His personality.* They confound the Christ with the form through whom He is manifested, the Divine Logos with the man Jesus. Some think of Him as the Man of Nazareth, who attained the human stature which raised Him up as one who had reached Sonship to God ; whilst others in varying ways view Him as the Son of God incarnate. By some He is loved as a hero and followed as a leader ; by others He is exalted to the seat of the Most High, and wor-shipped as only the Ever Blessed One should be wor-shipped. To the one class of adherents the real meaning of His Christhood is lost ; with the other class the Christ-hood is materialized.

To only behold Him as Jesus of Nazareth is to fail to understand His Christhood ; to make His Christhood personal is not only to limit it, but to change its nature. For Christhood is not a personal thing in the sense in which we would think and speak of the person of a man. The Churches have been accustomed to think of the Divine and Ever Blessed One as a person, evidently not knowing that such an interpretation cannot be put upon the Divine Hypostasis. The Divine Hypostasis relates not to the *persona* as of a man, but to the nature of the Divine. Even a man is only personal in relation to the form through which he makes manifest the real individuality; the latter is his own true being, and that is entirely spiritual. How frequently the real man is not known through the personal, he being better or worse than the manifestation, generally the former. But the Divine as such has no outward personal form. Whilst it may be helpful to many to think of God anthropomorphically, we must not forget that God is not a man.

THE MAN JESUS.

That the Master was the Man Jesus, surely none need doubt. By the man Jesus we mean perhaps more than at first appears. The very name is fraught with profound meanings for us. The name given Him in the Records was not His family name, but the name which represented His mission. We have a parallel case in Gautama having been named the Buddha because of his mission. The Master was called Jesus because He was the Saviour of the people from their sins, so that the name implied the mission. He had given to Him the name because He was in the spiritual state which it represented. He was to become the Saviour of the people because He was in a state of Redemption, both knowing and realizing the Redeemed Life. He was Jesus in Himself as well as in His mission. The mission of many men and women has been greater and purer and nobler than they have been in themselves : with Jesus it was otherwise ; He was what His mission represented. He knew from experience the life unto which He called the people, the life of the Redemption, the Redeemed Life. He became their Saviour when they followed that life ; when they did not follow it, He could not save them. That the following of Him was not meant personally, except that the personal life of the follower was influenced with Redemption, may be gathered from several statements in the Records. There were many who were said to be attached to Him who followed Him whilst they thought He was going to found a new kingdom, all of whom failed at the last because their hopes were not realized. It was said that the immediate disciples of Jesus found others who were not recognised as disciples casting out evil in His name, and that they requested Him to command them to follow with them ; but that Jesus replied, " They who be not against us are for us."

Men and women have confused two distinct things, the personal form and the spiritual signification of the name. They have understood the term as personal and so have missed its meaning. They have failed to discern that when the Master as the man Jesus invited men and women to follow Him, He was not asking for any personal attachment, but rather that they would follow the life implied in the name, the life which the Master beautifully illustrated. For the Redeemed Life made manifest by Him was that unto which He so earnestly counselled the people. And it has been one of the tragedies enacted in the history of the ages that the Records which purported to portray the Master as He was should have so presented His portrait that whilst He bears the name Jesus, He is not made to embody the spiritual state which it signifies. He is made to eat flesh and drink wine, to encourage customs and habits barbarous and degrading, to give His name to a system represented by the Abattoirs and Shambles which speak of pain, suffering and anguish on the part of the Creatures, and inhumanity on the part of man. That the writers of the Records did not know the meaning of the term Jesus is evident from the presentation ; or if they did, then they purposely misrepresented the life of the Master. And whichever it was, they have misled the whole of the Western World and done despite unto the beautiful life of the Master which was so pure in all its ways, so profoundly compassionate unto all Souls, and so universally pitiful and gentle unto all the Creatures.

JESUS THE CHRIST.

As the name Jesus signified the state of His own life and the redemptive mission on which He had come, so the Christ signified also a state in which the Master was spiritually, and His Divine office of Interpreter of the Divine Love and Wisdom. He was Jesus the Christ. It was neither a Christian name, as we designate the first name of any one, nor a surname; it was a glorious state of inward Divine realization which also fitted Him for the sublime mission. The very term is significant. Just as Jesus meant that the Master was a Saviour of men, so Christ meant that He was the vehicle of the Logos, the Adonai, the ever blessed Son of the Eternal One. The Christ was the Anointed One. To be anointed is to be Illumined from the Divine. To be illumined thus is to know the Divine through inward realization, to have the perfect consciousness of the Divine Presence dwelling within the Sanctuary of the Soul.

It was thus with the Master. He was Jesus the Christ, the anointed or illumined one from the Divine Kingdom. He was the vehicle of the Logos who is ever in the bosom of the Father, and who was with Him and in Him. He was therefore able to speak as one who knew the Divine Father, and who was in perfect harmony with the life and purpose of the Father. His Saviourhood was crowned with Christhood. He was the Redeemer of men through making manifest the Redeemed Life that they might follow it; He was the Christ or the Interpreter of the Divine Love and Wisdom which He showed forth in the Teachings which He gave to the inner group of the disciples. As Jesus He made plain for all the life that was to be lived; as the Christ He revealed the attainment of the Crown of Life as the outcome of the Redemption. As Jesus He taught men how to make their lives pure on all its spheres, as the Christ He taught Souls how to realize the Divine Love within themselves and come into the beautiful consciousness of the Divine Presence within the Sanctuary of the Soul. As Jesus He called all unto the life of Self-denial and Self-sacrifice; as the Christ

He constrained Souls to give themselves in beautiful Abandonment to the Divine. The one was the Office of the Redeemer, whilst the other was the Office of the Interpreter of the Divine ; both were divinely appointed, and both were Offices of the Cross.

His Christhood has been as little understood as His office of Redeemer. The Records that failed to show how He lived the life of the Redemption to save men, confused His Christhood and gave a false vision of it unto all who trusted these Records to be the true picture.

THE DIVINE LORD.

But there is yet one other title which was given unto the Master by the writers of the Records, which likewise was applied to Him personally, but which was wholly Divine in its significance. He was also spoken of as *The Lord*. In every instance in which it is made use of, the designation is applied to the man. It is the man who is thus spoken of as Divine. The inner significance of the appellation is thus entirely lost, whilst the mere form through whom the Divine has been manifested is exalted to the Divine Kingdom and made Divine. For the term Lord as applied to the Master implies Divine Kingship and speaks of the ruling power of the Divine Love. It speaks of the Christhood of the Master as having been crowned with the ruling power implied in the title of Lord. And in doing that it signifies that just as the Master's Life and Office of the Redeemer was crowned with the Christhood Estate, so His Christhood was the outcome of the Divine overshadowing. There is but one Lord, as the blessed Master taught, and His Name is One. He alone is the Lord of the Heavens and the Earth. He alone is the Ruler in High Places, the spiritual and Divine realms. He is the Adonai, ever blessed Son of God. He alone is King of Kings and Lord of Lords. But He is not personal, though He makes manifest the Divine within the Soul who has attained Christhood. When He is present, the Fear or Divine Awe of the Lord fills all Souls. Those who are disciples indeed of the Christhood need not to ask who it is, knowing that it is the Lord. It was not concerning the personal Jesus that the disciples made the inquiry, for they knew Him well. His form and ways were familiar to them. But there were times when the conditions were such that they were filled with wonder and awe, and made inquiry one of another as to the meaning of them, until they came to the blessed knowledge that it was the approach of the Lord, the overshadowing of the Divine Love.

The writers of the Records were unable to distinguish between personal and Divine things and so mixed them. They did not understand the vehicle nature of the personal life and so naturally applied all the beautiful terms to that life. They first gave the personal the title of Jesus, then Christ, and then the Lord, and so made the man the Lord Christ Jesus. They failed to perceive the significance of the titles as the Divine Presence, the Soul crowned with the fulness of that Presence through Christhood, and the Life of the Redemption made manifest. They beheld not how the terms expressed the way in which the Ever Blessed One communicated direct with the Human Kingdom as the Lord Christ Jesus ; nor how they showed forth the ascent of the Soul to the Divine Kingdom when the Divine Love alone rules throughout the whole being, as Jesus, the Christ, and our Lord. And thus did they crown their other mistakes by presenting the man as the Divine Lord to be adored and worshipped, and so led the whole Western World into another form of idolatry. J. TODD FERRIER.

THE VISION OF CHRISTHOOD.

*I saw the Heavenly Christ : Grace from His lips
    did flow
And find its utterance in the Master's life ; in Him
The Holy Wisdom of the Gods dwelt as Treasure
Precious in a treasure-house, and found an outlet
In His gracious words and deeds. These were as
    gems
Whose facets to illumine Souls threw out the
Radiance of the Gods, Wisdom of Heaven and
Love Divine, as light refracted, beautiful and
Glorious to behold, full of the images*

Of things Divine, the secrets of the Gods.
His words were fraught with Life Immortal, Life
For all Souls whose cherished aim it is to know
The Christhood, that Estate whose riches are so great
That they endow the Soul with wealth whose increase is
Of God, wealth which never makes impoverishment,
Nor tarnishes, nor gives those cankering cares which
Follow earthly gain, but riches great and holy,
Knowledge and Love Eternal, Wisdom Divine, Light
Whose glory is the reflex of the Lord, and Royal
Diadem, crown of the Sons of God.   Upon the
Master's brow there sat that royal dignity, emblem
     Divine,
Of one who had been namèd Son of God and sent
Forth from the Heavenly Kingdom by Him the
     Hebrews
Knew as Adonai, the Lord of Life, the Manifest
Of Him no mortal eye hath seen, the Invisible
And Ever Blessed One.   Within the Christ there
     burned
The Sacred Fires kindled by Elohim, the Seven
Spirits majestic from the throne of the Eternal,
Those sacred Spirits whom God giveth unto all
Who know His Fear, the Holy Awe, in Christhood ;
And these shone forth the Light of the Eternal Love
(Even as the Sun pours out his glory during day)
To shine upon man's pathway leading him to Heaven,
That Path by which all Souls must gain the goal,
Rising above things earthly to find their fulness
In the Life and Love Eternal : Such was the Christ.

Shall we not seek to follow Him, to share His Cup,
His Baptism and His Service ? To know Denial,
     Sacrifice,
Abandonment, perfect, complete, unto the will of
Heaven ? To follow on from Sphere to Sphere in
     service,
Glorious in nature, life-redeeming, until we too
Are crownèd Sons of God ? For such is Christhood.

J. TODD FERRIER.

THE HERALD OF THE CROSS.

Vol. v. New Series. December, 1909. No. 12.

THE ANGEL OF THE LORD.

(HIS MESSAGE UNTO JERUSALEM [THE EARTH].)

The Angel of the Lord spake unto me during the watches of the night, saying,

" Son of Man, prophesy unto the people and tell them that the day of the Lord is at hand."

So I arose and proclaimed that the Day of the Lord was near.

But the inhabitants of Jerusalem cared not to hear the message of the Angel who spake unto me.

Then the Angel of the Lord spake unto me again, saying,

" Go ye down into the City and cry aloud unto all the inhabitants, that the Day of the Lord is upon them in the which He shall appear in His Glory to redeem the Children of Israel from the Darkness, and to restore unto them the Ancient Heritage which He gave unto Abraham, Isaac and Jacob."

And I did as the Angel commanded me : and there were many who heard the Angel's words in gladness and went forth from the City to meet the Lord.

And with the break of day He came unto all who were looking for His coming.

THE ANGELIC VISION AND SONG.

I.

THE BREAKING OF THE VISION.

THE Angelic Vision is again breaking upon the Soul, that vision so full of Peace and Praise. The Heavens are again open unto all who are able to look up into them and catch the glory of the Divine Love. The poem of Bethlehem is being repeated, for its beautiful drama is now taking place in many Souls. The Christ-child is being born in many lives, even within those shelters where the creatures are ministered unto and which remain outside the Inns where the far-travelled seek their spiritual refreshment. The true Shepherds hear the Song of the Heavenly Hosts as they watch the flocks amid the night of the world. They understand the Glad Tidings of great joy which the Heavens proclaim unto all people ; for they have been expecting the advent of the Christ, looking for the signs of His coming, watching for the opening of the Heavens and the blessed vision of the Angelic Hosts. They are the Souls who belong to Bethlehem, the City of David, the ancient City of the Kings, and who first discover the new-born Christ.

WHAT THE VISION WAS.

The Angelic Vision associated with the birth of Jesus into this world was, as we have had occasion to show, not anything outward, not any objective picture like some heavenly landscape presenting itself to the eye, but a beautiful inward spiritual experience, a reality to the Soul far greater in its issues than any outward and visible phenomenon. It was the vision of the Soul itself, the opening of the Heavens unto it, the recognition of the Angelic ministry sent from the Father, the ever Blessed One. And it was the vision which proclaimed the birth of the Christ-child within it, the attainment by the Soul of the Divine Consciousness and its entrance upon the Christhood path and into the Christhood experience. And the Angelic Song heard was the heavenly harmonies heard within the Soul when it arrived at that stage of its spiritual unfoldment, harmonies none the less real because *within the Soul*; indeed more real because altogether spiritual. For when the Soul approaches the state when the Christ is born within it, it is not only able to have the Vision of the Angelic World within its Sanctuary, but to hear the harmonies of that world. And the message which it hears proclaimed is " Glory to God in the Highest, and on Earth peace and the good. pleasure of His will." For it is the message which Christhood brings with it unto the Soul and through the Soul unto the world. The glory of the Lord rests upon the Sanctuary and upon the earthly house abides His peace and the gladness or pleasure of His will. For the " Highest " is within the Soul ; there are the Heavens reflected ; there is the glory of the Divine seen when the Soul is in the silence and seeks to ascend. And the Earth is the lower or outward spheres of life, those spheres within which the noises of life and the world find their echo and reflection ; and those spheres are to be filled with the heavenly peace and the pleasure of doing the Divine Will. They are to know the peace shed by the Christ-spirit within, the peace of God which passeth all understanding, because it is born from the beautiful inward life of spiritual realizations, realizations of the Divine Presence within.

The Angelic Vision, song and message are, therefore, for all Souls who can behold and hear and receive them. They were not local experiences on the physical plains of the little city of Bethlehem in Judea, but universal in that they were wholly spiritual, and experiences which every Soul should enter into. They were those experiences which Souls who once knew the Christ-spirit and life had passed through, and who were called by the blessed Master to seek to enter upon them once more. It was unto that sublime end that the experiences were portrayed by the Master, that the setting of them forth might aid them to awaken unto the consciousness of that life and bring unto them its beautiful realizations.

IT IS A RECOVERED TREASURE.

How that wonderfully beautiful and blessed vision has been misunderstood throughout the ages of the Christian era ! How it has lain buried amid the materialized history of the Christ, like lost treasure buried amid the ruins of some ancient city overthrown by tremendous seismic conditions ! And how difficult it is to impress Christian men and women with the truth of its storied wealth for the Soul, and bring them into that blessed state when they themselves shall know it as the portion of their own experience, the sublime realization within them of the Divine Love, Life and Light ! For it is not an easy work to accomplish to restore that long-lost Soul-vision to its true place, to lift it up out of the debris amid which it has been buried, to let its beautiful image become once more pure and clean so that all who have the true willinghood to understand its meaning and realize its blessing may again behold it unto its full realization. So long has it been lost as a history experienced within the Soul ; so long has it been regarded as history upon the physical planes; so long has it been related to pastoral shepherds watching on the fields outside a town in Judea ; so long has it thus been made local rather than universal, outward instead of inward, material history in place of spiritual, that now it is most difficult to impress upon men and women that it is the blessed embodiment of the Soul's experience who has accomplished its Redemption from the dominion of the sense-life, interpreted that Redemption in the Redeemed Life which it lives in the world, and has arrived at that beautiful experience when the Christhood of the Soul has been born. It is almost impossible to impress upon men and women that it is *a most real experience within the Soul,* that the vision of the Angelic Life and ministry is actually beheld within the Soul, that the Angelic Song is there actually heard, that the things seen and heard are not imaginative, but tangible.

O blessed Vision of the Soul, how beautiful thou art !
O Song of the Angels sung by the Heavenly Hosts,

what glorious harmony may be brought into the life when thou art heard !

O Message of the Father through His Angels, have we not felt the heavenly influence of thy meaning, the blessed power which comes upon the life in whose "Highest" there is "Glory to God," and upon whose earthly parts there is the breath of a Divine Peace !

J. TODD FERRIER.

THE ANGEL OF THE LORD.

(THE DELIVERANCE OF ISRAEL.)

The Angel of the Lord spake unto me in the watches of the night when all the inhabitants slept unconscious of the intensity of the Darkness, and that even the Stars of the Heavens no longer shone, and said unto me,

" Son of Man, tell it all abroad unto the House of Israel that the Day of their deliverance is at hand when the Lord Himself will break the bonds by which they have been bound by the oppressor, and deliver them from their cruel bondage, and set them free to leave the land of their captivity that they may return unto their own land and have restored unto them all the sacred treasures which were taken from them when they went down into captivity."

So I proclaimed the message for many days within the City and all its gates.

But many even of the Children of Israel could not receive the message ; but those who did receive it found the chains of their captivity broken, and were able to arise and go forth towards the Ancient City of the Lord.

THE ANGELIC VISION AND SONG.

II.

IT WAS THE BLESSING GIVEN UNTO ABRAHAM'S SEED.

THE Angelic Vision which was said to have been seen by the tenders of flocks on the plains of Bethlehem in Judea on the night when the Master was born into this world, and which has throughout the whole of the Christian era been regarded as a true history in the experience of these shepherds and as a sure testimony to the Heavenly Nature of the Master, is now being repeated in the experience of many Souls. Many are coming from the East and the West, the North and the South to sit down within the kingdom of our Father Abraham, to behold the glory of the land given unto him for a possession and to his seed for ever, to know the joy of His salvation who hath caused the Star of the Day-spring to arise upon us ; for many are the Souls awakening all over the world to the realization of the Redeemed Life and the beautiful visions of the Christhood. The North and the South, the East and the West, represent the manifold states in which Souls are found—those who seek the inward spiritual or Eastern life, and those who seek the outward material or Western life ; those who find life in the cold Northern or intellectual conditions, and those who seek them in the volatile Southern atmosphere of the emotions. And they are all coming into the kingdom given unto our Father Abraham and to his seed for ever, the goodly land of Christhood on which the glory of the Lord never sets and which is full of the riches of His Love and Wisdom, for Abraham was and is the Divine Estate of this Planet, the state in which it was when the whole world was young, the golden age ere " the Gods slept " (the Planetary Systems of Sol), the state the Planet was in prior to what is now known as The Fall when all was pure and true and beautiful upon every plane and within every sphere, and the state unto which she is being redeemed with all her children.

THE COMING OF THE REDEMPTION.

The coming of the Son of Man upon the clouds of the

Heavens through the restoration within the Soul of the vision of the Christhood Life, is showing itself everywhere; for there is an awakening of the Souls of all peoples who once knew that vision and lived that life, to seek unto its realization once more. The descent of the Angelic Heavens to encompass the Earth is now a glorious reality; for the Christ-Soul has purified the intermediate kingdom (the Astral Spheres) so that the Angelic ministry is not only possible now, but is realized by every Soul who has unfolded its life through purifying its ways. The days of the Redemption are upon us; days full of great changes in and for humanity; days full of the separating fires of righteousness wherein evil is consumed and the gold of good is purified; days full of travail for the Soul as the breath of the Spirit passes over its life, winnowing the chaff from the true grain of good; days prophetic of the victory of truth over error, purity over evil, and love over lovelessness and hate. For the coming of the Son of Man is as the rebirth of the Christhood, the day of "glad tidings unto all peoples," the heralding from the Heavens of the coming of the Deliverer in the form of the Christ-child Jesus born within the Soul, the sure Redeemer of the life from all evil and the manifestor of the glory of the Heavenly Father. For the true Redeemer of the Soul is the Divine Love who by His approach unto it through the Angelic Heavens has not only heralded the coming again of the Son of Man, the Adonai, upon the clouds of the Heavens (or true Spiritual conditions which give true spiritual phenomena within the Soul), but has enabled all who were in a state to behold the vision to once more look into those Heavens of Angelic ministry and hear the harmonies which fill them. And the true Redemption of the Soul is the purification of all its ways, from the centre to the circumference of its experience, every sphere made to respond to the life and service of the Divine Love.

THE SIGNS THAT THE VISION HAS BROKEN.

The coming again of the Angelic Vision unto the Soul is the surest testimony we could have or desire of the

Second Advent or coming of the Son of Man. It is a
testimony transcending anything of an outward or personal nature such as is looked for by those who still
expect the return of the Master in the form in which He
lived the Christhood, more glorious in its results for the
Soul, and further-reaching in its redeeming and regenera-
ting effects upon the whole world. For if men and
women do not recognise the vision of Christhood when
it is shown them, and refuse the interpretation of the
Redemption as the path to Christhood which must be
taken by all who would truly follow the Master, we may
be quite sure that they would fail to understand or even be
attracted to the Master were He to again appear to live
the Christhood ; nor would they follow out the demands
which He would make upon them as preliminary steps
to their finding the Redemption which leadeth unto the
path of Christhood. If they hear not the prophets concerning purity in living, neither would they hear Him.
If they refuse the ways of repentance proclaimed by the
John the Baptists of our own age, they would not be
likely to accede to the high demands of the Master.
But if men and women have awakened to the sublime
reality of the life of the Soul, and have brought forth
fruits meet for repentance by changing their habits of
living, putting away every evil and impure thing, feeling
purely toward one another, acting compassionately unto
all Souls and pitifully towards all the Creatures, scorning
to wound any living thing or cause it hurt or suffering
in any way, making the body pure through pure food
and the mind through pure thoughts and feelings, seeking
only the truest, best and highest, then such Souls will go
on to know the Redemption as the blessed state in which
the life is redeemed from evil until all its impulses,
desires and purposes are to seek after and fulfil the Divine
Will. They will live on the fruits of the Earth. They
will have no creatures destroyed to find nourishment
or adornment for them. They will be the protectors of
the Creatures from cruelty wherever practised. They
will oppose the ways of Vivisection and Vivisectors.
They will require no creature to suffer to provide drugs

or serums for them. They will oppose all the unclean and degrading methods of the Medical Faculty, not requiring such impure protective aids themselves, nor believing them necessary for others. They will thus live the Redeemed Life, and influence others to go along with them. They will follow the Jesus-life until they also arrive at the vision of the Christ. And they will at last come into the blessed experience when the Angelic Heavens shall open unto them and they will behold again what the shepherds are said to have beheld upon the planes of Bethlehem. They will hear once more the glorious harmonies of the Heavenly Hosts in their Praise of the Ever Blessed One, and realize within themselves the beautiful and profound meaning of all that the Angels sang. And then they will know and understand the meaning of Christhood as the Crown of Life.

J. TODD FERRIER.

THE ANGEL OF THE LORD.

(UNTO THE HOUSE OF ISRAEL.)

The Angel of the Lord appeared unto me as I sat by the streams of Babylon, mourning because there was none found able to accomplish the deliverance of the people from the cruel bondage of the enemy; and He said unto me—

"Arise! Proclaim unto the whole House of Israel that the days of their oppression and mourning are ended; for my servant the Cyrenean will accomplish for them their deliverance from the land of sorrowful captivity:

He will command that all the people go free and return unto their own land full of joy and gladness."

So I proclaimed the glad tidings.

THE ANGELIC VISION AND SONG.
III.
THEIR PROFOUND MEANING.

HOW profound in their meaning were the words of the song which the Angels were said to have sung ! Who now pauses to inquire concerning their significance ? What is the true poetry of them, their full splendour ? Embodied are they in Litanies of Praise, and set by some of the great Masters of Harmony to music born in them of the overshadowing of the Heavens ; sung are they in many Sanctuaries, thrilling those who feel their sublime meanings though as yet they see them not, moving Souls to nobler impulses and more beautiful experiences ; yet remain they in their innermost meanings like sealed caskets whose outward form is rich and beautiful, but whose treasures are hidden from the beholders. For though the language is much thought of, yet is the real significance of them for the Soul unseen. And why ? Because men and women have been taught to regard them as words spoken only concerning the birth of the Master, whereas they are the language of Heaven unto the Soul itself when the Christ-spirit is born within it.

The story of the Angels' Song was not preserved unto us by the Shepherds who were said to have heard it ; it was told by the Master unto the inner group of His Disciples as an exposition of the experiences through which the Soul passed as it approached the beautiful realizations implied in the term Spiritual Christhood, when the Soul had found the Redeemed Life and attained unto it, and was following on to know the Divine. His birth-story was one told by Himself, but not concerning His own birth into this world, nor His own Christhood, but concerning the experience of every one who rose from sphere to sphere until the Angelic World found its correspondence within them so that its life could be imaged within their Heavens and the echoes of the Heavenly Song be heard.

How rich and beautiful the blessed Master's Teachings were, how profound in their far-reaching meanings and comprehensive in their scope, has yet to be made known. And this Angelic Vision was one of them. It was told by the Master not only to inform the Soul of those experiences which come to it when it has accomplished its Redemption and is in the path to the blessed realization of Christhood ; but it was told primarily to awaken within those who heard it memories of long ago, of a past whose history had written on it that very experience. For the Shepherds of Bethlehem were those spiritual teachers who were as the messengers of the Father unto the children of this world in the days prior to " the fall " or descent of the whole system from pure spiritual conditions to conditions largely and, in some instances, wholly material. The flocks upon the planes were the little human children who were being tended by these devoted Souls ; and Bethlehem itself was the planes of the Planet upon which the children dwelt. For Bethlehem originally meant the little House of the Lord, the state of such simple yet beautiful spiritual life that to live was to praise and to serve was to pray. The flocks upon the planes of Bethlehem were those Souls who had risen up in their true evolution before the Divine from the simple elementary life to the complex life of the first or highest sphere of the Human Kingdom, many of whom were almost ready to rise another stage unto the realization of the Angelic life. And the Souls who were spoken of as the Shepherds were Souls who had long ago been crowned with the Angelic Life, Souls who had once been as those within the little House of the Lord, or Bethlehem, upon another planet, but who had evolved and unfolded before the Divine until they had attained the high estate of sonship to God, and who were known as the Sons of God or His Christs upon the system of Sol. And some of these Souls were of the innermost circle of the disciples of the Master.

The story was not only the embodiment of the experience which comes to every Soul who is on the path to Christhood, but it was one which these Christ-souls had passed through when they were the Spiritual helpers of the children of Bethlehem. They had arrived at the

experience of the Angelic Vision and Song of the Heavenly
Hosts individually; but they had likewise had an experience of it collectively during the dark times which
overtook the Bethlehem when the elements of the planes
of the Planet were changed in their nature, so that the
evolution of the Souls of the children was interrupted
and at last suspended. Darkness had fallen upon the
Earth and the Night of the Soul resulted. The magnetic
conditions had become so changed that even the Christ-
souls or Sons of God found the Bethlehem to be other
than the little House of the Lord. They kept watch over
the flocks, but it was *night* with them. The Heavens
seemed far away—the Heavens of the Lord reflected
within the Soul with all their hallowed images and sacred
signs; for it was night around and within them.

It was at that time that the Heavenly Vision was sent.
They were all, as it were, lifted up on to the Angelic
Heavens where they beheld the Angelic Vision and heard
the Angelic Song. And the purpose of it was to inform
them of the coming of the Saviour and Deliverer who
would redeem them from the bondage imposed by the
darkness and deliver all who were made captive by the
enemy, namely, the changed elements; and that He
would be their Lord, made manifest in Christhood, and
born to be Jesus, the Redeemer from all evil.

The Vision was prophetic : it foretold the necessity
for a Redeemer, and that He would be forthcoming.
It was pathetic ; for it was the outcome of the endeavours
of the Angelic Kingdom to communicate with this world
amid most difficult conditions, after it had been for long
ages struggling on amid the darkness which had overtaken
it as the outcome of its descent from a pure spiritual
state to one in which the magnetic conditions were all
changed. And its meaning was profound ; for it informed the Shepherds or Christ-souls that it would be
necessary for the Divine to descend from the Heavens
to effect the necessary Redemption and Deliverance.
It was also prophetic in that it anticipated for the Shepherds the coming of that Life within them, which once
they knew ; those most blessed experiences which were

their constant heritage, the Angelic Visions, Communions, and Fellowships which they once had as their perpetual portion ; that inward knowledge of the Divine and consciousness of the Eternal Presence associated now with Christhood : it spake to them of the restoration of these through the work of the Redeemer. It was in this way likewise pathetic ; for its very prophecy of the restored conditions within them implied so much as to their past, showing what they once had been before the Night overtook them upon the planes, and all that they had lost amid the darkness arising from the changed conditions. And in this respect was the meaning of the Heavenly Vision profound, for it not only spake of all that they once had been, what they had lost through the changed conditions, but also how alone the restoration could take place both for them and the whole of the Bethlehem.

The Angelic Vision was, therefore, prophetic, pathetic and profound in its meanings for all Souls, and even for the Divine. It was glorious in its anticipations in looking forward to the time when Christhood should again crown the lives of all who once knew that blessed state, and when the planes of the Bethlehem or little (that is, in experience of Divine Consciousness) House of the Lord should all be redeemed back to their original state, when life for all the children upon them would be pure and beautiful ; when there would be Glory to God in the Highest states of experience through the Soul reflecting His Glory in the life and ministry of Christhood, and Peace on Earth, or the lower states of experience, through the restoration of all Souls unto the purity they once knew in their ways and the wonderful harmony and concord born of that purity in them and the conditions around them. For " Glory to God in the Highest " was not simply meant as a poetic expression of the glory rendered unto the Eternal and Ever-Blessed One upon the Heavens, but as the testimony of the Soul's true nature, function and service, and an injunction to render within the Soul wherein " The Highest " has His abiding-place, the glory of life and service : for *the Soul is the highest place for man*, and wherever the Soul is, here or in another system, it is always within itself that it must first give the Glory of the Divine Life in beautiful service. And through the giving forth of that real and blessed glory in " the highest," will the earth-spheres be filled with the Divine Peace ; for only through the restoration within the Soul of the Glory of the Lord as a realization can the Redemption be truly and fully accomplished.

The Christhood must be sought unto its blessed realization ; and unto this end must the Christ-child or Christ-spirit, be born again within the Soul.

J. TODD FERRIER.

THE ANGEL OF THE LORD.

(UNTO THE CHILDREN OF ZION.)

The Angel of the Lord spake unto me concerning all the Children of Zion, and their return unto the Holy City of the Lord, the Christhood Estate, saying unto me,

" Son of Man, go down to the Gates of the Holy City and stand at the entrances and proclaim unto all who are without that they may now enter in for the true worship and service of their Lord ; for the Gates into Zion have been opened and the Sanctuary has been restored so that all His Redeemed Ones may again possess the Holy City, and behold the beauty of the Lord within His Sanctuary."

So I went down and stood at the entering into the Gates, and proclaimed the message of the Lord which the Angel of the Lord gave unto me.

And those who were ready to enter as His Redeemed Ones passed up into the Holy City.

THE ANGELIC VISION AND SONG.

IV.

TESTIMONIES THAT THE VISION IS NOW SEEN.

BEHOLD the awakening in these latter days of many Souls to seek unto the Christhood life and service, and the descent of the Divine Love, in all the redeeming powers which are in operation upon the Earth ! Behold the outpouring of the Spirit of the Lord in the awakening unto a new consciousness within the Soul of its own nature and heritage, and the endeavour of many to find the meaning of these things ! Behold the signs of the coming of the Redemption in all the excellent endeavours put forth to reclaim those who have gone far afield in their experiences, and to restore men and women unto the true ways of living once more ! Behold how many of the most beautiful Souls amongst us have to pass through experiences of the strangest nature, alone and misunderstood, full of pain and often anguish, as if their lives were afflicted by some Divine judgment which had overtaken them, and see in these things the sure signs of the days of the Regeneration ! In all the true reform movements—Vegetarian, Anti-Vaccination, Anti-Vivisection, Social Purity, true compassion, pity and love manifesting themselves in the redress of great evils which have for ages been imposed upon the defenceless— we may behold the fruits of that awakening of the Soul to a higher consciousness of the meaning of life.

These are all testimonies to the coming realization of the meaning of the Angelic Vision and Song. They are like the shooting forth of the new life at the dawn of Springtime, and as such are the prophecies of great good. They are the testimonies to the passing away of the long Winter of spiritual coldness and impoverishment, during which the real life of the Soul has been almost quiescent, and the harbingers of the reawakening of the very Gods themselves (the Planets of the System of Sol), who have long slept because of the changed conditions which overtook the Earth ; the reawakening of all Souls from the sleep in which the Heavens were shut so that " no open vision " was vouchsafed, to the consciousness of the reality of those Heavens and to desire and seek after the Heavenly Vision ; the coming forth of all who went down into the graves of matter symbolized in the going down of Israel into Egypt and there finding sorrow and oppression, and the rising up into the light of a new and great hope of the whole House of Israel under the leadership of Moses, the name by which the Divine Love was known unto the most ancient Hebrews ; the first resurrection consequent upon the coming again of " the Son of Man " upon the Clouds of the Heavens and the entrance into the " resurrection life " of all who are able to ascend unto its most blessed realization

Such are the portents of the age in which we live, Planetary and Human, Spiritual and Social, Racial and National. The Heavens are telling of the dawn of the New Age in which all things shall be made new. The Angelic Visions are coming unto many to testify of the birth of the Christhood realizations which are to be. The Planetary influences are once more in favour of the true upwardness of the Earth, and all her children, notwithstanding the devastating magnetic storms which in these latter days have been filling many with fear and dismay and leading the students of the Heavens to all sorts of conjectures as to the cause of them.

J. TODD FERRIER.

THE ANGEL OF THE LORD.

(A VISION OF THE SOUL.)

There came to me in the night-watches when the City lay asleep, a vision of the Angel of the Lord.

I was lifted up, as it were, out of the Earth on to the planes of the Heavens and there beheld with open vision the Angel of the Lord.

His garments were glorious in fashion, more glorious than the fine raiment with which kings are clothed, and upon His head did He wear a Crown of pure gold.

The fashion of His Countenance was such that He reflected the glorious Image of the Invisible and Ever Blessed One, radiant with the Light of His Love.

With His presence He seemed to overshadow me like the Cherubim overshadowing the Mercy-seat.

And He spake unto me, saying,

"Son of Man, make it known unto the whole House of Israel that the promise of the Lord hath been fulfilled; for He hath sent unto them His servant Jesus to redeem them out of all their afflictions, to deliver them from the bondage into which they went down when the oppressor took them away, to establish again the throne of the House of David, and to lead them into the land which He gave unto our Father Abraham and to His seed for ever."

So I again was let down upon the earth where I proclaimed the message of the Angel of the Lord unto all who were able to hear and receive it.

THE ANGELIC VISION AND SONG.

V.

THE CELEBRATION OF CHRISTMAS.

THE return of the Christmas season is also the return of the time when the Angelic Vision, Song and Message are recited in the Churches of the West. For Christmas is the great time of joy in Home and Sanctuary, a time of great gladness shared more or less by all, a season of devotion when gifts are bestowed and the needy ones are specially thought for. The Home is the scene of very special festivity, and the Sanctuary of praise. And all these things are supposed to have their origin in the Glad Tidings heralded by the Angels concerning the coming of the Redeemer, the advent of the Christ.

It is very beautiful is the celebration in so far as there is good in its Joy and Praise, Devotion and Gifts : these are beautiful when true and pure. They are full of true poetry, are the expressions of the noblest feelings of the Soul, and should be prophetic of such wonderful fulness of spiritual realizations as to point to the attainment of the Redeemed Life crowned with Christhood. There is something sensuously delightful in hearing the recital of the Angelic Vision, Song and Message when set to inspiring music ; and good in the arresting of the mind busily engaged with material things to present to it the story of the Advent of the Redeemer, and to impress it with the reality of His having come in the life and ministry of the blessed Master. But that is not all the meaning of Christmas. If it be, then no wonder the Season has failed to lift Humanity up out of the depths of the evils associated with its celebration, the fearful tragedies of the Abattoirs and Shambles ; the unspeakable suffering thrust upon the defenceless creatures ; the indescribable shame presented in the streets where their mangled forms are exposed for purchase, and in the Homes of the people, even of many who profess that they are the friends of the creatures, where the mangled remains are served up as fitting diet and nourishment for those who would enter into the meaning of the Angelic Vision, Song and Message. Throughout the centuries of the Christian Era the celebration of Christmas has not been prophetic of the coming of the Redeemer and the Christ, but the awful carnival which it has been in these later ages. It has not been the harbinger of a coming Redemption for the Race, but the perpetuation of the most revolting cruelty to the creatures and degradation to Humanity. It has not foreshadowed the birth of the Christ-life and spirit, but an order of things which are the abrogation of any such experience. When a Redeemer brings Redemption to a people, the chains of their captivity are broken, and the means of their bondage are overthrown ; but the celebration of Christmas has only served to bind the Western World more firmly in the bondage of the flesh-pots. It has not brought Deliverance, but increased the Captivity. It has filled the Creature Kingdom with anguish unspeakable, and blinded the Soul to any true heavenly vision. So intense has the darkness been that those who truly desired to live the true and pure life have not been able to see the way. The would-be Humane and truly pitiful Souls, who in their innermost life love the creatures, have been so grievously misled that they too often have partaken of the terrible feast in the Western World's terrible way. Such have been the effects of the celebration of Christmas.

THE STAR OF BETHLEHEM HAS ARISEN.

But the hour has struck when the Redeemer was to make His appearance. The Star within the Eastern Heavens has arisen to herald His coming and proclaim the birth of the Christ. The Magi have beheld it and have sought out the Christ in Bethlehem. The Shepherds of the Planes have been awakened in the dead of the Western World's night through the approach of the Angelic World unto them ; and they have beheld the vision of the Heavenly Hosts and heard the Angelic Song. For the Christ-souls who once were the true Teachers upon this Planet have both seen and heard those Angelic things which mortal eye hath not seen nor ear heard ; to them the Heavenly Hosts have once more made themselves manifest, and the Song sung has been re-interpreted. The Magian Souls who have always sought to understand the movements of the Heavens of the Divine, who have sought their highest wisdom in the Heavenly knowledges gained through communion with those Heavens, who have longed for the realization of their beautiful aspirations and profound yearnings in the crown of Christhood, have beheld the arising in the Orient of the sign of the birth of the Christ-child, the Eastern Heavens signifying the Divine within the Soul. For the Star is the sign of Christhood within the Soul, " the bright and the morning Star " given unto all who overcome. The Redeemer has been born. The Redemption has been entered into. The Deliverance of many who sat in bondage has been accomplished. The cruel chains which bound many in slavery have been broken. For the Redeemer is the Divine within the Soul finding expression in the Redeemed Life, the life purified upon and within every sphere ; the Redemption is the attainment by the Soul of victory over all the sense-feelings, desires and affections, the mastery over the outwardness of life so that all the senses are under control from the Soul and are only its servants to do its service and not their own ; the Deliverance is the liberation of the whole being from the bondage in which it has been held by the sense-life, the snapping of the bonds or fetters which hold it down, the setting free for the true worship, service and life of the Divine Love the whole spiritual man.

The hour has struck that heralds His coming : the Star has arisen that proclaims the birth within the Soul of Christhood : behold how the Redemption proceedeth through the purifying and uplifting movements, and the Christhood may be beheld.

J. TODD FERRIER.

THE ANGELIC VISION AND SONG.

VI.

CONTRADICTIONS OF BELIEFS.

IT is sad to reflect that where the Angelic Vision and Song should have been most expected, it is almost unknown as an experience, and its meaning is misunderstood. The channels of Divine Communication to the World have, as a rule, been found outside the Churches, not within them. These latter have valued and stereotyped and guarded the letter of such Revelation as they have had handed down to them ; but the spirit of the things signified has most frequently had to find a dwelling-place elsewhere. From their own confession and claims the Churches should have been the means through which the Angelic Heavens communicated their messages from the Divine, and the interpreters of those messages for all Souls ; yet do they repudiate the very thought that it is even possible for a Soul to commune with those Heavens, and receive messages from them. They jealously guard all the records wherein accounts of Heavenly Visions are given ; yet they deny that such visions may now be the heritage of the Soul. To them the days of open vision are no more. The Visions of the Adonai seen by the Ancient Seers are accepted by the Churches, though they understand not either the nature of the vision nor how the vision is vouchsafed unto the Seer ; yet do they deny the possibility of such visions coming unto the Soul now or reject the vision when it is presented to them. They believe in the reality of these things in the past, and proclaim the glorious times which are to come ; but for the present they see not, neither do they believe in, these beautiful realizations. Their faith is still intellectual rather than spiritual, and looks along the planes of outward history rather than within the vail of the Spiritual World. They profess spiritually without realizing ; they confess faith in a Spiritual World which they do not know. They believe that Angels once visited this World and communed with

men and women ; but they do not accept the fact that
Angels even now are communing with Souls upon the
Earth, that the Heavenly Vision is being seen and the
Angelic Song heard. They believe (according to the
things they confess) that the Angels are ministering
spirits sent forth from the Divine to minister unto all
who are heirs of Salvation ; but who the Angels are,
what their nature is, and how they minister, are to them
things unknown.

O Churches founded upon the name of the blessed
Master as the means of communicating to the whole
world the vision of His most beautiful life and the Redemption which He brought to men and women, and as the
interpreters of the profound spiritual mysteries of the
Soul and the Divine Love and Wisdom, how great is·
the darkness which is still within ye ! How sad that
ye know not the vision which ye were ostensibly founded
to set forth to all men ! How grievous that ye understand not the Redemption ye proclaim ! How pitiful
that the interpretations of the Divine Love and Wisdom
made known by the blessed Master should be yet unknown
unto you !

What is it that hath overtaken those who should have
been, and who yet profess to be, the repositories and
interpreters and manifestors of the Divine Love and
Wisdom ? Whence hath it arisen that the altars upon
which the Light of the Divine should now be brightly
shining, have only those lights kindled by men and
women ? Why is it that the Redeemed Life which the
blessed Master so beautifully interpreted, has always
been unknown unto those who were its supposed interpreters and manifestors ?

O Church of the Living God, glorious in thy garments
and radiant with the light and beauty begotten from
the Divine ; truly Catholic because universal in the divine-
ness of the spirit of which ye are born ; Spiritual and not
Ecclesiastical, because ye are of the Soul ; wherein no
evil thing finds shelter nor cruel practices are condoned ;

through whose sympathy the Creatures are defended, and the Shambles, Abattoirs and Physiological Laboratories will be abolished: Church of the living Christhood, whose Light is from the Divine, whose Life is the Divine in manifestation, and whose Love is the Divine Love interpreted unto all men, in whom there is no schism, no sectarian strife, no impurity, but whose garments have been washed in the Blood of the Lamb (the Life-stream of the Divine flowing through the whole life of the Soul), when will ye be raised up upon the Earth once more to shed abroad the Glory of the Lord !

J. TODD FERRIER.

THE SHEPHERDS OF BETHLEHEM.

The glorious Sun had set, and all its afterglow
Had faded into night ; the Stars had lost their lustre
One by one till not a light hung anywhere
Upon the Heavens to tell what was the hour :
The heavy cloud-belts which had girt the Earth
Had blotted out her Heavens and clothed her planes
With desolation, sorrow, pain and woe :
Upon the planes of Bethlehem, sad and weary,
Some Shepherds watched their flocks in sorrow,
Mourning that the night prevailed so long ;
Beneath, the Ancient City slept unconscious
That the darkness had not passed but only deepened,
And what was the hour of night, and even
That all the Stars had long since ceased to shine :
The weary Shepherds yearned greatly for the morn
To break with roseate hues—blest herald of the noon

When all the planes would share with Hills and
    Mountains
The glory of the day, and make resplendent
With the garments of the Heavens the uplands of
The Soul, that splendour which once they knew before
The Sun went down ; and then, as if in answer
To their yearnings deep and true, and weary pain,
Visions most glorious appeared upon the Heavens ;
The curtain of the night was drawn aside,
The cloud-belts cloven in twain, and in the cleft
There stood the Angel of the Lord who spake
Of things to be accomplished, the Break of Day
Within the Soul, the Advent of the Christ,
Bethlehem restored to Royal Dignity,
(That little City wherein the Eastern Kings
Were born and crowned) : thus spake the Angel,
" Behold ! behold ! Tidings of great joy to you
Which shall be unto all peoples of the land ;
This day is born within the City of David
He who is Christ and Lord : in Bethlehem
Ye will find Him, so go ye there to-day."
Then suddenly the Heavens were thronged with
Visitants, Hosts of Angelic beings, whose
Garments were as Light dispersed and broken
Into colours such as those the Seer beheld
Within the Rainbow around the Throne of
The Eternal, radiant with purity, the
Imagers of God unto the Soul, reflectors
Of His Glory, through whom His Love is scattered
O'er the world : from these there fell upon the
    Shepherds
That glory in translucent stream, glory which

Once they knew as heritage upon the Heavens :
These sang this song, so wonderful in harmony,
" Glory be to God within the Highest
Where He reigneth King over all,
Making manifest His glorious Presence
In the Vision of the Beauty of the Lord ;
And upon the Earth-spheres His Peace,
And the willinghood of His good pleasure."

The vision passed, but left its blessed power behind ;
The Shepherds saw the breaking of the morn
And hastened into Bethlehem, the little City
Of the Ancient Kings, to find the Christ-child there ;
Whom, when they found, they loved, joy welling up
Within them, and, strength through hope arising,
They sought their flocks to minister unto them,
Made glad through having seen and known the Christ,
To know Redemption was at hand for Israel,
And even for Judah's land on which the darkness lay
In desolation, pain and woe, making it
Into a land of Light and Health and Joy
And glorious Harmony, restoring long lost Eden
With its Golden Age, its Purity and Good.

The Shepherds' Vision was within their Souls,
Where all Souls may behold the Heavenly Hosts,
And Angel of the Lord, and know the Christ-child
Born within when Bethlehem is restored.

J. TODD FERRIER.

A VOICE OF COMPASSION.[1]

MEN pray busily enough for mercy for themselves, but they forget to extend it to weaker creatures : they hear, but they understand not, the words of their Master, " Blessed are the merciful, for they shall obtain mercy." What Goldsmith wrote more than a century ago is still unfortunately true of to-day : " The better sort here pretend to the utmost compassion for animals of every kind ; to hear them speak a stranger would be apt to imagine they could not hurt the gnat that stung them. They seem so tender and full of pity, that one would take them for the nameless friends of the whole creation, the protectors of the meanest insect or reptile that was privileged with existence—and yet (would you believe it ?) I have seen the very men who have thus boasted of their tenderness, at the same time devour the flesh of six different animals tossed up in a fricassee. Strange inconsistency of conduct. They pity and they eat the objects of their compassion ! " " Good-will towards men, and on earth peace," sing the Christians at Christmas time ; but instead of peace on earth, they make the earth a veritable hell for other creatures, celebrating even the birth of the " gentle Jesus " by devouring the bodies of millions of sentient creatures whom they have slaughtered. At harvest time Christians devoutly place in their churches thank-offerings of their God-given food—but why do they not put pieces of meat there ? Instinctively the suggestion repels them ; but if, as they say, God gave them animals to kill and eat as well as the fruits of the earth, what should there be disgusting or repugnant in making a thank-offering of all such gifts ? Why make an exception of meat, the very food of all foods which so many of them assert is the most important of all, and the most essential for the life of man ? Again, why does the average Christian shrink from entering a slaughterhouse, when he does

---

[1] From " Food and Health," by A. E. Powell. Readers of the author will be well repaid for their trouble. The book is full of most valuable information on this great and vital question of Humaneness. 3/6 nett. Methuen.

not shrink from a grain-mill or a fruit-farm ? Why do Christian women of refinement delight in making with their own hands dainty dishes of fruit or corn, but shrink from dressing or handling the dead bodies of animals, and leave such work to menials and underlings ? Can any Christian picture the Christ, arrayed in a blood-bespattered smock, wielding poleaxe or knife in the shambles ? And yet He would surely not be ashamed to turn His hand to any useful and *necessary* work, *unless it were opposed to the spirit of His teaching.*

A VOICE AMID THE CHURCHES.[1]

WE might draw arguments from the Bible, as that in the state of man's innocence it is represented that he lived on fruits alone, and that this shows at least what was the ideal to which man's conscience, spirit-enlightened, witnessed when the description of Eden was written. And, again, in the prophetic fore-shadowing of the Messianic Kingdom in Isaiah, a part of the picture is the cessation of the violent slaying for food of one creature by another : " They shall not hurt or destroy in all my holy mountain." This also bears witness to the spiritual ideal. Clearly then the nearer we can attain to the innocuousness described, the nearer we shall get to the ideal of the Messianic Kingdom of Righteousness.

COMMUNINGS.[2]

MY Soul, if the Divine enlighten thee, wilt thou not obey the revealing ? It were folly for thee to choose thine own path in a land in which thou art but a pilgrim and a stranger—to follow the dictates of the mind rather than the illumination of the Spirit.

---

[1] " The Religious Aspect of Vegetarianism," by the Rev. A. E. John-ston, M.A., B.D. A brief but earnest plea for the practice of Vegetarianism and the manifestation of the true Humane Spirit. 2d. Irish Vegetarian Society, Dublin.

[2] " The Way of Understanding," by Geo. Black, M.B. It breaths the spirit of its author, Trustful, Hopeful, Pure and Reverent. 2/6 nett. Simpkin, Marshall & Co.

There are many things which concern thee that intellect
is unable to solve—that, indeed, it has no means of
solving.   There are laws governing thy existence that
mind is incapable of dealing with, but through the operation of which thou dost live and move and have thy
being.

Be not, therefore, disobedient unto the heavenly
vision. If God give thee inward discernment, and His
voice is heard by thee, follow its guidance, listen to it
and thy way will be the way of truth and thy feet will
move in the paths of righteousness.

They walk most surely who are guided by the eye of
God.   The light that is here is the light that was never
seen on sea or land : it is the light of the terrible crystal :
it is the illumination of Him before whom all things lie
naked and open.

SEEKERS AFTER TRUTH.[1]

The Eternal Light of Truth comes to us through the
Great Prism of Life, by which its white Brilliance is broken
into a thousand rainbows, from no two standpoints can
those broken rays appear precisely the same, and a great
danger exists in treating one such ray as if it were the
unbroken eternal Light itself. All the way along the
road the Seeker travels, he will find " camps " established,
round whose watch-fires many have gathered and will
call to him to join in their joyful possession of the fiery
light of Truth. For these watch fires are lit by some ray
from the Great Prism ; they are indeed flashes from the
Eternal Brilliance, but the mistake has been to accept
part as the whole. To the true Seeker these watch fires
will burn as vainly as those in the desert. They may be
messengers to him, or as direction posts along his way,
but no abiding place for one who seeks the true Light
of the World.

---

[1] THE SEEKERS, by Mrs. Philips Munn. The St. Catherine Press,
Ltd. A Booklet indicating the trend of thought amongst true seekers
after the Christ-life. It should prove very helpful to many who are
only setting out on the Path, and is a Sign of the Times.

WS - #0022 - 300425 - C0 - 229/152/22 - PB - 9781333855031 - Gloss Lamination